Anger Management

3rd Edition

by Laura L. Smith, PhD

A Wiley Brand

Anger Management For Dummies®, 3rd Edition

Published by: **John Wiley & Sons, Inc.**, 111 River Street, Hoboken, NJ 07030-5774, www.wiley.com

Copyright © 2022 by John Wiley & Sons, Inc., Hoboken, New Jersey

Published simultaneously in Canada

For general information on our other products and services, please contact our Customer Care Department within the U.S. at 877-762-2974, outside the U.S. at 317-572-3993, or fax 317-572-4002. For technical support, please visit https://hub.wiley.com/community/support/dummies.

Wiley publishes in a variety of print and electronic formats and by print-on-demand. Some material included with standard print versions of this book may not be included in e-books or in print-on-demand. If this book refers to media such as a CD or DVD that is not included in the version you purchased, you may download this material at http://booksupport.wiley.com. For more information about Wiley products, visit www.wiley.com.

Library of Congress Control Number: 2021944239

ISBN 978-1-119-82827-3 (pbk); ISBN 978-1-119-82828-0 (ebk); ISBN 978-1-119-82829-7 (ebk)

SKY10030417_101121

Contents at a Glance

Table of Contents

Introduction

Anger is part of life — no less than memory, happiness, and compassion. Anger says more about you, including your temperament, how you view the world, how balanced your life is, and how easily you forgive others, than it does about other people. You don't have to be a victim of your own anger; you can actually *choose* how you respond when the world doesn't treat you the way you want it to.

In fact, you have just as much choice about how you express your anger as you do about what color shirt you wear, what you eat for breakfast, or what time you go jogging this afternoon. Although it often *feels* like you don't have a choice about feeling angry, you do. You also have a choice about how much of yesterday's anger you carry into the future and how much anger you're likely to experience tomorrow.

No one is exempt from problematic anger. Anger is a very democratic emotion; it causes problems for men and women, kids and the elderly, rich and poor, educated and uneducated, people of all colors and ethnic backgrounds, believers and nonbelievers. Tens of millions of human beings needlessly suffer from *excessive anger* — anger that literally poisons — each and every day of their lives.

Anger isn't something that can or should be cured. But you'd be well advised to *manage* it at home, at work, and in your most intimate relationships. This book tells you how to manage your anger by focusing on the positive, get a good night's sleep, change your perspective on life, transform conflicts into challenges, and much more. Anger management has moved far beyond the simplistic (albeit well-intentioned) advice of years past to count to ten or take a couple of deep breaths every time you get angry, and that's good news!

About This Book

How do you know when you have too much anger? Do you determine that for yourself, or do you let other people make that call? If you're not physically aggressive — physically hurting other people or poking holes in walls — does that mean you're not angry? Does it really help to vent, to get things off your chest, or are you better off keeping your mouth shut to keep the peace? Can angry people really change, or do they have to go through life suffering because that's just the way they are? And what should you do if you're on the wrong end of someone else's anger? These are all important questions that *Anger Management For Dummies*, 3rd Edition, answers for you.

This purpose of this book is to present you with new ways to look at anger:

>> Anger is more than a four-letter word; it's an extremely complex emotion that has meaning well beyond the crude and hurtful words people use to express it.

>> Anger can, and does, adversely affect your life when it occurs too frequently and is too intense.

>> Managing anger is something that is within your power — if you're willing to make the necessary lifestyle changes outlined in this book: changes in thinking, behaviors, communication, and habits.

Fortunately, there are many skills for managing difficult situations without excessive anger. You may want to focus on the area in which you're having the most trouble controlling your temper — at work, for example. Or you may want to head straight for a chapter on jump-starting anger management. You don't need to read the whole book. That's up to you.

Note: Sidebars in this book contain interesting information, but they aren't essential reading. If you're someone who likes to cut to the chase, go ahead and skip the sidebars.

Foolish Assumptions

Here are a couple of assumptions that I have about you as the reader:

>> **You may or may not have a problem with anger, but if you don't have a problem with anger yourself, you know or love someone who does.** If you didn't buy this book for yourself, you bought it for your husband, wife, partner, brother, sister, son, daughter, father, mother, friend, or co-worker. Or one of those people bought it for you.

>> **You don't want to know everything there is to know about anger; you just want to know what you need to know to manage anger effectively.** Scientists have studied anger for years, but you won't find a bunch of scientific mumbo-jumbo in these pages. The book focuses on proven strategies to help you manage your anger, and that's it.

Icons Used in This Book

Icons are those little pictures in the margins throughout this book, and they're there to draw your attention to certain kinds of information:

REMEMBER

This icon alerts you to important ideas and concepts that you'll want to remember and that you can use even when you don't have *Anger Management For Dummies,* 3rd Edition, in hand.

TECHNICAL STUFF

Every once in a while, there's an interesting bit of information that may be a bit more than you need to know. You can read these paragraphs if you want, but the information they contain isn't essential to your understanding of the topic at hand.

TIP

The Tip icon suggests practical how-to strategies for managing anger.

WARNING

This icon appears when a cautionary note is in order, when you should pay particular attention to potential problems, or when you need to seek professional help.

Beyond the Book

In addition to the material in the print or e-book you're reading right now, *Anger Management For Dummies,* 3rd Edition, also comes with some access-anywhere goodies on the web. No matter how much you gain from what you read, check out the free online Cheat Sheet for additional ideas and tools. Just go to Dummies.com and type "Anger Management For Dummies cheat sheet" in the Search box.

Where to Go from Here

You don't have to read this book from start to finish to benefit from it. Each part and chapter is meant to stand alone in its discussion of anger management. Feel free to choose a topic that interests you, and dive in.

Whether you read *Anger Management For Dummies*, 3rd Edition, in its entirety or not, if you still find that you're struggling with anger, seriously consider getting the help of a professional. Anger management is a niche market, and you need to find someone who is both a licensed professional and has credentials (for example, PhD, MD, MSW, MA) and expertise in this area.

Even if you benefit from this book, many people find that anger management classes help too. You get the extra benefit of having other people share their stories and hear yours. Class members usually give useful feedback to each other as well.

1

Getting Started with Anger Management

Chapter **1**

Understanding Anger

What in the world is happening on airplanes? Instances of air rage have increased dramatically. Being a flight attendant has become a dangerous occupation, not because of plane crashes, but because passengers are attacking flight attendants. Despite a zero-tolerance policy, passengers are losing their minds on airplanes. Although alcohol is a factor in about half of cases of air rage, the other half of rage comes from supposedly sober passengers. What is going on?

For starters, the world is coming out of the largest pandemic in a century. Politics have never been more divisive. Economic disparity has never been greater. Changes in climate have produced more natural disasters. People feel frightened, stressed, and very, very angry.

REMEMBER

Anger forms part of the survival mechanism of human beings. When faced with a threat, humans, not unlike other animals, either run away, freeze, or attack. Anger fuels attacks. Angry people experience a surge of energy that helps them repel adversaries.

But anger can also have the opposite effect and lead to an untimely demise. Too much anger can cause heart attacks, precipitate disabling work injuries, ruin relationships, and lead to a variety of unintended negative consequences. Anger truly is a double-edged sword.

FINDING THE KEY TO ANGER MANAGEMENT

You'd probably like a simple answer to the question "Why am I so angry, and what's the single, most effective thing I can do about it?" You're hoping that one chapter in this book will provide that answer. But, alas, that's not the way it works.

Anger is a complex human emotion. By reading this book, you can come to understand where your anger comes from — that is, which and how many of those factors that are unique to you are at work here. It may be that you need better coping skills, to cut down on drinking, increase your social outlets, enhance your sense of purpose and meaning in life, or look for a new job. A few of these items, all of them, one of them, or perhaps more, may cause problems that result in your anger. The important thing at this point is to find the right recipe for your anger management and to use the information and resources in this book to bring your emotional life to a better place.

Defining Anger

If you're like most people, you know what anger is, or at least you think you do. For example, maybe your gut tells you that a friend of yours feels angry. So you ask him if indeed he feels angry, and he responds, "No, not at all." Of course, your gut could be wrong, and your friend really isn't angry. But usually your intuition will serve you well in such instances. You can tell by your friend's tone of voice, posture, and body language.

Anger is an emotion that involves certain types of thoughts that focus on other people's intent to hurt you, unfairness, threats to your self-esteem, and frustrations. Anger expresses itself in the body (for example, muscle tension, loud voice, and restlessness) and behaviors (such as threatening actions, pacing, and clenching). Anger is a strong emotion that attempts to express displeasure and disapproval.

Choosing Anger

Humans are the only animals that have a choice about how they view the world. Cats, dogs, squirrels, hamsters, goldfish — they're all creatures of instinct, which means they respond in predictable ways that are prewired into their nervous systems. Instincts are universal, so if you scratch a Goldendoodle's tummy, he'll instantly begin shaking his hind leg. All Goldendoodles do it, and they don't have a choice in the matter.

REMEMBER

The miraculous thing about being human is that you're not ruled by instinct. Not only do you have *choices* about how you respond to the world around you (for example, when someone mistreats you), but even before that, you also have a choice about how you *perceive* or think about that person's actions.

Do you think she did that on purpose? Was it an accident, or did he do it deliberately? Is the mistreatment specifically directed at you alone? Do you view this as a catastrophe or a life-altering event? Is this something that you think shouldn't have happened? These questions are all ones your mind considers, albeit unconsciously, before you have a chance to react — or, better yet, *respond* to provocation. Consider the following:

> You might say that **Mike** is a born pessimist, but actually that's not true. Human beings aren't *born* with attitudes; those attitudes come from life experience. What *is* true is that Mike is the product of an alcoholic home, where things could be going well one minute and fall into complete chaos the next. He found out as a child not to expect the good times to last and that he and the rest of his family were always just one beer away from a family crisis.
>
> So for all his adult life, Mike has expected that most things will eventually turn out badly, given enough time. No matter how loving his wife is or how cooperative his children are, in the back of his mind he harbors this expectation that any minute things will change for the worse, and he's ready to react in anger when that moment comes. Why will he get angry? It's Mike's way of defending himself against chaos, a way of feeling in control, which is a response that's different from when he was a child, hiding under the bed while his alcoholic father ranted and raved well into the night.
>
> Mike is unaware of how his early childhood influenced his view of the world. Like most children of alcoholics, he figures that because he survived those unpleasant years (physically at least), he's okay. He also has no clue why he loses his temper so easily.

TIP

Many people with anger problems have troubled childhoods. Their anger during childhood usually made sense at the time as a way of coping with the difficulties they faced. However, they bring their anger into the present when it usually doesn't work very well. You can acquire new, more effective ways of coping, but it takes patience and work.

Dispelling Common Anger Myths

Before you can manage your own anger, you need to be aware of what anger is and isn't. Unfortunately, myths about anger abound. Here are some of the myths to dispel from the get-go:

>> **If you don't express anger, you just might explode.** The truth is, the more often you express anger, the more likely you will feel angry in the future. On the other hand, appropriately, carefully expressed anger can help you. So keep reading!

>> **Males are angrier than females.** If by angrier you mean how often people experience anger, it's simply not true that men are angrier than women. Surveys show that women get mad about as frequently as men. Men and women may express anger a little differently, but research has been inconsistent on that issue.

>> **Anger is bad.** Anger serves a variety of positive purposes when it comes to coping with stress. When *controlled*, it can energize you, improve your communication with other people, and defend you against fear and insecurity.

>> **Anger is good.** When it leads to domestic violence, property damage, sexual abuse, drug addiction, ulcers, and self-mutilation, anger is definitely not good.

>> **Anger is only a problem when you openly express it.** Many angry people either suppress their anger ("I don't want to talk about it!") or repress their anger ("I'm not angry at all — really!"). People who express their anger are the squeaky wheels who get everyone's attention; people who repress or suppress their anger need anger management just as much (see Chapter 3 for more information about the costs of anger).

>> **The older you get, the more irritable you are.** It's the other way around: As people age, they report *fewer* negative emotions and greater emotional control. People, like wine and cheese, do tend to improve with age.

>> **Anger is all in the mind.** When you get mad, that emotion instantly manifests itself in muscles throughout your entire body, the hairs on the back of your neck, your blood pressure, your blood sugar levels, your heart rate, your respiration rate, your gut, and even your finger temperature (it warms up!) long before you're fully aware of what's happening.

>> **Anger is all about getting even.** The most common motive behind anger has been shown to be a desire to assert authority or independence, or to improve one's image — not necessarily to cause harm. Revenge is a secondary motive. A third motive involves letting off steam over accumulated frustrations — again with no apparent intent to harm anyone else.

>> **If you don't express anger, you'll be seen as weak.** Not so. In fact, a calm, measured, assertive response (see Chapter 8 for more information about assertiveness) not only works better but also is quite powerful.

>> **People with anger problems have low self-esteem.** In fact, sometimes they do. However, a much more common companion of anger is excessively *inflated* self-esteem (see Chapter 7 for more information about the role of self-esteem and anger).

ALEXITHYMICS: PEOPLE WITHOUT FEELINGS

Alexithymia is a word used to describe people who appear to lack emotions — including anger. Alexithymia is thought to be a fairly stable personality trait but isn't a formal, psychological diagnosis in and of itself. Although alexithymics actually do have feelings, they appear unaware and unable to learn from them. Alexithymics tend to

- Have difficulty identifying different types of feelings

- Appear stiff and wooden in relating to others

- Lack emotional awareness

- Lack enjoyment

- Have trouble distinguishing between emotions and bodily feelings

- Appear overly logical when it comes to decision-making

- Lack sympathy for others

- Appear perplexed by other people's emotions

- Be unmoved by art, literature, and music

- Have few, if any, emotional memories (for example, memories of childhood)

Don't disconnect from your feelings to manage your anger. You *want* to have emotions but you want to be in control of those emotions. You want to let anger move you to write a letter to the editor in your local newspaper about some social injustice. You want your anger to move you to stand up for yourself when your talents are being exploited in the workplace.

Anger that says to your spouse, "Hey, something is not working here" is good for a marriage. But if your anger only moves you to hurt others — or yourself — then you definitely have a problem. Think of anger as a tool that can help you throughout life if you know how to use it — and think of *Anger Management For Dummies* as a reference on how to use that tool.

>> **Only certain types of people have a problem with anger.** You can easily find angry truck drivers, college professors, physicians, grandmothers, lawyers, policemen, career criminals, poor people, millionaires, children, the elderly, and people of various ethnicities, nationalities, and religions. Anger is a universal emotion.

>> **Anger results from human conflict.** Sometimes yes, sometimes no. People get angry by being exposed to foul odors, negotiating traffic jams, aches and pains, computer problems, and hot temperatures — none of which involve (or can be blamed on) the direct, intentional actions of others.

Examining Emotions

Emotion can be thought of as a compound word. The *e* stands for "energy" and the *motion* means exactly what it says: "movement." Emotions *move* you to act in ways that defend you from threat, lead to social attachments and procreation, cause you to engage in pleasurable pursuits, encourage you to reattach after some type of meaningful loss, and push you to explore your environment. Without emotion, life would stand still.

REMEMBER

Emotions are, by their very nature, meant to be brief, transient experiences. Typically, they come and go throughout the day, moving you in various directions, as evidenced by changes in your behavior. Not acting on an emotion like anger is unnatural and, in some instances, can be unhealthy. Emotions reflect changes in physiology — elevations in blood pressure, heart rate, blood sugar, and muscle tension — that are usually harmless because they're short-lived (that is, if you express them in a reasonable way). Emotions that aren't expressed remain trapped within your body, causing a sustained state of physiological tension — and that can be deadly.

Suggesting that anger is either expressed or unexpressed is actually untrue. All anger is expressed. The question is how. You probably think that you're expressing your anger when you do so in a way that other people can see, hear, or feel. Otherwise, you figure, you're not expressing it. But the reality is that *all* anger is expressed — some of it in ways that aren't observable right away. For example, you may not *look* or *sound* angry, but your anger may be expressing itself in your cardiovascular system (through high blood pressure or migraine headaches), your gastrointestinal system (through irritable bowel syndrome [IBS] or a spastic colon), or your musculoskeletal system (through TMJ [temporomandibular joint pain] or tension headaches).

Or anger may express itself in negative attitudes — pessimism, cynicism, hopelessness, bitterness, and stubbornness — or some form of avoidance behavior (giving people the silent treatment), oppositional behavior ("I don't *think* so!"), or passive-aggressive behavior ("I'm sorry, did you want something?"). Anger may also sour your mood and leave you feeling down or depressed. You suddenly lose the enthusiasm you had previously.

Dr. Paul Ekman developed a list of seven primary emotions seen in all cultures around the world. Table 1-1 lists these emotions and some of the ways they express themselves.

TABLE 1-1   **The Seven Primary Emotions**

Emotion	How It's Expressed
Sadness	The eyelids droop; corners of mouth turn down; people withdraw from others; thoughts focus on negative, pessimistic issues, losses, and inferior self-views; body temperature rises; and heart rate increases.
Joy	Corners of the eyes wrinkle; smiles and corners of the mouth turn up; thoughts dwell on positive enjoyment; laughter.
Surprise	Eyes widen and become rounder; the mouth opens; expression occurs and recedes rapidly in response to an unexpected event; thoughts focus on the unexpected aspects of what occurred and why.
Disgust	The nose wrinkles; the upper lip curls; also a rapid response to something that looks, smells, or tastes unpleasant; thoughts focus on avoiding or removing oneself from the disgusting object.
Contempt	The muscles in the cheek pull back, which results in a "half" smile or sneer; the head often tilts a bit back; thoughts focus on the inferiority of others.
Fear	The eyes open wide; lips stretch out; heart rate increases; body temperature drops; thoughts dwell on how to deal with danger — whether to fight, flee, or freeze; posture slumps.
Anger	The eyes glare and narrow; lips press together; body temperature and heart rate increase; posture puffs up; thoughts focus on issues such as unfairness, revenge, injustice, attacking, and getting even.

Getting the Help You Need

REMEMBER

Everybody needs support; nobody can go through life completely alone. When you're embarking on a major change in your life, the help of other people is especially important. And managing your anger is a major life change.

Support comes in many forms. To manage your anger effectively, you need all the following kinds of support:

WARNING

>> **Carefully selected family and friends:** You need people who are behind you 100 percent, people who know about your problems with anger and are cheering you on as you figure out how to manage it.

Don't be too surprised if, at first, you have trouble getting support for your efforts at anger management. Realize that you've probably hurt a lot of people with your anger over the years — and they may have some lingering resentment, fear, and uncertainty. That's natural. But if you're truly committed to managing your anger, chances are they'll eventually rally to your cause.

>> **Informational support:** You can have the best of intentions, but if you don't have the information you need about anger and how to manage it, you won't get far. Lucky for you, you're holding all the information you need to get a handle on your anger in your hands.

>> **Self-help:** Most communities have anger-management self-help groups and classes. There are also online support groups. Be careful about online groups. Some are engaged in trolling and might even make you angrier than when you joined.

>> **Professional help:** People with anger-management problems generally don't think of themselves as needing psychotherapy. However, a trained, licensed therapist, counselor, psychologist, or psychiatrist usually has important skills that can help you turn away from anger. Therapy can help you identify your personal anger triggers, teach coping skills, and support you through the process. And therapists would gladly work with you on getting the most out of this book as well.

WARNING

Refrain from exploring medications for your anger management problems *unless* your difficulties are *extreme* and you haven't gotten very far with self-help and professional assistance. Most of the medications for anger issues are quite powerful and have serious side effects. If you do choose this option, make sure you go to an expert at prescribing medications for mental health issues.

Chapter **2**

Finding Your Anger Profile

How do you know when you have an anger problem? Some people say that any time you get angry, that's a problem. Others disagree, sometimes even arguing that anger is never a problem as long as it communicates that something is wrong in your life.

Gianna, Daniel, and Aria all work for a biomedical engineering firm. They have annual reviews scheduled for this week. All three experience some anger at work, but express it very differently.

Gianna's boss tells her that her work is amazing but that other staff members have complained about her frequent irritability. Gianna feels her pulse rate increase and her face redden. "I can't understand that; I never get angry with anyone," she insists. "I get everything done for everyone and this is the thanks I get? Look, I get my job done. Right? So what's the problem?"

Daniel expresses his anger at work by slamming doors and raising his voice at others. His boss tells him that his emotions are out of control. He recommends that Daniel attend anger-management classes or expect disciplinary action. Daniel slams the performance review on his desk and shouts, "How the hell do you expect me to act when everyone around me is an incompetent fool? I don't have an anger problem; I work with a bunch of idiots, and that includes you!"

Aria's boss gives her a solid review. He asks her whether she has any concerns or complaints. She hesitates for a moment and calmly remarks, "Actually, I am upset and even a bit angry that a couple of my colleagues suffer from anger problems that distract me and hurt our workgroup's morale. I think our team could be more productive if we address those issues."

Perhaps you can tell that Aria manages her anger effectively, whereas Gianna and Daniel have problems with anger. Whether you have a problem with anger or you interact with other people with anger issues, anger can impact the way you function every day.

This chapter takes the mystery out of trying to decide who does and doesn't have too much anger. First, you take a look at the many ways that people express anger. This information helps you identify your anger style. Next, see how anger isn't always bad. There are ways that anger can actually be constructive. Then discover what triggers your anger, and start tracking those triggers. Finally, see how anger is sometimes displaced to the wrong places and how anger can complicate other mental health issues.

The Many Faces of Anger

Everyone gets angry. After all, anger is one of those universal emotions — along with sadness, joy, and fear — that people throughout the world recognize when they see or hear it. But everyone experiences and expresses anger a little differently. The following sections describe many of the ways people show their anger or, alternatively, hold it in. Understanding your strategies for anger expression can be helpful before you work on changing how you show your anger. When people talk about anger, you'll hear various terms and words tossed around. While you read through these examples, think about the way you typically express your displeasure.

Getting annoyed

All people feel annoyed from time to time. Traffic jams, computers freeze, kids interrupt. Annoyance is a perfectly normal reaction to frustration, and annoyance is usually a fleeting emotion. However, some people get annoyed daily, too easily, and about small stuff. If you are constantly annoyed, either you have a problem, or your life needs some changes.

Being irritated

Irritability is an overly sensitive emotional and physical state. Irritability, unlike annoyance, tends to be more chronic. When irritable, you easily get upset (and annoyed) yet may not be fully aware of your emotions, thoughts, or feelings. Frequent irritability is not good for your emotional or physical well-being. You may not realize how aroused you are with irritability. Many times, other people detect your irritability better than you can. Generally, it is not fun to be around an irritable person.

WARNING

Irritable people, in addition to being easily annoyed or agitated, often experience trouble concentrating, have a rapid heartbeat, and may experience rapid or shallow breathing. Physical problems such as low blood sugar, hormonal imbalances, or lack of sleep can cause irritability. If you experience chronic irritability, consider a visit to your primary care provider to check for possible physical causes.

Complaining and gossiping

The strategy of complaining and gossiping feels safer than directly confronting someone with anger. Complainers and gossipers find sympathetic listeners that will hear their frustrations, woes, and anger about someone else. That way, they avoid actually confronting the person they're angry with. And, not surprisingly, little gets resolved in the process.

Passive-aggressive anger

People who express their anger in a passive-aggressive manner try to find "safe" ways of showing their anger. They like their behaviors to have plausible deniability of their actual angry feelings. In other words, they make excuses and claim that their motives were excusable. Here are some examples of passive-aggressive behaviors:

>> Chronic procrastination of promised tasks to get back at someone

>> Chronic lateness

>> Subtle sulking or pouting

>> Purposely performing a task for someone poorly

>> Purposely forgetting over and over to do a promised task

>> Indirect verbal expressions such as subtle sarcasm

The following story illustrates passive–aggressive behavior in action:

> **Nic,** a passive-aggressive fellow, was married to Sonya. Nic often felt irritated and upset with Sonya but rarely, if ever, expressed his feelings directly. One day, he decided that their house would look better in a different color. So he brought home samples of about 30 different paints to splotch on the walls throughout the house to see what color he preferred. Somehow, he failed to get around to actually painting the house for over two years. He always told Sonya, "I'm so sorry. I promise I'll get to it as soon as I can."

When confronted, passive–aggressive people always have an excuse in hand and inevitably deny that they feel any anger at all. People living with passive–aggressive partners get pretty tired after 500,000 instances of "I'm sorry" or "I forgot."

Holding grudges and resentment

Grudges and resentment often go together. Resentment occurs when you feel that you have been wronged by someone or by the world. Grudges are the deep feelings of anger that many people hold on to against those who have hurt them. Grudges and resentment contribute to living in the past and can have lasting impact on relationships. Holding on to these negative feelings make moving forward more difficult.

Expressing hostility, rage, or physical aggression

This section covers what most people think of as anger. The expressions of hostility, rage, or physical aggression range in intensity and can easily get out of control. *Aggression* is the intentional infliction of hurt or harm to people or objects. Not everyone who is aggressive feels anger. Some people engage in aggression because they actually like or feel pleasure from inflicting hurt. Others, like bank robbers, may be aggressive without being angry. As you may suspect, these folks aren't ideal candidates for anger management.

>> **Hostility** refers to long-standing, chronic, negative attitudes and beliefs about others or certain types of situations. For example, a gang member may feel hostility toward everyone in another gang. Generally, hostility is somewhat more diffused and less focused than anger.

>> **Rage** refers to out-of-control, especially intense levels of anger. Rage is almost always accompanied by an extremely high level of physiological arousal.

>> **Verbal bashing** includes yelling, arguing, insulting, and making threats. Hurting people with words sometimes works at the moment, but it usually leaves a trail of resentment, anger, and bad feelings. For example, parents who frequently yell at their kids sometimes get momentary compliance but usually end up with rebellious, resentful kids in the long run.

>> **Nonverbal bashing** clobbers people wordlessly. Examples of nonverbal bashing include unfriendly gestures, such as pointing, clenched fists, and "flipping the bird." Facial expressions of anger include dismissiveness, hostility, and contempt (through sneers, prolonged angry stares, and snarls). It's difficult to explain dirty looks, but you know one when you see one! Purposely ignoring and not speaking when spoken to also convey anger and hostility. Body language includes aggressive, puffed-up poses.

>> **Physical aggression** includes actions against objects or people. Slamming doors, punching holes in walls, and throwing dishes all fall under the category of physical aggression against objects. This type of aggression can feel very intimidating to those who witness it. Furthermore, these behaviors sometimes precede physical aggression against persons. Assaults can take the form of pushing or shoving, punching, and slapping, and they can even include the use of weapons. Obviously, physical aggression is almost always abusive to both recipients and witnesses.

TIP

Physical aggression with anger is only adaptive when you're actually under attack from someone else and your survival is at stake. Physical aggression doesn't lead to solutions.

Suppressing anger

People who suppress anger feel mad but work hard to hold it in. Usually, close friends and family members pick up on the anger that these people feel. However, some folks are masters at suppression, and no one truly knows how much hostility they hold inside.

Unfortunately, this type of anger often comes with physical costs, such as high blood pressure, digestive problems, and heart disease. Chronic tension, unhappiness, fatigue, and distress frequently occur as well. Therefore, suppressing anger doesn't constitute a good anger-management strategy. See Chapter 3 for more information about the costs of anger and anger suppression.

Expressing effective anger

Yes, *keeping your cool* can be one way of expressing anger. Of course, if you're reading this book, keeping your cool probably isn't your primary method of anger expression. Keeping cool means that you don't respond impulsively. You may take a slow, deep breath or two before saying anything. Then you directly express your feelings while trying to solve the issue or problem.

REMEMBER

Anger is an emotion that includes physical arousal, thoughts about threats, unfairness, injustice, intolerance, and unacceptable frustration. The emotion of anger may or may not be acted upon. When you feel anger, whether you express it or not, treat it as a signal to pay attention to what is going on around you.

Looking at your style of anger

I grew up in a home where anger was rarely expressed. Looking back, I'm sure there was plenty of anger, but yelling, cursing, or physical expressions of anger were simply not tolerated. I vividly recall one incident when my older brother slammed his bedroom door (my mother wouldn't let him get another dog). I also remember the one and only time my mother said the word "hell." That was when, at age 16, I declared that I wanted to move out of the house and live in an apartment down by the university. As a result of her uncharacteristic outward anger, I didn't move out.

My inexperience with overt anger expression at home did not always serve me well. I became frightened and overwhelmed when I encountered anger in the real world. And suppression was my go-to anger style for much of my young adult life. That did not always work to my advantage in decision-making and in relationships.

Take a few minutes and think about your early experiences with anger. Ask yourself the following:

» How did the adults in my family express anger?

» How did other family members express anger?

» How did we react to each other's anger?

» How did I express anger?

Now, think about your current ways of expressing anger. Most people find that the way they were exposed to anger in childhood influences their methods of expressing anger as adults. Look at the following list and check off the ways you handle frustration and anger:

» Getting annoyed

» Being irritated

>> Complaining and gossiping

>> Passively aggressive

>> Holding grudges

>> Getting hostile and aggressive

>> Suppressing anger

>> Effectively expressing anger

Is there a pattern to your anger expression, or do you use different styles at different times? Think about the times you get angry. How does your current anger expression relate to your early experiences?

REMEMBER

Most people believe that anger management is for those who are loud or aggressive when they get angry. But as you will see, anger management is also useful for people who don't know how to effectively get their message across and suffer in silence or feel chronically irritated.

Discovering When Anger Works

Typically, you associate anger with aggressive behavior or some other type of destructive outcome in your life. This is true only because no one has shown you how to use anger constructively. This section, illustrates the *positive* side of anger — the side that can be harnessed to resolve problems of everyday life, understand other people's point of view, and minimize future conflict.

Emotions aren't inherently good or bad. People have suffered heart attacks because of a joyful event, like being promoted, and they've suffered strokes when surprised by the unexpected news of a loved one's death. Does this mean that you should avoid joy and surprise at all costs? Of course not. And you shouldn't try to avoid anger because of some mistaken belief that it can only cause hurt and harm. It's what you *do* with anger — how you express it — that makes it good or bad.

Making anger your ally

If you choose to use anger constructively, you'll join the ranks of some notable folks — George Washington, Martin Luther King Jr., Nelson Mandela, Jesus Christ, Gandhi, and Mother Teresa. These people admittedly felt anger — about poverty, racial injustice, or occupation of their countries by foreign powers — but channeled their anger into constructive action that changed the world for the better.

The following sections cover a few reasons you should consider making anger your ally in constructing a new healthier, happier, and more productive life.

Anger can be a built-in resource

People are born with a capacity for anger. Mothers recognize anger in newborns as early as 3 months of age. Babies express anger with loud crying and red faces to tell their caregivers they're in distress: "Change my diaper!" or "Feed me!"

Anger isn't something that has to be learned or earned, like money or friendship. It's yours to experience as the need arises. Think of it as your birthright. Just as babies express anger to communicate a need, you can use constructive anger to do the same.

Anger can be invigorating

The *e* in emotion stands for "energy." Anger produces an instantaneous surge of adrenaline, which causes your pupils to dilate, your heart to race, blood pressure to elevate, and breathing to accelerate. If you're really angry, even the hairs on the back of your neck stand up! Your liver responds by releasing sugar, and blood shifts from your internal organs to your skeletal muscles, causing a generalized state of tension. You're energized and ready for action. Remember, though, that emotions are short-lived — they come and go. So it's imperative that you strike while the iron is (literally) hot, and use the angry energy to your benefit before it evaporates.

WARNING

The surge of energy from anger is beneficial only when anger is controlled and appropriately expressed. See Parts 2, 3, and 4 in this book for numerous examples of ways to express anger productively.

Anger serves as a catalyst for new behavior

The *motion* part of emotion has to do with motivating behavior. If you're like most people, you want to change some things in your life. But you're afraid, right? You're uncertain about what will happen if you let go of the status quo and move your life in some new direction, like maybe trying a new relationship or giving up an old one, leaving a toxic job, moving to a new city, or starting a new, healthier lifestyle (such as joining a gym, starting a diet, or giving up alcohol). So you do nothing — that is, until you get mad enough about the way things are that you spring into action.

Anger communicates

Anger tells the world just how miserable you are — how *un*happy, *un*fulfilled, *un*satisfied, *un*excited, and *un*loved you feel. Anger speaks the *un*speakable! Think about the last time you verbally expressed anger. Do you remember what you said?

Was it something like, "Get off my back," "You don't care about me," "I'm tired of living hand to mouth," or "I give, give, give, and I get nothing in return"? Others heard what you said, but did you? Did you listen to your anger and understand what it's telling you about what's wrong with your life and what you need to do to begin correcting it?

The most helpful emotional dialogue you have is the one you have with yourself. When you feel angry, ask what this feeling is telling you about your situation.

Anger can protect you from harm

Anger is a vital part of that built-in "fight-or-flight" response that helps you adapt to and survive life's challenges. Anger is the fight component, which is the part that moves you to take offensive measures to defend yourself against actual or perceived threats.

Do you ever get angry enough to stand up for your rights or for the rights of someone else? Do you ever use anger to set limits on other people's rude or inconsiderate behavior? Consider these expressions of anger:

>> "Hey, that's uncalled for."

>> "Just stop right there. I'm not going to sit here and subject myself any longer to this abuse!"

>> "You're insulting my friend. Stop it!"

>> "You may bully other people in this office, but you're not going to bully me."

These are examples of *adaptive anger.* If you don't express it, you may be well on your way to becoming a victim.

Anger can serve as an antidote to impotence

Impotence — lacking in power and ability — feels lousy. And impotence isn't just about sexual impotence. It's how you deal with the world around you: your relationships, your job, your finances, your health, your weight, the loss of loved ones, and so on. You feel weak and inadequate, not up to the task at hand.

Then you get angry, and suddenly, you're infused with a sense of empowerment, a feeling of strength, confidence, and competence. You're standing straight up to the frustrations and conflicts you've been avoiding. Anger, used properly, is a can-do emotion: "I can fix this problem," "I can make a difference here," and "I can be successful if I try."

TIP

Pay attention to your posture the next time you feel down, dejected, and impotent about some important aspect of your life. Then notice how your posture changes when you get fired up and begin to take charge of the situation. You'll be amazed at the difference.

Understanding the nature of constructive anger

Constructive anger differs from destructive anger in a number of important ways, including the following:

>> **The anger has the purpose of fixing a problem or wrongdoing.** For example, getting mad when a ballgame gets rained out isn't particularly helpful, but feeling irritated then feeling motivated to come up with an alternative activity works.

>> **The anger is directed at the person responsible for the wrongdoing.** If a salesperson treats you rudely when you ask for help but you ignore her rudeness and take your feelings out on the checkout person, your anger isn't helpful.

>> **The anger response is reasonably proportional to the wrongdoing.** For example, if your adolescent daughter rolls her eyes at you and makes a sarcastic remark, it's appropriate to take away a couple of hours of her screen time. However, your response would be wildly disproportionate if you slapped her.

>> **The anger intends to stop problems and doesn't seek revenge.** This is a tough one for many people. For example, Patty's husband revealed that he'd cheated on her off and on for almost ten years. If her anger leads her to leave the marriage and get counseling, she's using it productively. On the other hand, if she devoted her life to harassing him and trying to turn her kids against him, she'd be seeking destructive revenge that would hurt her and her children as much as her husband. Not a good idea.

Identifying Your Anger Triggers

Knowing your anger triggers — the events and situations that make you mad — is important because you'll respond more effectively to your anger when you feel prepared for it. Anticipating the possibility of anger increases your ability to express it more constructively. This section explores common anger triggers.

Being treated unfairly

Many people feel annoyed, irritated, or even enraged whenever something unfair happens to them. Unfortunately, unfair events occur to everyone and even fairly often. Here are a few common examples:

>> Someone cuts in front of you at the movie theater line.

>> A teacher gives you what seems clearly to be an unfair grade.

>> Your boss gives you an inaccurate evaluation at work.

>> A policeman gives you a ticket when you know you weren't speeding.

REMEMBER

No matter what response you have to unfairness, what matters is whether your reaction is mild, productive, or out of proportion to what happened.

Consider the example of what happened to 16-year-old Cameron:

> **Cameron** was driving during a well-publicized traffic enforcement sweep in Albuquerque, New Mexico. The police pulled him over for allegedly failing to use his turn signal, which he insisted he had engaged properly. He was a sincere young man with high principles and a strong belief in fairness. Therefore, he argued with the policeman who promptly wrote a ticket and told him to tell it to the judge if he wanted.

> Being a somewhat naïve citizen, Cameron went to court and argued strongly to the judge that he was in the right and that the policeman had unfairly targeted him for some reason. The judge sentenced him to 30 hours of community service and a $50 fine. Cameron spent the next few weekends collecting garbage in an orange vest alongside people who had committed more serious offenses.

Was Cameron's sentence unfair? Probably. But Cameron concluded that sometimes it may just not be worth it to let his anger and desire for fairness override his common sense. Life simply isn't always fair.

Responding to time pressure and frustrations

Today's world is a busy place. People feel pressure to multitask and constantly increase their work output. But things inevitably get in the way of making progress. Examples of such interruptions include

>> Leaving a bit late to work and running into a huge traffic snarl

>> Running late for a plane and getting selected for extra screening by security

>> Having family members or friends constantly text you while you're working

>> Having a contractor for your house project fail to show when you had set the whole morning aside to wait

>> Being placed on hold for 45 minutes and then having your call suddenly disconnected

Are events like these frustrating? You bet. However, they happen to everyone, and they happen no matter what you do to prevent them.

REMEMBER

You may be able to set limits in a useful way for some types of interruptions. For example, you may be able to tell family members you need to have them stop texting you at work. However, numerous delays and frustrations inevitably happen. Allowing anger to run out of control won't help; instead, it will merely flood you with unnecessary stress.

Experiencing dishonesty or disappointment

When people let you down, whether they renege on a promise or simply lie, it's pretty common to feel annoyed, upset, or angry. And most people encounter these events off and on throughout their lives. Here are some examples:

>> Your partner or spouse cheats on you.

>> Your boss fails to promote you or give you a raise as promised.

>> A close friend forgets your birthday.

>> A friend fails to help with moving as she said she would.

>> A co-worker makes up a lie to get out of work one day.

>> Your kid tells a lie about hitting his brother.

TIP

Of course, it's normal to feel irritated or even angry about all these triggers. However, try to figure out which types of events happen to you the most often and, more importantly, cause you the most anger.

Encountering threats to self-esteem

People like to feel reasonably good about themselves. Even people who have low self-esteem usually don't like to experience put-downs and criticism. Some people react to self-esteem threats with sadness and/or self-loathing, whereas others respond with anger. These threats can be either realistic and deserved or quite unfair, as noted in the earlier section in this chapter, "Being treated unfairly." A few examples of self-esteem threats include

>> Receiving a bad grade or evaluation

>> Getting insulted or disrespected

>> Making a mistake in front of other people

>> Spilling wine on your neighbor's carpet

>> Getting rejected

>> Not getting picked for the sports team

>> Losing an election

TIP

See Chapter 7 for how self-esteem and anger relate to each other. You may be surprised.

Struggling in relationships

Good relationships make life better. However, they can become toxic battle-grounds when one or both members have trouble with anger. You might get irri-tated at the person in front of you in the checkout line at the grocery store because she can't find her credit card. You then make a rude remark, but you'll probably never see that person again. So in the long run, your rude remark may have little long-term consequence in your life. However, when you make a snarky remark to your partner, your roommate, or your child, that remark won't be forgotten. Worse, it may spark a rebuttal or rebuke, and that can start a cycle of anger that will be difficult to break.

Running into prejudice and discrimination

In the earlier section of this chapter, "Making anger your ally," recall that a few special historic figures, such as Gandhi and Nelson Mandela, channeled their anger and rage into remarkable, world-changing movements. Most people who face discrimination and prejudice feel powerless and unable to change their world. They respond with irritation, anger, rage, or even despair. The nature of discrimi-nation or prejudice can be subtle or blatant. Here are the most common themes of unfair treatment:

>> Racial or ethnic differences

>> Sexism

>> Sexual orientation

>> Nationalism

>> Classism

>> Disability

>> Religious beliefs

>> Appearance (such as height and obesity)

You probably realize that this list of common prejudices could be endless. Some people even prejudge others based on the TV news shows they choose to watch. And today, anger can be activated simply by the "color" of your political party.

REMEMBER

Anger can be triggered either by being intolerant or prejudiced or being the victim of intolerance or prejudice.

Experiencing physical problems

Physical problems such as chronic pain or serious illness make people more susceptible to fatigue and irritability. That can lead to frustration and anger, especially when there are no quick solutions or cures in the near future.

People in these positions feel vulnerable and defenseless and occasionally lash out at others. Unfortunately, their anger may be directed to those who are trying to help them, such as caregivers or health professionals. This anger is often self-defeating and can increase isolation.

TECHNICAL STUFF

COVID survivors who continue to have symptoms many months after recovering from the initial infection are called "long-haulers." They may experience trouble thinking, difficulty catching their breath, or chronic fatigue. Studies have not yet been done on the psychological implications of being a long-hauler, but common sense would suggest that they may be prone to irritability, depression, anxiety, and anger over time.

Getting attacked

Violence permeates the world. Being the victim of violence or abuse naturally creates anger, although some people respond with anxiety and/or depression. Chronic abuse changes victims into abusers in some cases. Abuse takes many forms and ranges from subtle to blatant. The following are broad categories of abuse or attack:

- » Partnership or domestic violence

- » Partnership or domestic verbal abuse

- » Child abuse

- » Assault and battery

- » Rape or sexual abuse

- » War trauma

- » Verbal intimidation

- » Genocide

- » Random violence and accidents

WARNING

Like prejudice and discrimination, you may be the perpetrator or the victim, either one of which may involve substantial anger. Look into your heart to determine whether you've been an abuser, a victim, or both.

Existential threats

Face it, since the beginning of time, the world has suffered every imaginable disaster and tragic event: plagues, floods, earthquakes, wars, economic depressions, and so on. Many of these challenges have posed threats to the existence of all humans. So what makes today's world more difficult for many people to manage without anger, rage, and sometimes exhaustion?

Anger is a natural response to uncertainty and the feeling of powerlessness that inundate people during times of crisis. Anger can inspire constructive action when change is needed. The modern world is, however, plagued by a new threat: constant media coverage of all that is going wrong everywhere on the planet. Maybe that's why studies have shown that people are more anxious, angry, and depressed than ever.

Tracking your anger triggers

To get your anger under better control, figure out what sets you off. Table 2-1 lists the broad categories of common triggers. The first column lists the trigger categories.

In the second column, rate each trigger category from 1 to 5 in terms of *how often* it has occurred for you. For example, a rating of 1 means you rarely or never encounter this anger trigger. A rating of 3 means you encounter this trigger moderately often. A 5 means you run into this problem almost all the time.

In the third column, rate *how problematic* the trigger is for you. A 1 indicates you have little concern with this issue. For example, some people just don't get stressed out by time pressures. Others find time pressure moderately problematic and would rate the item as a 3. A few people blow their stack on a daily basis due to time-pressure problems, and they'd rate them as a 5.

Triggers that occur often, and that you feel are highly problematic, represent your personal hot buttons.

TABLE 2-1 ## Tracking Your Anger Triggers

Trigger	Rating of How Often	Rating of How Bad
Unfairness	1 2 3 4 5	1 2 3 4 5
Time pressures	1 2 3 4 5	1 2 3 4 5
Dishonesty or disappointment	1 2 3 4 5	1 2 3 4 5
Threats to self-esteem	1 2 3 4 5	1 2 3 4 5
Troubling relationships	1 2 3 4 5	1 2 3 4 5
Prejudice or discrimination	1 2 3 4 5	1 2 3 4 5
Physical problems	1 2 3 4 5	1 2 3 4 5
Getting attacked	1 2 3 4 5	1 2 3 4 5
Existential threats	1 2 3 4 5	1 2 3 4 5

In order to better understand how tracking your anger triggers can help you, consider the following example of a person who uses this technique.

Forty-six year-old **Timothy** teaches high-school mathematics. His physician tells him that his blood pressure has been quite high lately and wonders if he is under unusual stress. Timothy explains that recent changes in his school's curriculum and teacher-evaluation system have given him a lot of pressure. He's been feeling quite irritable as a result. In talking with his physician, he realizes that he's been berating his students excessively and has lost his joy from teaching. His physician prescribes two blood-pressure medications but also strongly recommends some work on anger management. Doing so may even help him reduce his medications at some point.

At the second anger-management class, Timothy discovers the common types of anger triggers and is asked to fill out a Tracking Your Anger Triggers form (see Table 2-1). He discovers that his most frequent and problematic triggers are time pressures, threats to his self-esteem (from teacher evaluations), and unfairness because he feels that the curriculum changes are unfair to those who haven't had time to assimilate and understand them. Just knowing his triggers helps Timothy feel a little more prepared and empowered. He finds that he is able to stop taking out his anger on his students, and that alone gives him more joy in the classroom. The return of enthusiasm in his work is evident in his improved teacher evaluations.

REMEMBER

Tracking what makes you angry is the first step in change. You have to be aware of the problem before you can do anything about it. As you continue with this book, you'll find more anger management tools that you can use.

Finding Anger in All the Wrong Places

After all, anger doesn't occur in a vacuum; it happens in specific places or contexts. The most frequent place for anger to erupt is in the home. That's because home is thought to be a safe place to express feelings, both good and bad. Unfortunately, the initial anger trigger often starts somewhere else.

> **Jennifer** has a high-stress job as an account executive. Her boss demands long hours and often resorts to verbal abuse. Jennifer steams and fumes when he does so, but she remains silent out of fear that she could lose her job. Unfortunately, she routinely takes her anger out on her children. While preparing dinner, she feels impatient, short-tempered, and yells at her kids. Jennifer's anger triggers occur at work, but the expression of her anger takes place at home.

TIP

Thus, in addition to understanding your anger triggers, knowing exactly "where" you usually express your anger is helpful. If there's a mismatch between where your anger starts and where it ends up being expressed, you have something to work on. Part 3 provides you with a plethora of tools for more effectively managing your anger where it really begins.

Common anger situations or contexts include the following:

>> **Home:** Sadly, many people save up their anger to express with their loved ones. They seem to believe that it's safe to do that. What they don't realize is that such behavior can be abusive and frequently causes emotional scars, divorces, marital strife, and even charges of abuse.

>> **Work:** People in power have a tendency to express excessive anger, generally at those who have less power. People on the bottom of the hierarchy either stuff their anger in or explode and get fired.

>> **Crowds, noisy places, and traffic jams:** Even people without major anger problems sometimes become irritable and frustrated in these contexts. Think

about people who have gotten into fist fights on airplanes over 2 inches of legroom or instances of road rage that result in bodily harm. (See Chapter 15 for specific ideas about dealing with road rage.)

>> **Social settings:** Parties and family functions can provide a tinder box for igniting anger. Sometimes that's because of alcohol, which can disinhibit people's anger expression. Other times, it's because of long-standing histories of hostility between friends and family.

Exploring Anger Feelings: Frequency, Intensity, and Duration

To understand how much of a problem you have with anger, you need to look at how frequently you experience the emotion, how long it lasts, and *how intensely* you feel it and how intensely you express it. Obviously, if you feel frequent, intense, and long-lasting anger, you have a problem, and your anger likely interferes with your life and relationships. Ask yourself the following questions:

>> **How frequently do I feel irritated, annoyed, or angry?** Generally, if you experience angry feelings more than two or three times a week, it's probably a good idea to look at whether you have situations or stressors that need to be addressed. However, your *anger intensity* and *duration* may matter more.

>> **Just how mad do I get?** Everyone gets annoyed from time to time. And frankly, most people experience anger here and there. But most people don't punch holes in walls or aggressively threaten people. The intensity of your anger is excessive if you become violent, hysterical, vicious, scary to other people, or out of control. There's no really simple, valid, numerical scale of how much anger is too much, but you get the idea.

>> **How long do I stay mad?** Some people get over their anger quickly. Others dwell and ruminate for hours, days, or even longer, sometimes for years. Once I took a cruise and had an Eastern European waiter. He bitterly complained about barbarians who had butchered his family. I expressed shock and concern. Then the waiter went on to say that this butchery had happened in the tenth century. That's a long time to hold onto a grudge!

TIP

Negative emotions like anger are normal parts of human experience. Anger becomes a problem when it detracts from the quality of your work, pleasure, and relationships.

Complicating Problems

Excessive anger, in and of itself, can seriously harm work, relationships, and daily satisfaction. However, when anger accompanies other emotional, physical, and/or social problems, chaos carries the day. Unfortunately, anger is, more often than not, associated with other problems.

Anger can be found as a symptom in many mental health disorders. It can coexist with anxiety, depression, obsessive compulsive disorder, borderline personality disorder, bipolar disorder, and post-traumatic stress disorder. In addition, anger is a primary sign of the following conditions:

>> **Intermittent explosive disorder:** A person with this problem has big outbursts such as tantrums, fights, tirades, physical aggression, or destruction of property. These outbursts happen frequently and are way out of proportion to the triggering incident.

>> **Conduct disorder:** This pattern of behavior is one of aggression to people or animals, rule violation, deceitfulness, or destruction of property. It often begins in adolescence but sometimes emerges in childhood.

>> **Oppositional defiant disorder:** Signs of this disorder usually begin to surface during childhood and involve being irritable, argumentative, defiant, and spiteful. Kids and teens with this disorder can be particularly challenging to parents and teachers.

>> **Disruptive mood dysregulation disorder:** This is a relatively new diagnosis that is thought by some to be a form of depression. Angry outbursts occur frequently and with little prompting. Irritability and anger also occur frequently, as in most days. This diagnosis must be given to children who experience these symptoms between the ages of 6 and 18. There is considerable controversy about this diagnosis in part because of the overlap with oppositional defiant disorder.

TIP

When your body is hurting and your mind is sad or worried, your anger buttons may be pushed more easily. If you suffer from significant emotional or physical problems, you need to address them to maximize your chances of managing your anger more effectively. Discuss any concerns you have with a mental health professional or primary care medical provider.

The world around you can also make managing anger more difficult. Sometimes you can make meaningful changes to the world or situations that you find yourself in. In those cases, you should take action. When you can't, look for sources of support, such as advocacy groups, friends, and even therapists. Review the following list to see how many of these issues apply to you:

>> Excessive anxiety, worry, or fears

>> Chronic low moods and/or self-esteem

>> Overwhelming fatigue

>> Overuse of alcohol, substances, or prescription medications

>> Chronic pain

>> Flashbacks to past traumatic events

>> Oversensitivity to criticism

>> Insomnia

>> Chronic moodiness from highs to lows

>> Beliefs that the world is against you

>> The world actually acts against you with prejudice or discrimination

>> Poverty

>> Isolation

>> Crime

>> War

If you have co-occurring emotional, physical, or social problems, be sure to address them along with your attempts to manage your anger.

TECHNICAL
STUFF

Sigmund Freud believed that depression is anger turned inward, and that belief remains held by many professionals to this day. Nonetheless, this hypothesis hasn't been proven despite many attempts to do so. Anger actually tends to activate and motivate people, whereas depression generally does the opposite.

Chapter **3**

Deciding Whether to Change

Why are you reading (or listening) to this book? Maybe your partner bought you a copy of *Anger Management For Dummies,* 3rd Edition, and told you that you'd better read it or else! You might have had some trouble at work with anger and you're hoping that understanding a bit more about the topic will help you get along better with your colleagues. Perhaps a judge or social worker assigned you to an anger-management class, and the instructor uses this book as a text. Maybe your partner has an anger problem and you'd like to understand more about anger. Or possibly you suspect that you have an anger problem, but you aren't sure you want to change because you believe anger helps you in many ways.

The bad news is that reading a book about anger management will not rid you of all of your anger. The good news is that if you want to change, this book provides lots of tools for you to work with. People don't change if they don't want to. Perhaps you've heard the old joke, "How many psychologists does it take to change a light bulb? Only one. But the bulb has to want to change!"

Actually, that joke contains a lot of truth. You have to make your own decision about anger. And if you don't want to change, you probably won't. But if you do, this book may help.

This chapter, lets *you* decide what you want to do about your anger. You see what benefits anger has for you as well as the many costs.

The Top Ten Reasons for Not Changing Your Anger

People have reasons for continuing to express their anger. They hesitate to change because of beliefs that they hold about feelings, anger, and change itself. These beliefs can be quite powerful, so it's useful to examine them. Then you can decide whether you want to consider alternatives to these beliefs.

REMEMBER

The *alternative perspectives* listed under each reason or belief for not changing your anger are exactly that: another way you can choose (or not) to look at the belief. I'm not trying to tell you how to think, but I want to offer something to consider.

People deserve my anger

This belief keeps the focus on blaming others for your anger. Let's face it; people do lots of things that deserve anger. They lie, cheat, steal, deceive, and generally screw up. So you have darn good reasons to feel angry.

Alternative perspective: Sure, people do all sorts of irritating, upsetting things. But does your anger change, prevent, or solve anything? Is it possible that better ways exist for addressing these problems? Or is it possible you can express your anger in a managed, constructive way?

I'm afraid to try changing and failing

This belief tells you that you can't successfully manage your anger differently. You may also worry that you'll look foolish if you try to change and flop. Therefore, you don't make the effort.

Alternative perspective: You not only might fail, you will! After all, habits die hard. But persistence and practice pay off on almost everything in life. Have you ever achieved much of anything without taking a few risks along the way? Probably not.

I don't like to be told what to do

People don't like having other people tell them what to do. Your mom tells you to eat your vegetables, stop running around, or sit up straight. And that inner 2-year-old self automatically says "No!"

Alternative perspective: This book doesn't tell you what to do. You may feel like others are making you do things, like attend anger-management classes, but at the end of the day, you have to make your own decision about how you deal with your anger.

Who would I be without my anger?

Anger may so thoroughly saturate your life that you wonder who you'd be without it. You may feel that you're an angry person and have no idea what it would be like to feel calm and controlled most of the time. Who would you be? Would others think something was wrong with you?

Alternative perspective: If you change your habitual ways of dealing with anger and don't like the results, you can always go back to your old behaviors. Anger doesn't have to *define* anyone. If you manage your anger, you'll probably have most of your same likes and dislikes and probably most of the same friends — perhaps you'll even discover that finding friends becomes easier.

Feelings can't be controlled

Many folks believe that feelings or emotions are unchangeable. They can't imagine how they could feel differently because situations beyond their control cause their feelings. They think that events directly lead to reflexive emotions. That's that.

Alternative perspective: Scientific studies have shown again and again that people can acquire new ways of thinking about, interpreting, or perceiving events in ways that then lead to different feelings. See Chapter 6 for help with understanding how to change the way you interpret anger-inducing events.

I have to express my anger or I'll explode

A highly common belief in our society revolves around the idea that anger is much like a pressure cooker without a safety valve. With enough time and heat (anger), the cooker will inevitably explode. So many people believe that they must express any anger they feel or risk going completely out of control.

Alternative perspective: Studies have consistently shown that calming down leads to better emotional, physical, and interpersonal functioning. There's no truth to the belief that you must express all angry feelings.

Anger makes people do what I want

This belief provides motivation for expressing lots of anger. And, in fact, anger often *does* get people to do what you want in the short run.

Alternative perspective: Unfortunately, what works in the short run usually back-fires in the long run. If you manage to bludgeon people into doing what you want, you're pretty likely to create resentment, bitterness, and hostility. Like other bad habits, such as smoking and drinking, the long-term consequences are worse than the short-term benefits.

If I don't show people who's the boss, I'll look like a wimp

This belief is based on the idea that only two choices exist in dealing with others — dominance and submissiveness. If you don't push around others, they'll see you as weak and take advantage of you.

Alternative perspective: Most people aren't trying to push you around. In fact, most of the time, they're too concerned with themselves to take much notice of you. Furthermore, you can express your needs assertively, which is neither overly dominate nor submissive. See Chapter 8 for information about the benefits of assertiveness.

Anger protects me

You may believe that unbridled anger keeps you safe from attack by others. Thus, you always feel justified in your angry responses, which you believe protects you from harm by other people.

Alternative perspective: Real attacks from other people aren't actually all that common. Even in high-risk professions, such as law enforcement, keeping anger under control leads to better decision-making and safer work conditions.

My anger gives meaning to the bad things I've experienced

Many people with anger problems have had terrible things happen to them. They've been abused as kids, they've been victims of a crime, or perhaps they were injured during a war. Victims of trauma often believe that feeling anger or rage about those events helps them cope with what happened to them. They think that their anger is the *morally righteous* response to horrible events.

Alternative perspective: Giving up anger doesn't mean that your traumatic experience was insignificant. You can give up your anger and move forward with your life. See Chapters 16 and 17 for information about letting go and forgiving while still remembering.

The Stages of Change

It's best to make an informed decision about whether you want to make changes. To do that, you need to understand what the process of change looks like. Drs. Prochaska, Norcross, and DiClemente, in their highly acclaimed book, *Changing for Good,* describe the process of changing human behaviors, emotions, and habits. They believe that people move through six stages of change. However, people don't necessarily go through each stage in a set order but instead may move forward or backward or even skip a stage or two. These stages are described in the following sections so that you can consider which one you may be in with respect to your anger.

Precontemplation

If you've opened this book and are reading this sentence, you're probably not in the precontemplation stage. That's because people in this stage of change *aren't even thinking* they have a problem that they want to change. They might know they have an issue with anger, but they have no plan to do anything about it. They aren't reading self-help books, and they aren't looking for therapists. If you ask them if they have a problem, they defend it, deny it, or blame someone else. So, someone who's overweight and in the precontemplation stage wouldn't consider weight a personally relevant issue.

Contemplation

This stage applies to people who are merely thinking about making a change. They haven't yet translated those thoughts into concrete plans or actions. They just have a growing sense that something is wrong that should be addressed. You could be reading this book and be in the contemplation stage of change.

A common example of contemplation is someone who sort of knows he should lose some weight but hasn't really thought about a diet, exercise, or other plans for getting there. In the case of anger, a person in the contemplation stage might say, "I should stop yelling so much at my kids," but has no ideas or plans for implementing that change.

Preparation

People in the preparation stage of change begin to create plans, make an appointment with a therapist, or write down steps they plan to take. During the preparation stage, people gather resources and start to imagine exactly how they plan to proceed. This is the stage that begins the process. You have made a commitment to work on decreasing anger.

Action

Here the rubber meets the road. During this stage, people put their plans into real actions. In the case of anger management, they may start writing down their anger triggers and use a variety of strategies described throughout this book for responding to their triggers in new, more adaptive ways.

You may find several techniques that seem to really help and practice them in real life situations. You find yourself becoming less angry and more able to handle life's frustrations.

Maintenance

After people have made most of the changes they want to, there's more to be done. They have to work at *maintaining* their changes, and that's not always easy to do. Increases in stress or other life changes can make maintenance tough. See Chapter 18 for ideas on how to keep your gains stable in the face of adversity.

Termination

Not everyone gets to this stage of change. Termination refers to the stage of change when new habits become so deeply engrained that they require little or no effort to maintain them. Therefore, relapse becomes much less likely at this point.

For example, some ex-smokers reach this stage and feel no particular temptation to ever smoke again. However, others succeed with a lifetime of abstinence but still struggle occasionally with difficult urges. So you don't have to reach this stage to be successful, but it's nice and easier if you do.

Working through the stages of change

To help clarify how the process of changes works, the following example of Caleb shows you how people don't always go through each stage in a neat, clean, straightforward manner. Rather, it's common to bounce around a bit.

> **Caleb** works for an interstate trucking company as a long-distance driver. Caleb drives longer hours than he should. He also has a hot temper, especially when he's fatigued. Caleb blows up one day at the loading dock. He swears and pushes a co-worker up against a wall for messing up an order.
>
> Following the incident, Caleb's boss tells him he's got to watch his temper. So Caleb tells his boss he will never do it again and gives his word on it. Caleb believes what he tells his boss and swears to his wife and friends that his angry days have come

to an end. Caleb has suddenly shifted from the precontemplation stage of change (not even thinking about it) to the action stage, but with no contemplation or preparation.

Two weeks later, Caleb makes a couple of obscene gestures to other drivers. Over the next few days, he gradually slips back to his old anger habits and quits thinking about the issue. He has now shifted back to the precontemplation stage of change. Unfortunately for Caleb, he has another major anger outburst at work. His boss tells him that he has put Caleb on probation for the next six months and tells him he must get help for his anger problems.

This time, Caleb starts giving the problem a lot of thought (contemplation stage). He then starts gathering as much information as he can about anger management (preparation stage). He buys a copy of *Anger Management For Dummies* and makes an appointment with a therapist. He and the therapist develop a set of specific actions and goals like those described throughout this book. He begins implementing these actions (action stage) and mostly succeeds, but from time to time, his old habits return.

Eventually, Caleb rarely loses his temper, and his friends see him as almost a new person (maintenance stage). He never gets to the point of never having to think about his anger impulses (termination stage), but his job performance and relationships improve.

Most people who attempt to change any habit or pattern, like Caleb, go through various stages of change. You might not think you have a problem with eating too much (precontemplation), but then something happens that makes you realize you do have a problem, like you step on a scale (contemplation). It's possible to ignore that problem until something else reminds you, such as the doctor telling you that you have high blood sugar (more contemplation). So you decide to go on a diet (action). That diet works great and you lose weight for a couple of years (maintenance). But you never reach the last stage (termination), because you always have to watch what you eat. And you might slip for a few months and find yourself having to go through the stages again. That's just the way habits are fought.

The Critical Costs of Anger

This section shows you the many ways in which anger can be costly. If you find yourself feeling like a battery that's losing its charge, if you can't seem to lose weight or stop smoking, if you have headaches all the time, if you're taking blood-pressure medication, if you're concerned about your relationships, or if your career seems like a train wreck, you'll find this section especially enlightening.

Harming your health

The link between emotion and physical health can be both direct and indirect. Anger, for example, has an instantaneous effect on your blood pressure — but that effect is short-lived and generally doesn't cause any immediate harm, although chronic anger appears to increase your risks of heart disease and possibly high blood pressure. Furthermore, anger elevates blood pressure through its link to smoking and obesity — and that effect is permanent.

Robbing your energy

Anger and fatigue go hand in hand. Emotions spend energy. The body requires energy to mobilize itself into an attack posture — heart pounding, blood pressure up, muscles tense from head to toe. By its very nature, anger excites you. Your adrenaline flows. And afterward comes the recovery, where you feel physically drained and exhausted.

Now, imagine that you suffer from chronic anger, like Colleen in the following example. You go through this vicious cycle of excitation and exhaustion several times every day. Consider how much of your energy is being robbed by this intrusive emotion.

> **Colleen** decides to go to her primary care physician because of overwhelming fatigue. Colleen's doctor runs some blood tests but suspects that the real culprit may be her anger. Colleen has often brought up problems with her husband who drinks too much. She's left to take care of her three kids all by herself in addition to working full time. Colleen feels hostility and resentment of her husband throughout most of her days. However, she says she's afraid to confront her husband because he gets really angry when he's drunk. Colleen's doctor happens to work in an *integrated health system* (which has a variety of practitioners providing a wide range of medical, rehabilitation, health promotion, and mind-body care), so he sends her to a psychologist down the hall.
>
> Colleen and her psychologist work together on ways to gently talk with her husband when he's not drunk. They also come up with a plan to help her find affordable daycare to take some of the pressure off of child-care responsibilities. Colleen's husband denies that he has a drinking problem in spite of overwhelming evidence to the contrary. Colleen eventually decides to leave her husband, who fails to respond to her appeals. Interestingly, a few weeks after they separate, her energy level slowly comes back to normal.

Smoking

Your risk for being a cigarette smoker is substantially higher if you typically experience intense anger and hostility.

ANGER, PREGNANCY, AND SMOKING

Researchers agree that smoking during pregnancy poses dangers to both the mother and her baby. Nicotine and other poisons a pregnant woman inhales pass directly into the baby's bloodstream. Smokers have a higher incidence of miscarriage, stillbirths, and premature births. Babies are more likely to weigh less, have lung problems, birth defects, and even sudden infant death syndrome when their mothers smoke during pregnancy.

Cigarette smokers report higher levels of hostility and aggression than nonsmokers. A study of pregnant, low-income smokers found that anger-management intervention given during pregnancy increased the likelihood of successful quitting. Just one more reason to consider managing anger better.

Surprisingly, using nicotine reduces the likelihood that you'll react aggressively when you're provoked to anger. That's the good news. The bad news is that smoking is linked to heart disease (and obviously, cancer). Angry smokers are far less likely to succeed in their attempts to quit smoking than non-angry smokers. Finally, anger is the second-leading cause of relapse among ex-smokers — less than stress/anxiety but greater than depression.

Being hooked on cigarettes may also mean that you're hooked on anger.

Drinking and drugs

Most illegal drugs and alcohol are numbing agents when it comes to emotions. People use substances to forget not only their troubles but also what they're feeling at the moment — sadness, anxiety, shame, guilt, and anger. The more you use, the less connected you are to those feelings. Most people don't drink or use drugs to make themselves feel good; they use to feel less bad.

If you plan to continue to drink alcohol but you're concerned about anger, consider the following:

>> **Drugs or alcohol can cause you to misperceive the motives and actions of others.** What might otherwise be viewed as unintended or accidental is now seen as intended to inflict harm.

>> **Mind-altering substances have a disinhibitory effect on emotions and behavior.** They lower the nervous system's threshold for emotional expression, allowing you to do things you otherwise wouldn't if you were sober. They also transform behavior and make you feel you have the "right" to act opposite to your normal self. So the quiet person becomes loud; the submissive person becomes dominant; the sweet person becomes angry.

>> **Alcohol and drugs affect mood in the aftermath of using.** In other words, if you're a heavy drinker or drug abuser, you can expect to feel more depressed after you sober up than before.

>> **If you are what's called an *angry drinker* (that is, you get angry when you drink), alcohol is probably a very bad choice for you.** No one really knows why, but some people act silly when drinking, some feel depressed when drinking, still others feel more sexual, and so on. But if you usually feel angry when drinking, you should stay away from alcohol.

TIP

One drink per day for women and two drinks a day for men is considered moderate drinking. Studies have shown that people who keep their drinking at that level may even have less cardiovascular disease and reduced memory loss in old age. However, anything more than this amount is excessive and usually harmful to your health. The bottom line: Some people simply can't stick to one or two drinks per day, and, in those cases, abstinence works better than moderation.

WARNING

Prescription drugs can be life-savers when they are, well, prescribed. However, some prescription drugs, especially pain medications, can quickly become addictive. When you or someone you care about has trouble maintaining appropriate prescription drug use, get help immediately. Postponing getting help can have deadly consequences.

Obesity

Do you head for the refrigerator or the nearest fast-food restaurant when irritable, upset, or angry? If you do, you're not alone. Food is, unfortunately, the solution that many people choose to quell their anger as well as other negative emotions. And, of course, obesity is yet another risk factor for heart disease and diabetes.

In fact, studies have shown that depression, anger, and hostility may increase the risk for *metabolic syndrome*, which is a condition characterized by high blood pressure, high triglycerides, high blood glucose levels, resistance to insulin, and excess weight around the waist. Metabolic syndrome often leads to heart disease, stroke, and diabetes.

High blood pressure

People who have high blood pressure have a much higher risk for heart disease. And people who are habitually angry have a much higher risk for high blood pressure. It should be noted that people who express their anger outwardly (yelling, screaming, and throwing objects, for example) as well as people who pretend they're not angry but actually harbor considerable rage are all at increased risk for developing high blood pressure and heart disease.

High cholesterol

Anger doesn't cause you to have high cholesterol, which places you at risk for heart disease. Family history contributes a lot to high cholesterol. But, anger can move you to eat high fat foods. And there is no question that obesity, anger, and stress aggravate the problem.

REMEMBER

When your physician tells you that you need to lose weight and start exercising to lower your cholesterol levels, you should follow that advice. But if anger is a problem for you, consider the potential benefit of anger management in helping you get to your goals.

On-the-job injuries

You'll probably spend most of your adult life working. So if you're injured, it's most likely to occur on the job, and that's true no matter what you do for a living. So what does that have to do with anger? It turns out that on-the-job injuries occur at a higher rate for people who have excessive problems with anger. Many accidents at work occur during or just following an episode of anger.

Road rage

Anger is hazardous to driving, and if you're a self-professed high-anger driver, do yourself a favor and get some help. Anyway, it's no fun to start every journey angry. High-anger drivers take more risks, drive faster, and have more accidents and injuries. Not a good combination.

REMEMBER

Many of the things in life called accidents really aren't accidents. And some people are really just accidents waiting to happen. Be honest with yourself about your own road rage — you could not only be saving your life but also the lives of everyone else on the road with you. See Chapter 15 for ideas on managing road rage.

Sabotaging your career

Not only can anger rob you of energy and end up making you sick, it can also drastically affect your career — and not in ways you want.

> **Liam,** a 35-year-old unemployed man, called in to a syndicated talk show that offered career advice, telling the host that he needed advice on how to get a good job. The host asked him about his educational background (he was a college grad) and inquired about his last job. He described what sounded like a pretty good job as a town administrator in a small community.
>
> "How long did that job last?" the host asked.
>
> "About 18 months, and then I quit," said the fellow.

"Why did you quit?" the host asked.

"They wouldn't give me the big raise I felt I deserved, so I got mad and resigned," was the answer.

"And what did you do before that?" the host asked.

"Same thing: city administrator for another small community."

"How long were you at that job?" the host inquired.

"I think about two years, but again they wouldn't meet all my demands, so I got mad and quit."

The conversation continued until the caller had described four good jobs since he graduated from college, all of which he had left in anger.

Finally, the host said, "I get the picture, but I think you're wrong about what your problem is. Your problem isn't how to get a good job. You've had four. Your problem is your inability to control your temper whenever your employer either can't or won't give you exactly what you want."

Liam was furious, shouting, "You don't know what you're talking about. I'm not the problem. They are. You're not giving me any help here." Then he hung up. Obviously, what had started out as a highly promising career was now stalled and heading down the toilet — fast.

The following sections cover some other ways anger can sabotage your career.

Getting off track early

In today's world, more than ever before, if you hope to succeed at work, you need an education. Without an education, your choices are extremely limited, and you'll be lucky if you get what amounts to back-breaking, low-paying, here-today and gone-tomorrow jobs.

What does this have to do with anger? Well, it turns out that men and women who were ill tempered as children and adolescents drop out of school before they graduate from high school a lot more often than even-tempered youngsters. They enter the job market already at a distinct disadvantage and they never catch up.

Heading in the wrong direction

Most people want to have a better life than their parents and grandparents had. You want to make more money, have more creature comforts, drive a better car, live in a nicer house, wear more expensive clothes, eat in gourmet restaurants, and take more elaborate vacations. Those are the incentives that may spur you to work longer, harder, and smarter year after year.

JOURNALING TO GET BACK TO WORK AND GET OVER RAGE

Losing a job often makes people angry. In fact, over many years of research, Dr. James Pennebaker from the University of Texas found that one of the primary emotions experienced by those who are laid off their jobs is outrage. He also discovered that a simple strategy helped those unemployed folks with their emotions while increasing their probability of finding re-employment. Simply put, he had laid-off workers randomly assigned to one of three groups. He asked the first group to spend 30 minutes a day for a week writing about their thoughts and emotions. He told the second group to spend the same amount of time writing about neutral topics, such as time management. The third group wasn't given any writing assignment.

The consistent, stunning results indicated that merely writing about thoughts and emotions decreased emotional distress and increased the likelihood of the workers finding new jobs. In fact, those given the task of writing about deep thoughts and emotions obtained new jobs at a rate that was five times greater than those in the other two groups. That's quite a return on the worker's investment of time.

But not everyone is following that dream. Some people are experiencing just the opposite, so by the time they reach midlife, they're actually worse off in terms of job security, job status, and income than their parents. Why? For some, the answer is anger. It turns out that easily angered people have more jobs over a lifetime, get fired or quit more often, are forced to take whatever jobs are available (instead of logically pursuing a career), and have a much more erratic employment history as compared to those who are slow to anger.

To add insult to injury, many ill-tempered adults seek out jobs that tolerate their angry outbursts as long as the job gets done. In effect, they've found a niche for their anger. (Unfortunately, most of these jobs are physically dangerous and low paying.)

Engaging in counterproductive work behavior

Have you ever engaged in any of the following behaviors while at work?

>> Come to work late without permission

>> Made fun of someone at work

>> Found yourself daydreaming rather than doing your job

>> Behaved rudely to a client or co-worker

>> Refused to assist a colleague at work

>> Blamed someone else for a mistake you made

>> Tried to look busy while doing nothing

>> Taken a longer break than you were entitled to

>> Avoided returning an email to someone at work

>> Intentionally wasted supplies

>> Stolen something that belongs to the company

>> Hit or pushed someone

>> Made an obscene gesture to a co-worker

If you answered yes to any of these questions, you've engaged in what's called counterproductive work behavior. *Counterproductive work behavior* is any act at work that is clearly intended to hurt the organization you work for or other employees. And which employees are most likely to engage in such behavior? The angry ones, of course. See Chapter 12 for ideas about improving work behaviors.

Ruining your relationships

Angry people are difficult to live with, and anger is powerful enough to kill any positive feelings that married couples, domestic partners, or friends have for each other. The idea that "love conquers all" is a myth. Anger is contagious. Anger, much like COVID, can make you sick by just breathing the air around someone who has it.

TIP

If you feel anger toward anyone and try to keep it inside, it's not likely to work. Anger follows you around like a dark cloud. Generally, people detect your anger even if you don't think that's the case.

And you might not see the effects of your anger on your partner, co-workers, or friends right away. People with angry partners quite often keep their upset inside of themselves, and resentment builds over time. Eventually, they decide they've had enough and terminate the friendship or leave the relationship.

TIP

You should look at what role anger may have played in your relationships. Has it cost you more than you've realized?

A Cost-Benefit Analysis of Your Anger

Earlier in this chapter, I review a range of possible perceived benefits for anger. That's because it's crucial to understand that all emotions (including anger) have benefits at various times to varying degrees. The preceding section covers an extensive array of possible costs of anger.

Business people use what's known as a *cost-benefit analysis* all the time to improve their decision-making and increase their odds of success. A cost-benefit analysis involves a systematic approach for evaluating the strengths and weaknesses of any kind of option under consideration. This technique has, in fact, become a cornerstone of cognitive behavioral approaches to anger as well as depression, anxiety, worry, and substance abuse.

A cost-benefit analysis helps you form an objective picture of any important decision. You can use one to decide whether to change your approach to anger and also to make better decisions about what you want to do with things like the following:

>> Whether to refinance your house

>> What school to send your kid to

>> Which car to buy

>> Whether you want to quit drinking

>> Whether to change your job

>> Whether you want to change the way you spend money

>> Whether a particular belief you hold helps or harms you

>> Whether to stay or leave a relationship

Seeing how a cost-benefit analysis works

Conducting a cost-benefit analysis is pretty easy and straightforward. This technique helps you see conflicting thoughts side by side. The following two examples show how it works.

Rosalyn marries **Todd,** who has an unusually close-knit family. She loves her in-laws who are caring, warm, personable, and kind. Although her in-laws live across the country, during the first four years of marriage, they shower her with thoughtful gifts, frequent texts, and favored recipes. She can't believe how lucky she is to marry into a family like Todd's.

No wonder Rosalyn feels excited and thrilled when her in-laws announce their retirement and decision to move just a few blocks away from them. Immediately after her in-laws move into their new home, they start dropping by frequently and unexpectedly. Sometimes they even plop themselves into Rosalyn and Todd's living room for an entire day on the weekend. Rosalyn feels she can't go out and run errands. She finds herself feeling restless, irritable, angry, and invaded. She isn't even sure why.

Rosalyn asks Todd to intervene, but he can't seem to set any limits with his parents for fear that their feelings will be hurt. She can't do anything about the problem for the same reason. Todd and Rosalyn start bickering with each other. Rosalyn starts thinking perhaps she has an anger-management problem. Table 3-1 shows what Rosalyn's anger cost-benefit analysis looks like.

Rosalyn concludes that her anger costs her a lot. However, it comes with a couple of benefits. The most important benefit is that anger helps her see that there's a problem that calls for action. She and Todd discuss their need for more privacy with his parents. Surprisingly, his parents realize that they haven't done enough to develop new friends and activities since moving.

TABLE 3-1   **Rosalyn's Anger Cost-Benefit Analysis**

Costs	Benefits
I feel on edge all the time.	My anger is at least helping me see that something is wrong.
I'm arguing with my husband too much.	My anger is pushing me to take action.
I don't appreciate my in-laws anymore.	I took up jogging, which I like, although it's to avoid my in-laws.
I can't sleep at night.	My house is cleaner because I clean when they're around.
I want to take up smoking again, but that's not a good idea.	
I'm not having fun anymore.	

Rosalyn figures out that she doesn't really have an anger–management problem other than needing to become more assertive. Her anger is fully justified and understandable. She also concludes that if she expresses her anger more effectively, she can solve her problems and still keep the benefits of having a cleaner house and continuing her newfound love of jogging. And she can notice when things are going wrong and take actions sooner.

On the other hand, some people do have an anger problem. Consider the following example:

Geraldo gets into a shouting match with another fan at a football game. Tempers flare, and the conflict escalates into shoving. Geraldo throws a single punch, and other spectators intervene — and so do the security guards who have him arrested, and he's subsequently charged with disorderly conduct.

Geraldo has never done anything illegal in his life but is well known as a hothead among his friends. He shows for his court appearance and starts to argue when the judge gives him a fine of $500. Geraldo tells the judge in a loud voice, "The other guy started this; I don't deserve a fine!"

The judge responds, "Well, not only is a fine reasonable, but now you've talked yourself into 12 weeks of anger-management training. Do you have anything else to say?"

Geraldo reluctantly stops arguing with the judge and goes to anger-management classes. At the first class, he marches into the room and slams his notebook on the table. His face radiates rage. He says, "I don't belong here."

He is surprised to be told that "Maybe you don't belong here, and, for your information, no one will actually *make* you change if you don't want to. The decision is up to you."

The class leader describes a cost-benefit analysis and suggests that perhaps Geraldo would find a cost-benefit analysis of his anger useful. Table 3-2 shows what Geraldo came up with.

Geraldo reviews his cost-benefit analysis and still doesn't quite feel inspired to change his anger, but he does realize that it's costing him something. He figures that he has to come to these classes anyway, so maybe he'll actually listen to what they have to say.

Geraldo attends a few more classes. At that point, he realizes that he's no longer in high school and that he needs to deal with his emotions in a more mature way.

TABLE 3-2   **Geraldo's Anger Cost-Benefit Analysis**

Costs	Benefits
Well, my temper and my anger landed me here at anger-management classes, which don't sound like fun to me.	No one pushes me around!
My anger cost me $500.	My anger is a way of getting my way on things.
I lost a really good friend last year over an argument.	Most of the people I get angry with deserve it, and it feels good to let them know that.
My boss said I have a bad attitude and that I'm not management material.	When I used to play high-school football, my anger made me more aggressive.
Sometimes I get so mad that I have to wonder if my high blood pressure isn't fueled by my anger.	

Considering your own cost-benefit analysis

You may want to experiment with a cost-benefit analysis of your anger issues. Take your time. Simply draw a line up and down dividing a piece of paper into two columns. Label one side *Costs* and the other *Benefits*. Put down everything that occurs to you for each side. Then put it away and come back to it after a while — you just might come up with a few more items.

Here are a few questions to consider:

>> Has anger impacted my health; if so, how?

>> Does anger keep me from getting hurt?

>> Has anger helped or hurt me at work?

>> What has anger done to my relationships — good or bad?

>> Has anger gotten me into trouble?

>> Has anger truly gotten me more of what I want?

>> Has my anger served to punish people in a way that they learn from?

>> Has anger affected my family — in good ways or bad?

TIP

After you complete your cost-benefit analysis, review the perceived benefits once again. Ask yourself whether addressing your anger truly means that you'd have to lose all those benefits. Many times people find that setting limits and expressing their anger more effectively help them maintain the benefits of their anger without the old costs.

When reviewing your cost-benefit analysis, also consider whether the items represent short- or long-term costs or benefits. For example, yelling at someone may feel good at the moment, but usually costs occur over the longer term.

REMEMBER

The absolute number of costs versus benefits isn't the key; what matters is how *important* the items are to you as a whole. For example, a single cost, such as being sent to jail, just might override a list of 20 seeming benefits.

2

Rethinking Anger

IN THIS PART . . .

Find anger in your body.

Learn some quick tips for anger management.

Look closely at anger triggers.

Untwist twisted thinking.

Give up being perfect.

Chapter **4**

Jump-Starting Anger Management

The initial thing to do when you feel anger coming on is to stop yourself from taking immediate action. The old saying, "He who hesitates is lost," doesn't apply here.

The idea that emotions need to just run their course is a myth — and a dangerous one at that. The sooner you take control of your anger, the better off you are (and that goes doubly for those around you who may end up on the receiving end of your wrath).

This chapter gives you a first-aid kit for your anger. You turn to first-aid kits for immediate help. Band-aids and gauze stop the bleeding. More intensive treatment comes later.

First, discover how to immediately tune into your internal anger signals in the form of physical sensations and emotions. Only after you're aware of those signals will you be prepared to do something different about them. Second, take advantage of some simple techniques for quickly quelling anger flare-ups. Finally, decide to avoid anger triggers in the short run. Later chapters give you more permanent solutions.

Increasing Awareness of Your Angry Feelings

Anger involves a complex mixture of bodily sensations, feelings, thoughts, and behaviors. Many folks with anger problems go from 0 miles an hour to 100 in an instant without knowing how they got there. This seemingly instantaneous process is reminiscent of the phrase *blind rage*. Blind rage involves striking out without any thought or conscious processing about what's going on or the possible future consequences for the behavior. By the way, court room judges don't usually consider blind rage as adequate justification for violence.

So, for many people with anger problems, the first steps are to slow the process down and increase awareness of anger's earliest warning signals. Those signals usually come in the form of bodily sensations and feelings. When you're aware of the early warning signs, you can pull out your first-aid kit.

TIP

Although the chapters in this book are designed to be read in any order you like, consider proceeding with this chapter soon *after* you feel ready to make changes with your anger issues. If you're conflicted about your desire to change, read through Chapter 3 that discusses the pros and cons of change.

Tuning into physiological responses

Your body is the *first responder* to anger triggers. These responses happen almost instantaneously, often without awareness. People all have their own unique pattern of physiological responses to anger triggers. Here are two examples of different responses:

Melissa notices her palms getting damp on her commute to work. Initially, she thinks that maybe her drive through traffic is causing her to feel tense. However, as weeks go by, she notices other physical signs, such as tightness in her throat and feeling excessively cold in the afternoon even though the building temperatures are ideal. Gradually, she connects these sensations to an awareness of various emotions.

On the other hand, **Bob** works at the same office and has different sensations on his way to work. He begins to notice tension throughout his body, an increased heart rate, and frequent stomach upset on his commute. At first, Bob has no idea why these feelings consistently accompany him on his drive to work. However, he, too, begins to connect his sensations to various feelings of unease.

So you may wonder what other kinds of physical sensations accompany the emergence of anger. The following list gives you a guide to many of these sensations, although the list could be endless. Be on the lookout for sensations like these:

- » Rapid breathing
- » Dizziness
- » Blushing
- » Face draining of color
- » Sweating
- » Body trembles
- » Hands trembling
- » Stomach upset
- » Tightness in throat
- » Clenched jaw
- » Clenched fist
- » Puffed-up posture
- » Teeth grinding
- » Headache
- » Feeling too hot or cold
- » Grimace
- » Glaring
- » Rapid pulse
- » Voice volume and tone changes

Circle the sensations you notice occurring repeatedly. Or list them in a file on your smartphone. You may recognize these physical responses also frequently go along with emotions other than anger. Good observation! To know what's what, you need to first become aware of these sensations in your body. Then you can connect them to various emotions and feelings.

TIP

If you discover that other emotions like anxiety, sadness, fear, or depression connect to these sensations, you may want to read the latest editions of *Depression For Dummies* and *Anxiety For Dummies*, both by yours truly and published by Wiley.

Finding angry feelings

You can think of feelings and emotions as the labels that apply to your various bodily sensations at any given time. Getting in touch with your emotions can help you understand and cope better. To see how this works, return to the examples of Melissa and Bob (discussed in the previous section). You may recall that they work together in the same office:

Melissa realizes that her bodily sensations are trying to tell her something about what she feels. She recognizes that she feels unsupported, unappreciated, and disrespected by her boss. Furthermore, these feelings lead to additional feelings of discomfort, irritation, and resentment toward her boss. She concludes that she needs to give thought to appropriate actions she can take, which may include confrontation and/or quitting.

Bob finds that tracking his bodily sensations alerts him to the fact that something is going dreadfully wrong, but he's not sure what at first. After a while, he grasps the idea that he's been feeling exasperated, especially after the weekly staff meetings where he believes his opinions are routinely dismissed. He's irritated and angry that he was recruited from a position he'd previously found greatly satisfying. He's also extremely frustrated and incensed that his boss monopolizes discussions and digresses into irrelevant trivia. Bob also examines his options.

Melissa and Bob avoid the temptation of acting impulsively on their feelings without forethought. They listen to their bodies and consider what feelings connect to those physical sensations. Then they begin to ponder options, but they have not acted as yet.

Start by reviewing the following list of emotions or feelings. This list, like the preceding list of sensations, is just a beginning. Feel free to add to it:

Aggravated	Frustrated
Agitated	Fuming
Annoyed	Fury
Baited	Goaded
Cranky	Hateful
Exasperated	Incensed
Flustered	Incited

Inflamed	Resentful
Infuriated	Riled
Irritated	Tense
On edge	Upset
Peeved	Uptight
Perturbed	Vicious
Provoked	Wound up
Rage	

As you go over the list, ask yourself which feelings capture the bodily sensations you're having. Again, circle or keep track of the feelings you experience frequently. Practice this exercise repeatedly, and you'll find yourself much more aware of when your mind and body are trying to tell you something's wrong.

You may not think all the feelings in this list relate to anger. For example, words such as *cranky, on edge, tense, frustrated*, and *uptight* may not conjure up an image of rage. However, upon examination, many people find that these feelings provide the kindling for more intense fire of anger.

Philosophers, psychologists, and scientists have debated for a few hundred years whether body sensations cause or precede feelings and emotions or the other way around. Some believe that feelings can exist completely independently of bodily sensations. The debate doesn't need to be solved here. For the current purpose, it doesn't matter. The important thing is that it's useful to separate feelings or emotions from bodily sensations when working with anger problems.

Rethinking Your Reactions

When bodily sensations and emotions tell you that you're feeling some degree of anger, you have a choice. You can continue to react in your same old ways — whether exploding, seething inside, becoming passive-aggressive, or whatever. Or you can stop, back up, pause.

Ask yourself the following questions:

>> For the rest of your life, do you want to simply react to your anger in the same mindless, predictable way you always have?

>> Do you want to always be a victim of your emotions?

>> Do you want to continue to apologize for your angry reactions by telling those you hurt, "I'm sorry, I don't know what came over me. I promise I won't act that way ever again"?

>> Do you want others to begin to judge you by your angry reactions (for example, "Stay away from that guy; he's got a bad temper!")?

Probably, your answer to each of these questions is a very clear "No." More than likely, you're ready for a change. So before you do anything else, you need to make the decision to *respond* rather than *react* to your anger. Granted, this strategy is a mental one (as all choices are), but it nevertheless *is* a strategy and a crucial one at that. To begin to understand the basic differences between reacting and responding to anger, consider Table 4-1.

TABLE 4-1   **Anger Reactions and Responses**

When You <u>React</u> to Anger, You Are . . .	When You <u>Respond</u> to Anger, You Are . . .
Reflexive	Thoughtful
Impulsive	Deliberate
Unpredictable	Predictable
Out of control	In control

What happens, you ask, if I choose to continue reacting as I always have to my anger? Don't I have a right to react to my anger any way I want to? Of course you do, as long as you're willing to keep paying the same consequences you always have, or worse. You can keep apologizing, trying to undo the harm your anger has done. Or you can choose to quit reacting and start choosing how you want to respond.

Your first-aid kit for anger contains the following suggestions: Be patient, be quiet, and lighten up. However, there are a few very rare exceptions to following these suggestions.

TIP

If you're being attacked by a black bear, experts usually suggest you roar and puff yourself up. (Grizzly bears are another matter that may call for other techniques like playing dead.) Actually, with either kind of bear, you're in deep trouble! Or if attacked by another person who's trying to throw you into a car trunk, the more noise you make, the better. Nevertheless, the suggestions in the following sections help in most circumstances.

Be patient

Emotions, including anger, are by their very nature transient experiences. Each episode of anger has a beginning point (onset), a middle phase (where it peaks and begins to recede), and an end point (resolution). Emotions also work on the principle of gravity: What goes up must inevitably come down.

Anger always resolves itself and will actually do so without any effort on your part. The average adult is over anger within five to ten minutes. You don't have to react in an attempt to make anger subside. The relief you're seeking from the tension and thoughts that accompany anger will come if you just give it enough time to pass. In fact, time is your ally. The real paradox here is that the more time you allow yourself to be angry, the sooner you'll be free of this emotion.

TIP

To give yourself enough time, follow these tips:

>> **Remind yourself that time is on your side.** No one, not the angriest person alive, stays angry very long.

>> **Remember that patience is a virtue.** No one ever had a heart attack or died an early death as a result of being too patient.

>> **Repeat to yourself as many times as necessary, "This, too, shall pass."** Sometimes a little wisdom goes a long way.

>> **Say to yourself repeatedly, "Less is more."** In managing an episode of anger, it often pays to take a more passive posture.

>> **Pull out grandma's old trick:** Ever so slowly, count to 10 in your mind. If you don't feel better, go all the way to 100.

>> **Take a few long, deep breaths:** Inhale to a count of 3 and exhale to a count of 5. Repeat as needed.

Be quiet

Quiet is the natural state of the body at rest. Venting your anger verbally only adds more tension, further elevating your heart rate, blood pressure, and so on. Just by being quiet for a few moments, while you continue to formulate your response to anger, helps you begin to calm down. This band-aid is a great anger-management tool, too. The moment you feel angry, close your mouth. Don't let a single word escape. The odds of saying something useful or productive are calculated as *exactly* 1 out of 1.483 billion!

Lighten up

If you want to stay angry (or worse yet, get even angrier), then by all means stay serious. Remind yourself that anger is no laughing matter. Don't even think about smiling. And, for goodness' sake, do *not* try to find the humor in whatever situation provoked your temper.

On the other hand, if you're trying to calm yourself down, you need to lighten up. For example, if you feel compelled to say something to the person at whom you're angry, start by saying, "You know it's funny that. . . ."

Mastering the Art of Avoidance

Rarely is it a good idea to avoid your feelings, especially for the long term. Generally, that's a very bad strategy. However, when it comes to anger, most people need time to learn anger-management skills. While you're learning, you may profit from staying out of trouble by avoiding trouble in the first place.

Avoiding the avoidable

In most people, emotions are situational. Something in the here and now irritates you or makes you mad. The emotion itself is tied to the situation in which it originates. As long as you remain in that provocative situation, you're likely to stay angry. If you *leave* the situation, the opposite is true: The emotion begins to fade as soon as you move away from the situation. Moving away from the situation prevents it from getting a grip on you.

Psychologists often advise clients to get some emotional distance from whatever is bothering them. One easy way to do that is to *geographically* separate yourself from the source of your anger. For example, if you get enraged in traffic, take a longer route if you need to or try to get flex time and commute when the traffic lessens. Or if you usually find yourself losing your cool around Aunt Beatrice, make sure you don't sit next to her at the next family gathering.

Avoiding the company of other angerholics

Your attempts to stop reacting and make the choice to respond to anger may also be difficult because you're surrounded by people with excessive anger. You know what they say about birds of a feather: They tend to flock together, which means you've probably actively sought the companionship of others with the same temperament.

What you need instead are some anger allies, the kind of people who can help you form *new* habits of responding effectively to anger. Look for people who . . .

>> Show by personal example how to express anger in a healthy way

>> Will actively listen and support your efforts to bring your anger under control

>> Are nonjudgmental

>> Have conquered their own anger demons

>> Are patient

>> Are compassionate, appreciating what a burden excessive anger is

>> Don't assume that what worked for them in bringing their anger under control will necessarily work for you

>> Are willing to be there for you at a time of emotional crisis

>> Don't pretend to have all the answers

>> Are willing to help but aren't willing to be responsible for your anger (that's your job!)

WARNING

You may have to distance yourself from a flock of companions, whether that represents a group of angry peers or angry family members. Walking away from your angry friends takes a good deal of courage and a lot of willpower, but you can do it, and you'll see the positive benefits in your own life very soon!

Engaging in Anti-Anger Actions

Early anger-management strategies include behaviors that delay or distract from impulsive, angry responses. Most anger diminishes if you give it a little time. The next three sections give you easy-to-use tools for delaying your angry reactions.

Finding distractions

You experience whatever captures your brain's attention. If you get aroused with anger, your brain turns its attention to that and away from other things. That's why anger can be such a disruptive emotion. The stronger the emotion, the more captivated your brain becomes. You can be irritated and continue to at least partially attend to other things. But rage, now that's a different story.

Intense emotional experiences — positive or negative — override your senses. The good news, however, is that the brain can be distracted, meaning it can turn its attention elsewhere at any point in time. So the trick in anger management is to give your brain something else to attend to besides anger. Here are a few ideas to distract yourself when you feel anger coming on:

>> Play a game on your phone.

>> Repeat a word or phrase such as "calm down," "peace," or "chill."

>> Think about a vacation you're planning or start to plan one.

>> Count the freckles on the person's face you're talking to.

>> Either squeeze an ice cube in your hand or rub it on your face.

>> Try some aerobic exercise like jogging or jumping jacks.

>> Clean your house for a few minutes.

>> Go for a walk.

REMEMBER

Distraction strategies usually work within a few minutes. So you don't have to go jog for half an hour or clean your house for an afternoon — just five or ten minutes will likely do you a lot of good.

Doing the opposite of anger

Another great strategy for getting an early jump on anger is to find ways of acting quite the opposite of how you're feeling. Your brain has a way of observing your behaviors and often starts to make you *feel* the way you're behaving. Furthermore, all these techniques usually hold anger at bay for a long enough time for it to start coming down on its own. Try these ideas:

>> **Practice a facial expression that looks like Mona Lisa.** Practice before you actually get angry. Put a slight smile on your face. Then pull it out of your toolkit when anger strikes.

>> **Intentionally speak more slowly and softly.** Again, practice ahead of time helps prepare you for when you need it. You might repeat "slow and soft" inside your mind as you speak.

>> **Walk much more slowly.** Most people have a natural rhythm to their walking. Anger speeds you up. Whatever your pace tends to be, slow it down.

>> **Practice adopting a calm posture.** Use a mirror to help you with this one. Start by practicing an angry posture. Puff yourself up, grimace, and tighten up. Then try an opposite, relaxed posture. Let your shoulders soften a bit and your eyes and forehead relax. Think of a gentle flower.

>> **Start breathing in a slow, rhythmic pattern.** This technique isn't the same as taking extremely long, deep breaths as suggested in the earlier section, "Be patient." Instead, here we're suggesting you practice breathing at the pace you would while lying on a pristine beach in the Bahamas. Imagine feeling tranquil and serene and have yourself breathe the way you would there — yes, even if something has led to angry feelings.

Crushing candy

A simple, inexpensive, handy way to take immediate action when you find yourself getting angry is to suck on some type of hard candy until it's all gone. Unlike in the game Candy Crush, you should *not* crush it, but suck on it. (*Note:* If you have diabetes or metabolic syndrome, be sure to use sugar-free candy.) Sucking on candy takes only about five minutes, but it short-circuits the natural progression of anger.

TECHNICAL
STUFF

So why does it work?

>> **This technique takes advantage of the link between the sucking reflex and achieving a state of calm that is evident in all newborn infants.** Any mother knows that giving an infant something to suck on alleviates the baby's distress. That's why pacifiers are so popular — and difficult for some children to give up as they get older.

>> **The technique involves the ingestion of something sweet — sugar — and sweet sensations are associated at the level of the brain with pleasure, which is the antithesis of anger.** The candy literally sweetens your disposition! However, some people thoroughly enjoy a sour taste; that can work, too, because it's pleasurable for you.

>> **It buys you enough time to formulate a response to your initial anger instead of just reacting to it (see Chapter 6).** An angry reaction is immediate, impulsive, thoughtless, predictable, and typically leads to consequences that are later regretted. An angry response, on the other hand, is more deliberate, engages the mind, takes advantage of past experience, isn't always predictable (what works in one situation may not work in another), and more often has positive consequences.

>> **Patiently sucking on candy runs counter to the combative, behavioral tendencies that characterize many people.** Sucking is a passive response, not an aggressive one. And anger is essential only if you're moving against the world after you're provoked.

>> **By putting something in your mouth to suck on, you can't immediately verbalize your anger in ways that escalate the conflict between you and others or cause you regret later on.** Telling someone "I'm sorry" after you've assaulted her with your angry words and tone of voice is useless and ineffective — it doesn't help you and it certainly doesn't help the other person.

REMEMBER

Don't bite the candy. It defeats the purpose of the exercise by shortening the length of time before you act on your anger and, more important, by indulging your aggressive personality. (Aggressive personalities seem to want to constantly "bite" life rather than savor it.)

Chapter **5**

Connecting Events to Thoughts and Feelings

Have you ever noticed how some people seem to fly off the handle over almost anything? Other people remain calm in the middle of a hurricane. Does that puzzle you? Consider the following examples:

Shelley inserts her credit card into the metro card ticket machine. She enters the amount for a 30-day pass. Nothing happens. She tries again — same result. Meanwhile, the train pulls into the station. She realizes she'll miss this train and arrive late to work. She shoves the machine in frustration. She stomps over to the ticket booth, and a disinterested metro worker takes his time getting her ticket. When she finally boards the train, she finds it packed. Her senses recoil at the smells and tight space. A passenger getting on at the first stop runs into her and grabs her shoulder to steady himself. She's furious and growls, "What the f*&@ is the matter with you? Keep your hands to yourself!"

Brian has the same trouble that Shelley did with the metro card machine. He, too, has concerns about running late for work but knows there's not much he can do about it. He boards the same train and encounters the same smells and the same crowded jostling. He calmly takes out his e-reader and opens an engaging novel. People push him and his body sways, yet he remains calm and unperturbed.

Why does Shelley lose her cool while Brian goes with the flow? This chapter, helps you understand why people respond to similar events so differently. First, it reviews the typical triggers for anger. Then it explains why those triggers don't directly cause angry reactions, even though many people think otherwise. Finally, the chapter illustrates how to connect specific events to feelings and interpretations of those events. Armed with this knowledge, you can begin to change the way you think about the things that happen to you.

Reviewing Anger Triggers

Chapter 2 describes in detail the major categories or themes of people's hot buttons. When specific events lead to angry feelings, they can usually be classified under one or more of the following general categories:

>> Being treated unfairly

>> Responding to time pressure and frustration

>> Experiencing dishonesty and/or disappointment

>> Encountering threats to self-esteem

>> Troubling relationships

>> Running into prejudice and discrimination

>> Experiencing physical problems

>> Getting attacked

>> Existential threats

When events lead to anger, try asking yourself which of these broad themes capture what just happened. Were you treated unfairly, frustrated, disappointed, or discriminated against? Were you frustrated with chronic pain? Were you verbally or physically attacked? Did someone lie to you or insult you or your family? Were you disturbed by world events that you had little control over?

The next three sections show you how your anger may focus on the past, present, or future. All three start with some *specific event* (when you feel angry, it's usually related to one of the previously listed trigger categories). Some anger occurs when you look back at events; other anger happens immediately following an event. Some people look to the future and get angry.

Holding onto anger from the past for dear life

When anger invades your head in response to thoughts about events that happened a few weeks, months, years, or even decades ago, you're still dwelling on something that happened to you in the past. Examples include thoughts like these:

>> "I'll never get over how my parents abused me; they've ruined my life!"

>> "I can't stop thinking about how unfair my third-grade teacher was."

>> "My last job was the worst experience of my life; I'll never forgive them!"

>> "If only I'd been treated as well as my brother, I might be a success today."

>> "I'll never be whole again after the trauma I went through."

>> "I can't get past having lost my home in a hurricane."

Bad things happen to almost everyone at one time or another — it's part of being alive. Holding on to anger from the past is a not-so-great way to ruin your present life. When you *ruminate* incessantly by going over the same old event again and again, nothing gets solved, nothing gets fixed.

You simply can't change the past no matter what you do. So stop trying! Okay, that's not always so easy to do. Therefore, consider looking at Chapters 9, 10, 16, and 17 for information about dealing with ruminations and anger from long ago.

Looking at anger in the here and now

Most of the time, the events that precede people's angry reactions happen in real time, in real life. Here are some specific examples:

>> Someone calls you stupid, thereby threatening your self-esteem.

>> You don't get the raise you deserve and thus feel treated unfairly.

>> Your boss demands a report in an hour, and you feel there's no time.

>> You open an angry text message from your cousin.

>> Your partner forgets to take out the trash, and you feel disappointed and let down.

My guess is that if you start tracking your anger reactions, you'll see that they largely happen in the present. But that clearly isn't always the case. See Chapters 11 through 15 for more information about anger in present, everyday life.

Looking ahead for something to feel angry about

Sometimes, the event that angers you hasn't even happened. You're just sitting around daydreaming and *wham* — you're hit with a blast of anger. You suddenly start anticipating something that *might* happen in the future. Possibilities of such future-oriented anger include thoughts like these:

>> "I just know that the meeting tomorrow will blow up, and I'll get blamed."

>> "My ex-wife and her lawyer are out to screw me; I'm sure they're going to try to take my kids away."

>> "They're going to be working on road construction on my commute for the next decade."

>> "I'll never get ahead in this firm."

>> "My father-in-law will never approve of my decision, and we'll get into a huge argument like always."

>> "When I go to that anger-management class, it will be a huge waste of my valuable time."

TIP

None of these things have happened yet. Some of these events may occur; others no doubt won't. Anger about conceivable future events isn't likely to solve anything or help you. Try to stay focused on the present rather than letting the future ruin your present moment. See Chapters 9 and 10 for more information about how to deal with future-oriented anger with present-day strategies.

Knowing the Difference Between Events and Causes

People naturally respond to their own anger by chalking it up to whatever happened to them. In effect, they're saying to themselves that events directly cause their anger. They truly believe that they have no ability to control their anger. After all, they say, emotions and feelings are created by events. So you may hear them declare the following:

>> "She made me so angry I had to tell her off!"

>> "I absolutely can't stand it when people cut me off in traffic!"

>> "My boss expects the impossible; he really sets me off!"

>> "My teacher said girls can't do math; he makes me so mad!"

>> "He put me down, so I had to retaliate!"

>> "My husband cheated on me, so I had to get back at him!"

>> "I blow my top whenever my kids don't do what I say!"

>> "Those damn security agents made me miss my plane!"

>> "That referee really ticks me off; that was an obvious foul!"

>> "That stupid vending machine took my money!"

In all these cases, the angry people attribute their reactions to what *happened* to them. They take no responsibility. Furthermore, they believe that anger, irritation, annoyance, or rage was the only reasonable thing to feel.

The fact is, if you believe that you've never said something similar to this list, you're probably kidding yourself. Everyone gets mad and blames someone else from time to time. It's human nature.

To dig a little deeper, consider the first example: "She made me so angry that I had to tell her off!" There are a couple of problems with that statement. First, no one can actually "cause" someone to have one feeling or another. Whatever the person did in this situation, you could respond in a number of different ways. Say, for example, that the offense in this case was someone insulting you. One response, of course, is getting angry and telling the offender off. Another response, believe it or not, is to walk away. But that response would probably require a different way of *thinking* about incidents like these.

What does *thinking* mean? Thoughts refer to the way you interpret or perceive what's happened to you — in other words, the *meaning* that the event holds for you. Sometimes, you're even aware of specific things you're saying to yourself about the event. For example, consider the item, "That stupid vending machine took my money!" When people call machines stupid, they may not be aware of having specific thoughts, but they feel angry. However, they're probably interpreting (or thinking about) the event in one of the following ways:

>> "Machines *should* work!"

>> "I *should* get what I want, and I'm not!"

>> "The machine was out to get me!"

But you can respond in other ways to a machine that takes your money. For example, you could have thoughts like these:

>> "I guess machines malfunction like anything else in life."

>> "Machines don't think or feel actual feelings so I guess they're not really out to get me."

>> "It's a little frustrating that it took my money, but it's hardly the end of the world."

>> "On a scale of 1 to 100, this happening is about a 3. I need to get over it and not let it ruin my day."

Connecting Events, Feelings, and Thoughts

Connecting the dots helps you form a more complete understanding of what's going on when you feel angry. In this case, the dots consist of events, feelings, and thoughts. This method uncovers your own personal pattern of anger.

Many people assume that their feelings are caused directly by the things that happen to them, such as the way people treat them (for more on this, see the earlier sections in this chapter). But there's an important go-between — specifically, the thoughts people have about those events. This section walks you through two scenarios with different interpretations and responses.

REMEMBER

You can view most events from various angles. If you habitually feel angry, annoyed, and irritated, you may want to consider how your interpretations may be to blame rather than actual events. When you start to feel angry, consider taking that feeling as a signal to slow down, back up, and rethink what's happened.

Rethinking helps, but sometimes people need assistance in figuring out how to do that. Chapter 6 guides you through a process that enables you to adopt new, more adaptive ways of thinking about or interpreting the things that happen to you.

Playing poker with John and Dave

John and Dave provide a nice example for illustrating precisely how changing the way you think about or interpret events changes the way you feel.

Here's the deal. **Dave** is playing poker with his buddies. He's winning by a wide margin, even though he isn't exactly a great poker player. He and everyone at the table are surprised at his success this night. **John** starts getting increasingly annoyed as his pile of chips dwindles. When Dave rakes in another pot, John complains, "Geez, Dave! How many cards do you have up your sleeve anyway?"

Tables 5-1, 5-2, and 5-3 show how the same event — John's comments — results in three different feelings because of the different thoughts that Dave could have about John's comments. Each table shows the same event, a different thought (or interpretation), and the feeling associated with that interpretation.

TABLE 5-1   ### Dave's Event, Thought, Feeling: Example 1

Event	Dave's Thought	Dave's Feeling
John says, "Geez, Dave. How many cards do you have up your sleeve anyway?"	"Wow, how dare he accuse me of cheating! He's no friend of mine anymore."	Angry, rageful

In this example, Dave thinks about John's comment as a personal attack on his integrity. In this case, the trigger categories are a *threat to self-esteem* and a *verbal attack*. However, there are other ways he could have thought about this event, one of which is shown in Table 5-2.

TABLE 5-2   ### Dave's Event, Thought, Feeling: Example 2

Event	Dave's Thought	Dave's Feeling
John says, "Geez, Dave. How many cards do you have up your sleeve anyway?"	"I'm a horrible card player, and he's really saying I'm just running a streak of dumb luck."	Insecure, embarrassed

In this example, Dave interprets the comment as a put-down about his lack of poker skills. That thought leads to feelings of insecurity and embarrassment. Note another interpretation in Table 5-3.

TABLE 5-3   ### Dave's Event, Thought, Feeling: Example 3

Event	Dave's Thought	Dave's Feeling
John says, "Geez, Dave. How many cards do you have up your sleeve anyway?"	"John's a funny guy and probably jealous that I'm winning for about the first time in my life!"	Amused, content

In this example, Dave interprets John's comments as a joke. Therefore, his feelings remain positive. Dave realizes that he's winning and other people at the table are noticing and maybe feeling a tad jealous, but that's okay.

One event with three different interpretations leads to three completely different reactions.

Banking with Rebecca

Rebecca's story provides another example of how the same specific event can lead to various interpretations resulting in quite different feelings or emotions.

> **Rebecca** drives to the bank on her lunch hour. She doesn't have a lot of time, but she thinks she can get back to work by 1:00 p.m. The line moves more slowly than she expects. She finally gets to the teller window and expects to be remembered because she's been there frequently for the past five years. The teller looks up at her and asks for her identification.

Tables 5-4, 5-5, and 5-6 illustrate how this event could play out in various ways depending on Rebecca's perceptions or interpretations of the request.

TABLE 5-4   **Rebecca's Event, Thought, Feeling: Example 1**

Event	Rebecca's Thought	Rebecca's Feeling
Bank teller asks for Rebecca's identification.	"That teller knows me perfectly well. She's intentionally slowing things down. This is insulting and outrageous."	Angry, furious

Rebecca already feels a bit irritated and pressured about time. That sense of time pressure primes her to interpret events with a negative bias. And, in fact, she does. Her *interpretation* of the event in Example 1 leads directly to her feelings of anger and fury. The trigger categories (see Chapter 2 for more information about common triggers for anger) for her thoughts about the event are *time pressure* and thinking she's *being treated unfairly*. But there are alternative ways to look at this event. See Table 5-5 for another possible reaction.

TABLE 5-5   **Rebecca's Event, Thought, Feeling: Example 2**

Event	Rebecca's Thought	Rebecca's Feeling
Bank teller asks for Rebecca's identification.	"What a pain! Tellers have to ask everyone for ID, even though they absolutely know who people are. I hope I make it back to work on time."	Mild frustration, worry

In Example 2, Rebecca views the situation in a different manner. She understands that tellers have to ask for ID, but she doesn't take it personally. She has feelings of mild frustration and worry about getting back to work on time, nothing more. Table 5-6 shows Rebecca perceiving the event in one more way.

TABLE 5-6   **Rebecca's Event, Thought, Feeling: Example 3**

Event	Rebecca's Thought	Rebecca's Feeling
Bank teller asks for Rebecca's identification.	"Poor Cindy. She works so hard. Why do they make her ask a stupid question when she knows the answer? I'm glad I don't work here."	Empathy, compassion

In Example 3, Rebecca's thoughts exhibit an entirely new perspective. She actually puts herself in the teller's shoes. By doing so, she avoids personalizing the event and actually feels a positive, warm feeling for someone she knows. This reaction puts her in a much better place than the previous two examples.

Chapter **6**

Reexamining Angry Thoughts

This is not exactly the first book to discuss the effect that thoughts have on feelings and emotional reactions to events. In fact, a guy back in the first century spoke about this same issue quite eloquently. Epictetus, a slave born in 55 A.D., who was later freed and became a philosopher, declared, "People are not disturbed by things, but the view they take of them."

His wisdom has truly endured the test of time. In the 20th century, this essential philosophy inspired the founders of cognitive therapy who put Epictetus's insights into concrete, easy-to-understand practice. In doing so, these founders transformed the foundations and practice of psychology. And numerous studies have confirmed the value of this transformation. Simply put, cognitive therapy works to decrease anxiety, depression, anger, and other emotional problems by helping people change their perceptions.

This chapter lays out how to apply a cognitive therapy approach to the problem of anger. It centers on Epictetus's stance that when you find yourself feeling upset, disturbed, or angry, it's often not what *happened* to you so much as how *you're looking* at the situation or event. However, taking this perspective isn't as easy as it sounds. That's because most people believe that their thoughts are inherently accurate. Hang in there, as you'll see how to question your thinking to discover possible distortions.

REMEMBER

Everyone has distortions in thinking. People acquire these inaccurate perceptions from life experiences, parents, peers, and culture. They *don't choose* to have twisted thinking, but they can discover ways to untwist their thinking.

People with anger problems don't distort everything that happens to them all the time. Sometimes, with some events, they see things quite accurately. However, when anger rears its ugly head, more often than not, one or more distortions cloud their vision.

Uncovering Distortions in Thinking

This section guides you through the most common distortions of thinking that easily lead to anger. If you struggle with anger, you may think that your spin on things clearly represents reality and that no other view makes sense. Of course, you have a right to feel angry about issues such as unfairness, threats, frustrations, and put-downs. But what if you were given a path that leads to another way to view issues that have been making you angry over and over again? Would you consider taking it? If you're reading this book, you're probably searching for something new. So take a look at what follows. See what path you want to take.

Filtering

The angry mind has a pair of glasses that allows certain information in while filtering out other important data. This type of mind zeroes in on insulting, unfair, irritating, and frustrating aspects of events. I walk you through how filtering works and examine an example of it in the next two sections.

Discarding positives and focusing on negatives

Most events contain a complex array of positive and negative implications. The brain naturally wants to simplify things. So, for example, when people run into traffic, most will have a simple, straightforward perspective — one that, more often than not, dwells on negatives. The following are some examples of simple thoughts in response to heavy traffic:

>> "This is a bit annoying."

>> "This is horrible."

>> "I can't expect traffic to always run smoothly."

>> "Hmm, time to kick back and listen to music."

>> "I have to be at an appointment in three minutes; I'll never make it."

>> "I like the challenge of driving in heavy traffic."

>> "If people in this city would just drive right, this would never happen."

>> "I don't like to be late, but it's not the end of the world."

>> "The traffic is congested, but it's because of the booming economy here."

Which thought accurately interprets the event? Well, they all have an *element* of truth to them. The angry mind is likely to go to only those viewpoints that are negative, over the top, and upsetting. And it filters out any possible positive aspect of the situation.

Now, no one expects you to believe that heavy traffic is particularly a good thing! But if you can include a positive aspect, or at least a neutral element, or focus on milder ways of thinking about it, you may calm down just a bit.

Looking at filtering in action

The following dialogue between a customer and an automobile service technician demonstrates filtering in action.

Technician: Welcome to our service center; how can I help you?

Customer: I'd like an oil change.

Technician: No problem. You can wait in our lounge — there's WiFi, coffee, and doughnuts.

Customer: Great. I have some email to catch up on.

Thirty minutes later, the technician returns.

Technician: Excuse me. Our service manager noticed that you have 53,400 miles. You're overdue for the 50,000-mile scheduled maintenance. Do you want us to go ahead and complete that for you?

Customer: Well, I guess. How long will that take?

Technician: Actually, I think we can get it done in another 45 minutes to an hour.

Customer: Okay, if you think it will be done on time, go ahead.

Ninety minutes later, the technician returns.

Technician: Okay, we have everything done. Come over to my desk, and we can settle up.

Customer: I thought you could have this done in under an hour. I've been here for a total of two hours.

Technician: Yes, I'm sorry about that. We got behind. Your bill comes to $786.

Customer: Are you kidding me? No one said anything about hundreds of dollars when I just came in for a damn oil change!

Technician: I know it seems like a lot. As you should know, the scheduled maintenance is a set price. And you can see all the services and parts on the bill.

Customer: Look, I came in here for an oil change and planned to be out of here in 30 minutes. This feels like bait and switch. And what do you mean, "I should know"? Are you calling me stupid?

Technician: Of course not. Tell you what, you've been a great customer; I think I can knock 10 percent off your bill. We really didn't mean to deceive you, but I hope you understand that you were due for the 50,000-mile service.

Customer: So you admit that you did deceive me — you just didn't mean to.

Technician: No, actually, I don't think we did deceive you. I did ask your permission, and I am offering you a 10 percent discount.

Customer: When you asked my permission, you didn't tell me it would cost a small fortune. And I sure didn't come in here to be told I don't understand things and that I'm stupid.

Notice that the customer engages in several instances of filtering out positives and focusing on negatives. First, the customer zeroes in on the service taking longer than expected (even though that's a pretty common experience). The customer also dwells on the bill, even though he filters out that he didn't ask for a quote. When the technician tries to explain the bill, the customer is offended by the phrases "hope you understand" and "as you should know," while interpreting them as insults.

The customer ignored the technician's statements about being a good customer, offering a discount, and asking for permission to do the service. The customer also focused on the word *deceive* and filtered out the technician's words *didn't mean to*.

Catastrophizing

Catastrophizing refers to the habit of exaggerating the negative consequences and the meaning of events. The old saying, "making mountains out of mole hills," captures the essence of catastrophizing. Three different ways of catastrophizing appear in the following sections.

Awfulizing

Those who "awfulize" look at events as *horrible, terrible,* and *dreadful.* Actually, that's not the problem per se. When you call genocide, massive earthquakes, pandemics, violent crime, and tsunamis awful, you have a good point! But people with anger problems have a way of using those terms to refer to everyday hassles and bothers. Here are a few awfulizing statements:

>> "The 9-percent drop in the stock market is going to *ruin* me!"

>> "The frosting on the wedding cake has a smashed flower. That's *horrible!*"

>> "I can't believe I have a stain on my shirt for the interview. That's *dreadful.* I'll never get the job now."

>> "This heat is utterly *unbearable.*"

Global ratings

This form of catastrophizing involves sweeping, negative labels that you put on yourself or others. These judgments condemn and vilify. So inevitably, you end up angry with yourself or others. Some examples of global ratings include

>> "I'm a *total failure.*"

>> "He's a *complete idiot.*"

>> "That sales person is *nothing* but a *screw-up.*"

>> "My sister is an *absolute loser.*"

Magnifying

Magnifying represents the final type of catastrophizing. When people distort events with magnification, they're exaggerating the amount of distress or upset that's called for. In a sense, this mental strategy adds an *-est* to *awful, horrible,* and *terrible.* In other words, magnifying turns events into the absolutely worst ever. Here are some examples:

>> "That's the *nastiest* meal I ever ate!"

>> "She's the *vilest* person in the world."

>> "That kid is the *cruelest* bully ever."

>> "That politician is the *most corrupt in history.*"

>> "That office is the *sickest* place ever, and the director is the *craziest* person I've ever dealt with."

Looking at the wrong source

The angry mind also has a knack for attributing the cause of upsetting events to the wrong person or reason. This distortion comes in two types. The first looks inward and the second looks outward as described in the next two sections.

Personalizing

This distortion leads people to get very angry at themselves. Perhaps you've done it yourself. Something goes wrong that could be due to lots of different things, but somehow you manage to blame everything on yourself. Personalizing also takes place when people take neutral comments personally. Following are a few examples of personalizing:

>> "My son doesn't turn in his homework. It's *all my fault.*"

>> "My supervisor tells the staff we need to increase productivity; she's *really talking about me.*"

>> "Someone tells me, 'the picnic got rained out,' and I conclude that *I never should have scheduled it for this day.*"

>> "My wife left me because I obviously *wasn't good enough.*"

>> "My friend is unusually quiet today. He must *not like me anymore.*"

>> "My workgroup gets a bad evaluation, and the boss must think *I messed up bad.*"

>> "My car got dinged in a parking lot. *I never should have* parked there."

Blaming

This type of distortion points the finger away from the actual source or sources of the problem and blames someone or something else. Usually people blame that person or happening entirely, even though other causes of fault exist.

Angry people do a lot of blaming. Blaming gets the blamer off the hook and puts responsibility elsewhere. Examples include

>> "The mess this country is in is totally the _____'s fault." (You fill in the blank.)

>> "You always ask me to watch your kids, and I end up having no time for myself."

>> "My car's blind spot sensors didn't warn me about the car in the other lane, so I got into a wreck."

> » "I could be happy if it weren't for my husband's insensitivity."

> » "Your phone call made me late to work."

WARNING

If you blame others for your misfortunes, you're generally not seeing that you own *at least a piece* of the problem. Look carefully for all the possible contributors to the issue, and don't forget to include looking in the mirror.

Overgeneralizing

This type of thought distortion takes a single event and imagines that it applies to an excessive range of possible events in the future. For example, someone who encounters rudeness by a checker at a grocery store starts assuming that all checkers are rude. Take a look at Jill's story next.

> **Jill** was brought up in an abusive family and has a tough time opening up and trusting anyone. Now an adult, she leads a pretty restricted life. However, over time, she gets to be friends with a co-worker named Stephanie. They go out for a weekly lunch and gradually begin to confide in each other. Jill reveals to Stephanie the details about her abusive childhood. She feels relieved to finally share her story. A few weeks later, another co-worker remarks to Jill, "Wow! I heard about your childhood. No wonder you're so uptight."
>
> Immediately, Jill knows that Stephanie broke her promise to keep her story confidential. She vows never to trust anyone ever again. She concludes that clearly people can never be trusted.

Jill has good reasons for not trusting people. After all, her childhood consisted of broken promises and abuse. Now, her first friend in years shatters her fledgling belief that perhaps a few people could be trusted. No wonder she doesn't want to believe in anybody again. However, her *overgeneralization* costs her a lot by isolating her almost completely from potential friends and intimacy.

Judging

You may notice that some of the types of thought distortions are a bit similar to one another. You're right. Often, a single thought involves more than one distortion. For example, you may think that blaming, judging, and global ratings sound rather overlapping.

The critical, distinguishing characteristic of *judging* is that people assume that others' behavior and actions are immoral, offensive, and inappropriate. A sampling of judging thoughts include

>> "He *should* never have acted that way."

>> "Her behavior is way out of line."

>> "You lie!"

>> "I'm furious that she cheated; that behavior corrupts the whole system."

Black-and-white thinking

People engage in black-and-white thinking *all the time*. And that statement is a perfect example. When black-and-white thinking comes into play, people see few grays or middle ground. Clues to this type of thinking can be found easily simply by examining a few extreme words, such as the following:

>> Always (as in, "you *always* argue with me")

>> Never (as in, "you *never* show me affection")

>> Totally (as in "you're *totally* wrong")

>> Absolutely (as in "she has *absolutely* nothing to offer")

Mind reading

Family members and close friends resort to this thought distortion frequently. In fact, human beings engage in this strategy almost naturally. And, at times, mind reading has some value — for example, when people try to empathize or figure out whether someone is a threat.

On the other hand, mind reading sometimes gets you into trouble. For example, if you automatically assume that someone's frown indicates displeasure with you, you're simultaneously engaging in personalizing (covered in the earlier section on personalizing) and mind reading. Consider the following example:

Sam and **Pete** sit down with their laptops after dinner. Sam says, "Pete, did you see that story about the latest crisis in Asia? Where's the world going anyway?"

Pete remains silent, focused on his screen. Sam interprets Pete's silence as disinterest and rejection. He says with sarcasm in his voice, "Wow. You sure do care about what I have to say. Thanks a lot."

Pete looks up from his screen and says, "What? What did you say?"

Sam says, "This is what's wrong with our relationship."

Pete responds with annoyance, "What are you talking about? I was reading some important email and didn't process what you were saying. Let's try again from the top, okay?"

This conversation probably repeats itself over and over with Sam and Pete as well as in countless other relationships. When you make assumptions about what other people are thinking (in other words, try to read their mind), those assumptions may erupt in conflict that needn't happen.

TIP

When you *think* someone is thinking something, check it out before you launch an attack. Doing so just might save you considerable grief.

I-can't-stand-its

It's surprising how many people go to this thought distortion. They predict that they can't handle or manage to get through all sorts of events. In other words, they say something to the effect of "*I can't stand it.*"

Almost everyone makes this statement here and there. Unfortunately, if taken too seriously, this distortion prevents people from actively coping and finding solutions. Instead, they moan, groan, complain, and give up. Here are some examples:

>> "I can't stand it when people don't agree with me."

>> "I can't tolerate long lines."

>> "I can't stand doctors who won't listen to me."

>> "I can't stand disrespect; I go berserk when that happens."

TIP

"I can't stand it" goes along with low frustration tolerance. That's unfortunate because life presents just about everybody with lots of frustrating experiences. The good news: You can increase your frustration tolerance just like you can exercise to increase your strength and physical fitness. But it does take lots of practice. See Chapter 10 for strategies to help foster increased frustration tolerance. Also see the section "Becoming more tolerant," later in this chapter.

Feeling entitled

A sense of *entitlement* frequently accompanies anger. Entitlement refers to a belief in an inherent, deep-seated *right* to get what you want and that you're more deserving of special treatment and privileges than other people. Those with a sense of entitlement believe that they're exempt from many rules that apply to other people. Thus, when entitled people don't get what they want, their anger flares. Consider these indications of entitlement:

>> "My interests and agendas are more important than other people's."

>> "It's okay for me to be late for meetings or to cancel appointments because I have important reasons for what I do, but I get enraged when others try to pull that on me."

>> "It's okay for *me* to drive at 138 miles an hour on a public highway because *I* know what I'm doing."

>> "I have no problem with offending other people when I'm right, and I usually am."

>> "People should pitch in to help with my projects, and I have little interest in theirs."

>> "I find it deeply offensive when people don't do what I want, and I feel furious when that happens."

Smoothing Out Distortions in Thinking

REMEMBER

Most distorted thoughts involve more than one distortion. The preceding section differentiates subtleties among various types of distortions, but they often overlap.

Distortions contaminate your thinking. Knowing about distortions helps you *reconsider* the absolute, unquestioned accuracy of your thoughts.

Don't assume that all your thoughts are wrong or, for that matter, right. Rather, take out a magnifying glass and start looking at your thoughts like an objective, skeptical detective. The following sections show you how.

Checking the evidence

Take the perspective that your thoughts or interpretations of events may or may not be true. Checking the evidence helps you consider information that can help sort things out. The following ideas and questions serve as guides for accomplishing this goal:

>> Is there any solid evidence for the absolute truth in my thought?

>> Do I have experiences that would contradict this thought?

>> Is it possible I am exaggerating?

>> Am I filtering out information that could alter my thought?

>> Have I ever handled something like this without getting angry?

>> Are there sources of blame other than the target of my anger?

Using a few of the anger-arousing thoughts from earlier sections in this chapter, Tables 6-1 and 6-2 weigh the evidence.

TABLE 6-1   **Checking the Evidence: Example 1**

Anger-Arousing Thought	Checking the Evidence	The Evidence
I'd be happy if it weren't for my husband's insensitivity.	Do I have experiences that would contradict this thought?	Well, I was happy with him for six years. I'm guessing he was just as insensitive then.
	Am I filtering out information that could alter my thought?	Actually, I am pretty happy with him most of the time; I just get really annoyed when he's insensitive.

TABLE 6-2   **Checking the Evidence: Example 2**

Anger-Arousing Thought	Checking the Evidence	The Evidence
I can't tolerate long lines.	Is it possible I am exaggerating?	Okay, I admit I've lived through hundreds of long lines in my life so I guess it's annoying, but I can tolerate it.
	Are there other sources of blame than the target of my anger?	Actually, I guess I get this way when I'm running late and haven't left enough time for myself.

Moderating extremist words

Toning down extremist words tamps anger down. Anger is a big emotion, and anger requires truly powerful words to keep it fueled. Extremist words appear throughout the earlier section "Uncovering Distortions in Thinking."

Benjamin Franklin reputedly recommended doing everything in moderation, including moderation. Those words have also been credited to a variety of other folks, so it's not clear who really said it first. Nonetheless, the advice is terrific.

Tune into words you're saying to yourself that go over the top and unrealistically depict situations as bigger and more important than they really are. Table 6-3 shows you how typical, angry thoughts contain loads of extremist words and how the thoughts change when you substitute moderate terms.

TABLE 6-3   **Moderating Extremist Words Example**

Angry Thought	Moderate Thought
I can't believe I have a stain on my shirt for the interview; that's dreadful. I'll never get the job now.	Oops, I have a stain on my shirt for the interview. That's too bad. I hope the interviewer doesn't notice.
My sister is an absolute loser.	My sister often disappoints me.
You always argue with me.	You argue with me more than I'd like.
I'm furious that she cheated; that corrupts the whole system.	I'm upset that she cheated; that can encourage others to take advantage of the system.

Taking the perspective of a friend

When people bog down in irritation, anger, or rage, rarely do they stop and reflect. Anger tends to be impulsive. This technique suggests that you try stepping back and delay any reaction for a few moments. Assume a friend comes to you describing an incident similar to the one that is making you angry. Now ask yourself the following questions:

>> Would I suggest that my friend respond with anger?

>> What alternative to anger might I suggest to my friend?

>> How would I tell my friend to look at the event?

>> If I told my friend to react with anger, would that really be the best option?

Consider how one person uses this technique during an annoying interaction with a plumber.

Ellen calls for a plumber because there's no hot water coming out of her shower-head. She's a bit irritated because she'd had a complete remodel of her bathroom less than six months ago. She had an instant hot water feature installed that she really likes. The plumber tells her that the system was installed improperly and will cost $325 to fix. She's about to explode, but she's learned to stop and back up.

So instead, Ellen asks herself what she might recommend to a friend in this situation. She realizes she'd probably tell the friend that the system should be under warranty and suggest calling the original contractor. So she calmly asks the plumber to hold off until she checks with the contractor. In the end, she saves herself both money and grief by taking the perspective of a friend.

Becoming more tolerant

Anger is the emotion of intolerance. Intolerance means you don't accept another person's viewpoint or behavior. Anger says that you think you're right and the other person is wrong. It can't be any simpler than that.

Anger defends listeners against any change in their ways of thinking. Instead of accepting the challenge of an honest difference of opinion, intolerant people resort to intimidation, insult, or withdrawal — all fueled by anger — as a way of rigidly holding on to their beliefs.

REMEMBER

The more intolerant people are, the more intense their anger.

The next time you find yourself getting angry about something another person says or does, do the following:

TIP

>> **Remind yourself that if you're secure in your way of thinking, you have absolutely nothing to defend.** Just because someone else thinks differently from the way you think doesn't mean you're wrong or that you necessarily have to justify your own beliefs and actions.

>> **Instead of being defensive (that's what intolerance is all about!), gather more information.** Say to the other person, "Tell me more about that. I'd like to understand how you arrived at that opinion. This is your chance to educate me."

>> **Don't personalize the conversation.** Focus on issues, not personalities. Direct your commentary to the matter in dispute (for example, "I disagree that we should make voting difficult for people") rather than the *person* on the other end of the debate ("You're stupid for thinking that way").

>> **Look for points of agreement.** Parents, for example, who are in a discussion about whether to furnish birth-control pills for their daughter can begin by agreeing (out loud) that they are, of course, both concerned about the ultimate safety and well-being of their kids.

>> **Avoid the use of expletives.** Swearing and cursing only demeans the other person and stifles any productive exchange of ideas. You're better off saying, "I really don't know what to say when you act like that" rather than saying, "You're an ass, and you know it!"

>> **By all means, avoid contempt.** Contempt — sighing, rolling your eyes — not only conveys a sense of intolerance, but it also tells the other party you think he (and his ideas) are utterly worthless. It's just a way of saying, "I'm better than you!"

Seeking diversity in all things

Babies are not born intolerant. It's an *attitude* that is mostly developed through life experience. If you grow up in a family that tolerates differing points of view, you tend to be like that yourself. The same is true if you're raised in an intolerant family.

One antidote to intolerance, which is a black-and-white approach to life, is diversity. Intolerance is one way of trying to simplify what is an ever-changing, complex world. Diversity helps you expand your horizons and see that the "sea of ideas, beliefs, and behavior" is vast and endless. There is, in fact, far more gray than black and white. Truth, typically, is somewhere between what *I* think and what *you* believe.

TIP

Diversity is easier to achieve than you may imagine. Here are some tips on how to become worldlier — and thus a more tolerant — person:

>> **Read about religions different from your own.** You can find *For Dummies* books on the major world religions — and most bookstores are filled with all kinds of religion titles.

>> **Read news from places other than where you live.** If you're from a small town in the Midwest, subscribe to the *New York Times*. If you live in New York City, have your aunt in upstate New York send you her hometown paper. Play around with websites that don't simply validate how you look at things.

>> **Every other time you go into a restaurant, try something new.** This forces you out of your comfort zone.

>> **When you go to a party, look for the person you don't already know and start up a conversation.** If you talk to only the people you know, you're less likely to discover something new.

>> **Travel as extensively as your pocketbook and current health orders allow.** And if you can, try to go to different regions of the country (or the world). When you're there, spend some time talking to the locals.

>> **Make a point of socializing with people from racial and ethnic backgrounds other than your own.** You can find people from different backgrounds at various churches, synagogues, mosques, and community groups.

>> **Read lots of editorials online or in the newspaper — not just those you agree with.** You might also consider watching the news from different channels than the one you're used to.

>> **Visit museums and art galleries.** Consider taking a "staycation" in your own state and see the various wonders. For example, go to a local museum that you haven't been to in a few years. Many states have reduced rates for their own citizens.

>> **Hang around with people of different ages.** You'll be amazed at how differently folks much younger and older than you think. Some cities have multi-generational centers where you can interact with people of all ages.

>> **Attend free lectures by local and out-of-town authorities on various subjects.** Most communities offer lecture series or similar cultural experiences. If you live in a very small town, look to a bigger town nearby and make a point of traveling there to take advantage of these things.

>> **Keep your eyes open and your mouth shut.** Learn now, debate later. It's hard to learn anything new while you're talking.

Many of the preceding tips suggest social activities. It's a sad reminder about how much people around the world lost during the pandemic. I hope that by the time this book comes out, the world has defeated the pandemic, and we can all learn to connect again.

Reevaluating intentions

Reevaluating intentions helps you figure out whether your anger at someone else actually makes good sense. People with anger problems tend to see other people as having malicious intentions — that is, they take perfectly normal, understandable situations as somehow inspired by spiteful motives. Consider the following example:

> **Walter** is in his early 60s; he's likeable, intelligent, and educated but always quick to see some evil intent in the actions of others. If he calls someone and leaves a message asking him to call back right away and if that person doesn't call right back, Walter's initial thought is, "Damn him! He has absolutely no respect for me!"
>
> It would never occur to Walter that the person with whom he's now irritated has other important things to do as well, or that he's stuck somewhere in traffic, or that he's home sick with a cold. Nope. As far as Walter is concerned, there's only one possible explanation for his phone not ringing — a lack of respect — and that's why Walter is angry. He's angry almost all the time.

If this were an isolated situation, it wouldn't be a problem. But if you're like Walter, this is the way you view everything that comes your way throughout the day. Every time someone cuts in front of you in traffic, every time you have to wait more than two minutes before a waiter appears at your table in a restaurant, every time your spouse forgets to pick up your dry cleaning, it's just one more example of *evil intent* — and one more occasion for what you consider as 100 percent legitimate anger.

Seeing evil everywhere doesn't work out so great. It leads to excessive anger and all its associated costs (see Chapter 3 for information about the costs of anger).

Ask yourself the following questions when you see yourself ready to pounce on what seems like the evil intentions of others:

>> Is it possible that I'm misreading this person's intentions?

>> What are other possible reasons this person might have done what he did?

>> Which of those other reasons are the most *likely* to account for what happened?

>> Am I taking something personally that I really shouldn't?

>> How would I behave differently if I assumed that no evil intentions were involved?

>> If I had been that person, what might *my* motives have been?

If Walter were to take this advice, he'd likely come up with various non-angry scenarios about why someone didn't call him back. He would probably just pick up the phone and dial the person's number back again. He would remain calm, not angry, and assume no malevolence.

REMEMBER

People who have problems with anger often look at life through a suspicious, distrustful lens. They erroneously believe that everyday events somehow involve them personally. They're quick to react with anger or aggression when they feel wrongfully attacked.

Reformulating Distorted Thoughts

This section describes a couple of tough life stories. These people have good reasons for feeling angry. You see how each of them could look at the thoughts they have in response to various challenging situations. I show you how to analyze those thoughts for distortions, and you use the techniques described in the section "Smoothing Out Distortions in Thinking," earlier in this chapter, to develop more reasonable, adaptive thoughts.

Dwelling on pain

The following example shows how one angry guy tragically never addressed his anger and focused on pain instead. Later, this section shows you how he might have responded differently and possibly even saved his life.

> **Dwayne** injured his back at work 11 years earlier and had been unemployed and in constant pain ever since. He was also a very angry man — angry about being hurt, angry that his doctors couldn't fix his back, angry about being mistreated by his employer, angry at family and friends who he felt weren't sympathetic enough, and even angry at God for allowing this whole unfortunate circumstance to occur so early in his life.
>
> Dwayne had his first heart attack at age 36. He was walking down the street when he saw one of his "enemies" from his old job, and he instantly fell down clutching his chest. He was taken by ambulance to the local hospital, where he told his family physician that he had gotten intensely angry when he saw that person and then felt a sharp pain in his chest. The doctor didn't believe that anger had triggered his heart attack.
>
> Dwayne continued his angry ways and had a second heart attack at age 41. Surrounded in the hospital by his cardiologist, psychologist, minister, brother, and wife, Dwayne was given an ultimatum: "Let go of all this anger, or you're going to die. Your heart can't take it anymore." Once again, his face took on that all-too-familiar look, his eyes teared up, and he forecasted his own death by saying, "Never. I'll never stop being angry. I'll die first."
>
> Three weeks later, while shouting angrily into the telephone, Dwayne had his third and final heart attack. Moments later, his wife found him dead on the floor, the phone still in his hand.

Unfortunately, it's too late for Dwayne to benefit from anger management strategies. But, if he had the opportunity and desire, discovering different ways of thinking may have saved his life.

Table 6-4 shows you how to put this process into practice, using one of Dwayne's anger-arousing situations as an illustration. If only Dwayne had been able to listen to his angry thoughts over time, identify his thought distortions, and use that information along with various change strategies (covered in the earlier section "Smoothing Out Distortions in Thinking") to develop more reasonable thoughts, his life may have not ended so soon.

TABLE 6-4 **Dissecting Anger: Dwayne's Example**

Dwayne's Angry Thoughts Collection	Dwayne's Thought Distortions
I can't stand my pain.	I-can't-stand-its
The doctors are totally incompetent.	Catastrophizing
They don't care about me at all. My employer screwed me over.	Looking at the wrong source
None of this was my fault, damn it. Life is unfair. I don't deserve this; I worked hard and now I get this.	Entitlement
I can't do anything but sit around and let the world go by.	Overgeneralizing
My wife and my kids don't believe I'm suffering.	Mind reading

Here are more reasonable thoughts that might have kept Dwayne alive:

>> I can stand my pain; I don't like it, but I can stand it.

>> The doctors largely know what they're doing, but I wish they had more ideas. They probably care about me as much as any of their patients, but they aren't my mother.

>> My employer did what many employers do, and they did allow some unsafe job conditions to save money. I probably could have been more careful, but the job conditions did contribute a lot to the problem.

>> Life is unfair, but I guess it is for everyone from time to time. I worked hard, but at least I get disability insurance.

>> I probably could learn a new skill.

>> My wife and kids are understandably frustrated, but they still love me, and they know I'm hurting.

It's too late for Dwayne, but it's not too late for you. Do you think Dwayne would have felt as angry as he had if he examined his thoughts for distortions and used various change strategies to formulate more reasonable thoughts like the preceding ones? If so, it's hard to imagine that his anger would have remained as intense. Perhaps he might have felt somewhat upset and maybe a little angry but not so constantly enraged.

Probing life's circumstances

In the following example, Paula demonstrates how someone with a difficult life situation engages in seriously distorted thoughts that lead her to feeling angry, resentful, and hopeless. This section shows how she uses awareness of her thought distortions to rethink her situation more adaptively.

> **Paula,** a probation officer of 35 years, returns from a mandatory computer system training workshop. She's lived through three previous computer overhauls, and all of them fell way short of their promises of increased efficiency, improved communication, and ease of use. They cost the state millions of dollars and most ended up no better than the old paper filing systems of many years ago. She concludes that this system will be a complete waste of time and do nothing useful.
>
> Paula's had it. She feels angry and resentful of everything around her. She sits at her desk, pulls up a screen to her personal financial account, and feels enraged looking at what she assumes is a pathetic 401(k). She knows she can't retire until she's Medicare-eligible (if then), and that's another seven years into the future. Paula thinks she can't stand waiting that long. She totally hates her job and feels her clients are all entirely worthless scum. None of them ever seems to remain out of trouble for long, and she's furious at them for wasting her time.

Paula has a list of topics that she turns to whenever she feels frustrated. She has thoughts like the following:

>> My husband left me 15 years ago; he was contemptible, just like all men.

>> Left with two kids and a mortgage, I had to refinance my house twice to raise cash; now I'm completely broke. Life is so unfair.

>> Just because I'm a single mom, I've been passed over for promotions again and again in this out-of-control, failed system.

>> I have nothing to look forward to.

At the age of 58, Paula's life is hardly over. But the way she's currently thinking keeps her from finding meaning, purpose, direction, or joy in her life. She feels bitter, resentful, angry, and miserable — hardly in a place to fix what's wrong with her life and move forward.

So imagine that Paula goes for help with her anger. Her therapist realizes she's not exactly depressed (although she is indeed unhappy). Paula's thinking is highly contaminated by anger and numerous distortions that keep her fuming.

Table 6-5 shows a summary of Paula's old thoughts, their distortions, and new thoughts she acquired slowly by using change strategies shown in the earlier section "Smoothing Out Distortions in Thinking."

TABLE 6-5   **Dissecting Anger: Paula's Example**

Paula's Angry Thoughts	Paula's Thought Distortions
I hate my job and can't stand waiting for retirement.	I can't stand it.
My clients are scum.	Overgeneralizing
I have nothing to look forward to.	Catastrophizing
The computer system is a total waste of time.	Extremist words

Here are Paula's more reasonable thoughts:

>> I don't like my job, but the benefits are pretty good and I get four weeks of vacation a year.

>> Most of my clients reoffend, but a few do well over time.

>> I enjoy spending time with my kids.

>> And the computer system is rather clunky, but it's not worthless.

Practicing Rethinking

The examples in the previous section represent a summary or compilation of two individuals who had multiple incidences of anger over time. If you want to put rethinking anger into your life, you'll likely do so most effectively by taking one or two difficult life events at a time.

To start, get out a pen and paper or, of course, some electronic device. Either dictate, write, or type — your choice. But seeing your thoughts on a screen or paper helps you view them more objectively and dispassionately. Only then can you step back from your typical immediate emotional reactions.

Then follow these steps. Feel free to review preceding sections in this chapter for more details and ideas about distortions, smoothing out distortions, and clinical examples of new, more reasonable thoughts that lead to new, more adaptive responses.

1. **Write down an event or situation that precedes an angry response.**

   Be clear and include all the details you can recall. See Chapters 2 and 5 for information about common triggers and events that often link to anger.

2. **Record your thoughts about the situation.**

   Don't hold back. Even if you realize a thought may be distorted (and you may be able to recognize distorted thoughts if you've read earlier sections in this chapter), put down whatever it is that was in your mind. If you're not aware of any specific thoughts, ask yourself the following questions:

   - How am I perceiving or interpreting this event?
   - What meaning does this event have for me?
   - Why am I feeling upset about this event?

3. **Review your thoughts for any possible distortions that they may involve.**

   Here are some examples (see earlier sections of this chapter for details about each thought distortion):

   - Filtering
   - Catastrophizing
   - Looking at the wrong source
   - Overgeneralizing
   - Judging
   - Black-and-white thinking
   - Mind reading
   - I-can't-stand-its
   - Feeling entitled

4. **Consider using one or more of the change techniques.**

   The change techniques discussed earlier in this chapter include

   - Checking the evidence
   - Moderating extremist words
   - Taking the perspective of a friend
   - Becoming more tolerant
   - Seeking diversity in all things
   - Reevaluating intentions

5. **Record one or more new, reworked thoughts that more accurately reflect reality.**

These thoughts should be less extreme and more supportable by actual evidence.

TIP

If you have problems with anger, go through these steps whenever anger crops up. Occasionally, you may find that your thoughts are pretty accurate. But, more often than not, I suspect you'll have no trouble discovering a few distortions in your typical responses. You'll get better at coming up with more reasonable responses the more you practice. Be patient.

Chapter **7**

Taking the Focus Off Yourself

O kay, I confess: I really am a geek. One of my favorite activities is to read interesting social psychology research (and, of course, write books). Some of the most fascinating research has looked at the role of what's called *self-absorption* and its effects on moods, aggression, and irritability. Self-absorption refers to focusing attention on your "self." Here are a few interesting tidbits from this research:

» Students perform worse on tasks when there are a lot of mirrors placed in the room, which causes them to dwell more on themselves. Future research may find similar results of students doing worse on tasks while looking at themselves on video calls.

» When asked to write essays containing as much use of the word *I* as possible, people's negative feelings increase.

» People previously assessed as highly self-absorbed felt more distress following a traumatic event than those who didn't focus on themselves so much.

» Self-centered people have greater fluctuations of happiness (going from depressed to euphoric) than people who are less self-centered. Those who are less self-centered have more stable moods.

So, specifically, what do these findings have to do with anger? It turns out that self-absorption and all negative emotions, including anger, are significantly related to one another. This chapter, discusses how self-absorption connects to self-esteem and perfectionism, which have unexpected effects on anger.

Reviewing Self-Esteem and Anger

Social workers, counselors, therapists, psychologists, and probation officers for decades believed that the root cause of anger was *low* self-esteem. Many people agree with this idea to this day. Therefore, they have logically recommended programs and classes aimed at raising the self-esteem of violent offenders, whether they be juveniles or adults. Just one problem: They were, for the most part, wrong.

So what exactly is *self-esteem* anyway? Here's a list of a few synonyms of self-esteem to give you an idea:

>> Self-image

>> Self-regard

>> Self-worth

>> Self-concept

You don't need to worry about the nuances that distinguish these terms from one another. Here's a definition of self-esteem that captures the essence: Self-esteem is a perception or observation accompanied by an evaluation or judgment on the qualities you value. The specific qualities that self-esteem rests on differ from one person to the next.

For example, an attorney may value her ability to articulate an argument and feel good about herself if she possesses this quality. A therapist may value her ability to avoid arguments with her clients and feel good about herself if she excels at this skill. A gangster may value his ability to lie to get out of trouble. And a pastor could value honesty above all else. In other words, the traits that self-esteem rests upon vary from person to person.

Flying with balloons of self-esteem

Think about self-esteem as similar to a balloon. For example, if you take a balloon right out of the package and lay it down in front of you, what does it look like? Flat, wrinkled, no air. In fact, a bit ugly and rather useless. That's what having low self-esteem looks and feels like. It's no wonder that people with exceptionally low self-esteem don't do much as they lack energy and bounce.

If you think about it, does the image of a deflated balloon make you think of someone at a high risk of flashing anger, physical aggression, or plotting elaborate revenge? Not so much because those acts require a lot of vigor, which people with deflated balloons (low self-esteem) don't have.

Now, blow that balloon up, almost to the bursting point. Okay, now blow another couple of puffs of air into it. Now, imagine that you *really* want to keep that overly inflated balloon out of harm's way, and you have to carry it around with you all day long. Not only that, but if you keep it safe, there's a million-dollar prize waiting for you! Would you push someone out of the way if they started coming after your balloon? Would you yell, shout, scream, or counterattack? Would you obsess about the dangers of your balloon popping and stay vigilant for any possible risks?

Okay, so there's not actually a million-dollar prize for carrying out this task. The point is that people with overly inflated, excessively positive self-esteem are burdened with protecting their fragile balloons inflated to the bursting point. They stand at great risk for anger and aggression to keep their balloons safe.

When people are all puffed up, it's pretty easy to puncture and threaten their self-esteem. For example, some frenzied sports fans find that their egos feel threatened when a game begins to go sour. A few of those frenzied fans even erupt in violence. Do those fans sound like deflated, empty balloons or too-full balloons ready to burst at the slightest provocation?

TIP

Think about the last couple of anger outbursts you may have had or witnessed. Did they occur when something threatened someone's ego? Numerous studies have confirmed that people who believe they stand far above other people (also known as narcissists), become more easily aroused and exhibit more aggression than others.

Now, go back to the balloon metaphor. Imagine a balloon with just the right amount of air. You can toss it around, bounce it, and not worry about the balloon popping. In other words, the balloon has resilience. Thus, solid self-esteem is steady and not easily disturbed. Solid self-esteem is based on reasonable self-evaluations and actual accomplishments that aren't blown out of proportion. Solid self-esteem doesn't lead to excessive self-criticism and derision. And solid self-esteem generally remains pretty stable.

Stabilizing self-esteem

One of my favorite pieces of advice that I've given to clients, students, audiences at workshops, and even members of my family (though I should know better about advising family members!) is to *put your ego on the shelf.* You, like others, may wonder, "What the heck does putting your ego on the shelf mean?"

Putting your ego on the shelf means that the less you evaluate and judge yourself — based on the opinions of others — the less your emotions will go up and down like a yo-yo. You'll be able to hear criticism and disapproval, which everybody receives here and there, objectively and appropriately. You won't get bent out of shape because your ego isn't on the line. When you keep your ego on the shelf, your self-esteem remains stable and unharmed. Look at the next three examples to see this process in action.

Sadie is a 20-something-year-old. From the moment she was born, her parents and family told her she was beautiful, special, and meant for great things. Basically, she was spoiled rotten. Her parents praised her for simply breathing and excused any wrongdoing while blaming others. Lucky for Sadie, she has always been fairly attractive and rather smart.

Sadie finishes college with a degree in political science. She thinks that politicians will hire her for a special position, such as press secretary or at the very least as an assistant campaign manager, immediately upon graduation. So Sadie feels outraged when numerous applications fail to capture employers' interest. She finally gets an interview, but her resentment, sense of superiority, and entitlement come through in her tone and her body language. She's insulted when offered a low prestige job, believing that it's beneath her education and social status. She turns down the offer and remains smugly unemployed.

Sadie's bad attitude wrecked her early career possibilities. People sense that she feels better than them, and they don't like her. She needs to figure out how to put her ego on the shelf and pay her dues.

Don's upbringing had a different tone than Sadie's. His parents also praised him for the smallest of accomplishments. However, they berated and humiliated him whenever he messed up in the slightest way. Understandably, he vacillated from feeling wonderful about himself to thinking he was a complete loser at the drop of a hat.

Don graduates from college; like Sadie, he has a degree in political science. He, too, finds the job market challenging due to economic conditions. Unlike Sadie, his response to initial rejection is despondency and despair. He predicts that he'll never get a job and feels that college wasted his time and money. Then he gets a call to an interview with a national political campaign. His ego soars. He confidently strides into the interview. The interviewer tells him that he's a very good candidate, but all he has to offer right now is an errand-running job. Don flies into a rage, throwing his résumé across the room and stomps out.

Don is an example of someone with a highly *unstable* self-esteem. He flips from thinking he's nothing to believing he's superior to others. This unstable self-esteem puts him at risk for both depression and problems with anger.

> **Cliff** was raised by parents who set firm, tough limits but with love and affection. His self-esteem rests on a solid, stable foundation. He, too, graduates with a degree in political science and finds the job searching process frustrating. He finally gets an interview.
>
> The interviewer says he's had a couple of applicants who didn't work out. After reviewing Cliff's résumé, the interviewer says, "You look like a really qualified candidate, but right now all I can offer you is an errand-running job."
>
> Cliff feels disappointed but realizes that it's his first job offer. He doesn't take it personally. Instead, he switches into problem-solving mode and says, "Well, that is a bit discouraging, but I can do anything for a little while. Is there any chance that this job can turn into something more after a while?"
>
> The interviewer says, "Oh, of course. In fact, many of the high-level staffers started as unpaid volunteers and worked their way up rather quickly. It's funny; the last two applicants basically walked out before they could learn that. I think I like you already."

Cliff put his ego on the shelf and discovered positive possibilities without letting anger get in his way. Like anyone who finishes school, he hoped for a good job and felt disillusioned when his first offer fell short of expectations. But because *his ego wasn't standing in his way*, Cliff allowed himself to take on a job that will probably pay off nicely in the longer term.

Becoming Less Competitive

Self-absorbed people (who focus on themselves excessively) also regularly go down a path toward extreme competitiveness. This is much more than normal, fun indulgence in sports and games or doing a really good job at work. Rather, it's about people who want to win at all costs. They *stop at nothing* to ensure that they end up at the top.

These people set challenging goals for themselves, which is fine, up to a point. But if they fail to get there, they may blow up in anger aimed at others or, sometimes, themselves. So one way to reduce problems with anger is to modify your approach to competition.

TIP

The following is a list of ways in which you can modify your competitive nature and engage in *healthy* competition:

>> **Try playing a round of golf without keeping score.** Here's something you may not know: Some overly competitive golfers not only keep their own score, but they also keep the other players' scores — to ensure that the other players don't cheat. And if the other players make a mistake, you can bet these folks will tell them about it.

>> **Let your children win at family games at least half the time.** Let them win even more often if you want them to love you 40 years from now.

>> **If you feel like you have to compete with your partner over ideas and decisions, be sure to let your partner win half the time.** If you do, you'll stay together longer!

>> **Never ask co-workers how much they get paid, how well their stocks are doing, or how much "face time" they have with the boss.** Just do your job and make your own investments, and you'll be fine.

>> **If you're going somewhere, don't try to see how fast you can get there.** Go the speed limit and enjoy the ride. Life isn't meant to be a race.

>> **Practice meditation.** If you've never meditated or you don't really know where to start, check out Chapter 9 to learn a bit about meditation and mindfulness. If you want even more information, pick up the latest edition of *Meditation For Dummies* by Stephan Bodian (Wiley).

>> **Walk on a track with someone who walks slower than you do and go at that person's speed.** Walking — without competing against your partner — does wonders for your heart.

>> **Alternate between competitive activities and noncompetitive activities.** For example, one Saturday afternoon, play tennis with your friend (and allow yourself to keep score), and the next Saturday, visit a museum.

>> **The next time a group you belong to holds an election, raise your hand and nominate someone else.** You don't have to be the head of every committee; you can trust other people to take charge and follow their lead for a change.

Come up with other creative ways you can reduce your competitive nature. If you're a little less competitive, you won't be as likely to get angry, and that's probably a good thing.

CULTURAL INFLUENCES ON ANGER

Culture influences how and when people express anger. Obviously, within any given culture, you can find a wide variability in how different people express their anger. Many social scientists have divided cultures into two major categories:

- **Individualism:** This emphasizes the importance of independence, self-reliance, personal achievement, and individual interests over those of the culture at large. Individualism is typically associated with western societies.

- **Collectivism:** This focuses on the needs of the group over that of the individual. These societies value cooperation, sharing, and collaboration. Eastern societies tend to embrace collectivism over individualism.

Some research suggests that those in collectivist societies restrain outward expression of anger. Individualism has been associated with increased levels of narcissism. And narcissism is a risk factor for excessive anger. However, people living in individualistic cultures report greater life satisfaction than those in collectivism societies.

So I'm not saying that taking an individualistic or a collectivist perspective is better, just different. Individualists are most likely to become angry and frustrated over infringements on their own personal goals and desires. Collectivists, on the other hand, may become angry more readily over perceived insults to their group or culture. Both extremes likely lead to having excessive sensitivity and perhaps greater anger overall.

Watching Out for Perfectionism

What the heck does perfectionism have to do with anger? Perfectionism also involves a focus on the self. A perfectionist is determined to do and always be perfect, a form of self-absorption. That standard is utterly impossible to maintain and frequently leads to frustration followed by, you guessed it, anger. Perfectionism, like an overly inflated balloon (see the earlier section "Flying with balloons of self-esteem"), is easily punctured.

Perfectionistic anger is usually directed inward. People with these standards all too readily dump on themselves whenever they fail to adhere to unrealistic goals. They say to themselves, "I am horrible because I can't be perfect."

Alternatively, some people direct their perfectionistic standards onto others. When that happens, co-workers, friends, and family members find themselves unable to meet the demands of the perfectionist. This situation easily leads to anger going both ways, back and forth from perfectionists to their targets.

> For example, **Suzanne,** a mother of two boys, was a consummate perfectionist. She repeatedly and harshly admonished her children, "If something isn't worth doing right, it isn't worth doing at all."
>
> She concentrated on pointing out errors and paid little attention to their considerable accomplishments. The boys grew up feeling insecure and diminished. They also felt resentful and angry toward their mother but feared expressing it to her. Instead, they expressed excessive anger toward others.

REMEMBER

I'm not saying that high standards are a bad idea. Most worthy achievements require pursuit of excellence. But it's important to realize that irrational, unbridled perfectionism leads to inevitable disappointment and, all too often, anger.

Embracing mistakes

Perfectionists hate making mistakes. Mistakes manage to crush their self-esteem and send them reeling.

One way out of perfectionism can be found by *embracing mistakes*. Embracing mistakes means discovering that mistakes have much to offer you. They teach you to be less self-focused and more self-accepting. Consider *intentionally* bringing mistakes into your life. Here's a list to get you started:

>> Wear two different-colored socks one day.

>> Put a small smudge on a document.

>> Pretend to trip over something.

>> Park slightly over a line in a parking lot.

>> Go in an "out" door.

>> Wear something with a small stain.

>> Say something stupid.

>> Mess up your hair.

>> Put a stamp on an envelope crooked.

>> Misspellll something! (This one might drive editors crazy!)

>> Press the wrong floor on the elevator and say, "Oops."

After you do these things, notice how people respond. Do they laugh at you? Do they criticize and insult you? Does your world fall apart? Probably not. But, with luck, you may just start feeling more self-accepting.

REMEMBER

You're not the center of the universe. Most people really aren't paying a lot of attention to you when you mess up. And if you pay less attention to yourself, you're likely to feel less angry.

Pummeling procrastination

Procrastination partners with perfectionism much of the time. Because you can't do anything to absolute perfection, you do nothing at all. When you don't get things done, you end up angry with yourself and irritable with other people.

Procrastination occurs when there's a gap between the time you decide to do something and the time you actually get around to doing it. Procrastinators want to avoid criticism, frustration, and even success. Success? Yes, because success leads to pressure to accomplish more. Here are a few signs that may indicate you're in a procrastination episode:

>> You have a difficult task, and you keep checking your email.

>> You wait for feeling in "just the right mood" for doing something.

>> You don't do things until the deadline threatens to engulf you.

>> You start compulsively cleaning your house rather than engage with the task at hand.

>> You undertake a weeklong office reorganization rather than deal with something you dread.

>> You start searching online for just one more piece of information over and over, even though it scarcely has anything to do with your project.

To battle procrastination, consider trying out a few of these strategies:

>> Turn off your devices and all connections to the outside world — yes, all!

>> Use Grandma's law: First, eat your green beans, and then you can have dessert. In other words, reward yourself but only after you've done a piece of your task first.

>> Carve out a space where you try to do most all of your productive work. Use it for work alone. It could even be a spot on your dining room table or a coffee shop. Exclusivity is the key.

>> Use visual cues like signs hung on your cubicle or door asking for privacy.

>> Break tasks into small pieces and let yourself savor each one as it's done.

>> Use a schedule or calendar, especially electronic ones that provide reminders.

>> Keep a to-do list on your calendar or somewhere that you can't avoid.

Today's world provides lots of distractions that facilitate procrastination. Procrastinators struggle with self-control, as do those who have anger problems. With hard work and diligence, you can tackle these problems.

3

Equipping Yourself with Anger Management Tools

Chapter **8**

Communicating Assertively with Compassion

N*ews flash:* Not everyone gets along all the time. Even the nicest people have occasions when they disagree with friends, family, neighbors, or co-workers. The dog next door barks every morning at 4 a.m., you babysit your grandchild and his parents routinely come back later than you expect, the boss throws a load of work on your desk on Friday afternoon, or your best friend stands you up for lunch at the last minute.

Like everyone in the world, you'll have times that you feel irritated, annoyed, or even angry. How you express your feelings under these circumstances can make things better or worse. This chapter describes the process of *assertive* communication. With assertiveness, you can let your needs be known without anger and get more of what you want.

Discovering Assertion

Assertive communication is direct and respectful. It allows you to express your views but in a way that can be heard by others. Assertive communication usually involves three elements: expressing feelings, saying what went wrong, and sharing what you want. The following sections explain.

Expressing feelings

Assertive communication requires you to *own* your feelings. Other people don't actually *make* you mad, sad, annoyed, or anxious. You choose to respond to situations with those feelings. With assertive communication, you want to provide a clear message about your feelings. So admit to them without blaming the other person. For example, instead of saying "You annoy me . . .," reword your statement and own your own feelings and try "I feel annoyed when . . ." Here are a couple more examples:

>> "You make me angry . . ." becomes "I got angry when . . ."

>> "You upset me when . . ." becomes "I was upset when . . ."

This technique is often referred to as *making "I" statements*. An easy way to remember this strategy is by simply starting your sentence with, "I feel. . . ."

Saying what went wrong

The second part of assertive communication involves giving a matter-of-fact, calm statement of what you believe isn't working for you. This part of assertion can be pretty hard for some people. Shy, passive, or reserved people typically avoid expressing displeasure to other people. On the other hand, aggressive people have a hard time turning their complaints into calm, reasonable, easily heard statements.

Assertive communication involves confronting other people about behavior that you find disturbing. The key to this part of assertive communication requires describing the problem behavior in clear, factual, unemotional terms. Here are a few examples:

>> Your boss is piling work on your desk on a Friday afternoon just before quitting time. You say, "I feel stressed when you give me work that I can't get to until Monday."

>> Your partner waits to the last minute to pack and is frequently late leaving for trips. You say, "I feel annoyed when you don't pack ahead because we are both rushed at the last minute."

> » Your neighbor leaves her children's bikes and toys in front of your house. You say, "I worry that I might trip on your kids' toys when they're left in front of my house."

TIP

You don't have to be assertive about every little thing that disturbs you. Sometimes you have to let hassles roll off your back. If you're unlikely to encounter a problem or see someone again, or if the issue is minor, you have to decide whether the effort to be assertive is worth it.

Sharing what you want with compassion

You've expressed your feelings and stated what went wrong; now you have to *share exactly what you want*. This part of assertive communication necessitates planning. It requires thinking ahead to figure out what you want and to consider what is practical and possible.

TIP

In addition to stating what you want, adding a compassionate statement helps build a bridge between you and the person you are talking to. When being assertive, search for some understanding and empathy for the other person's position. Most of the time, people are not trying to be difficult. They have their own struggles. Making a compassionate appeal increases the likelihood that you will be heard.

If your boss is giving you what you believe is too much work, something like the following example might *backfire*.

> "I feel annoyed when you give me extra work to do on Friday afternoons.
>
> I want you to stop doing that."
>
> Your boss may say, "Fine, I won't give you any more work at all. You're fired."

A more *reasonable*, compassionate, assertive approach may be

> "I feel stressed when you give me extra work to do on Friday afternoons. I understand that you have a lot of extra work to get through. That's got to be difficult for you. Can we get together and talk about how to solve that?"

Another example that would probably *not* work would be a mother telling her 9-year-old son the following:

> "I feel irritated when you don't clean your room. I want you to clean your room without reminders for the rest of your childhood!"

A mother could assertively revise that to

"I feel irritated when you don't clean your room. I know that cleaning your room is not a particularly fun activity. I think I can help you organize the task so that it doesn't take so long. How can I help you get it done so we can both feel better?"

TIP

When you describe what you want, use words like *prefer, desire,* or *wish.* Words like *demand, must,* or *require* sound like ultimatums and may result in a defensive response.

Seeing how assertive communication works

The following example illustrates how a difficult situation improves after an adult taking care of her elderly parents uses assertive communication.

Amy, a 58-year-old physician, attributes much of her success to her upbringing. However, she doesn't have fond memories of her childhood. Her parents were cold and verbally abusive. She turned to books and school to escape unrelenting criticism and contempt she experienced at home. Over the years, she has worked through her early abuse and enjoys good mental health.

Amy's parents are getting more and more frail as they age. Amy's cultural background dictates that she care for her elders. When her parents reach a stage that they need constant care, Amy brings them into her own home.

Despite their illness and dependency, Amy's parents treat her with disrespect and complain about everything she tries to please them. Amy ignores most of their assaults but becomes increasingly irritated and annoyed. Her husband and children suffer from the stress. Amy finally gets the courage to use assertive communication to give her parents feedback, "I feel unhappy and irritated when you criticize me in my home. I feel like I am doing everything to take care of you. I understand this situation is difficult for all of us. I would like you to be polite and courteous in my home."

Amy's parents feel stunned by her statement, and they also feel deeply ashamed. They vow to do what they can to change their ways and ask for Amy's forgiveness. She gladly agrees, and the three plan to talk about their progress.

TIP

A single assertive statement won't immediately change most other people's long-standing habits like it did in Amy's example. However, if you keep using assertive communication, you can open up a dialogue for creating lasting change. Persistence is the key.

Avoiding Sudden Escalation

The previous section lays out some initial ideas about how to use assertive communication. What happens when assertion, despite your best efforts, leads to elevated emotions and anger? Here are a few things *not* to do to prevent that from happening.

WARNING

Clearly, you need to avoid some things like certain gestures and behaviors if you're going to use assertive communication. By all means, do *not* do the following:

>> Roll your eyes when the other person is speaking.

>> Sigh audibly.

>> Engage in finger-pointing.

>> Lecture the other person when it's your turn to speak.

>> Use critical language (words like *stupid, idiot, crazy, ignorant,* or *ridiculous*).

>> Repeatedly interrupt or talk over the other person.

>> Personalize your message (for example, "What a fool you are!").

TIP

Consider the value of taking a timeout in your conversations. For example, don't be afraid to say to the other person, "I think we've gone as far as we can with this issue right now, but I really think we should continue our discussion at a later date. Do you agree?" Some issues take longer to solve than others — just as some destinations are farther away than others.

REMEMBER

This strategy works only if you actually do resume the discussion later. Otherwise, all your constructive efforts were in vain!

Realizing That No One Owns All of the Truth

When people criticize you or simply disagree with your views, do you automatically assume that they're wrong and you're right? That's pretty much the default assumption that too many folks carry around, especially those who have problems with anger. Although it's hard to do, it's a good idea to step back a little and actually consider the possibility that those who disagree with you may actually have a point or two.

You don't have to fully endorse perspectives that differ from your own. Rather, merely mull over the idea that *no one has a complete corner on all truth!* Can you think of times in your life when you felt fairly certain about something and later discovered that you didn't have all the correct information and thus, came to an erroneous conclusion? If you can't, you're not thinking hard enough! Everyone gets it wrong sometimes.

The following three sections present strategies based on a different assumption: More often than not, most people's views and opinions contain some truth and some element of erroneous ideas. Other times, you may not be incorrect per se, but you may not have all the information at your disposal. And if you discover those bits of truth or information gaps, you may even find yourself able to empathize with that person a bit.

Defusing disagreements and criticism

Defusing is a powerful way to de-escalate and calm down rather than engage in the automatic habit of striking back without thought or reflection. With defusing, you actively seek a way of finding at least *a sliver of truth* in what other people are saying, regardless of how much you feel certain that they are incorrect, irrational, or unfair.

WARNING

You may find defusing pretty tough to do. If so, think about reading Chapter 7, which shows you how to keep your ego on the shelf and out of the fracas. Putting your ego on the shelf helps you hold back natural tendencies to get defensive and resort to aggression and attack.

Take a look at the example of Cade that follows. First, he responds to criticism with his usual, reflexive, angry style. Then Cade replays the dialogue using a defusing approach.

> **Cade** is 27 years old and works at an auto body repair shop. He and his close friend, Jake, work on a commission basis and compete for clients. Usually, they manage to avoid serious conflict. However, Cade comes to work on Monday after a tense weekend with his wife. He and Jake quickly fall into an escalating conflict.
>
> **Jake:** So, Cade, I'm not so sure I appreciate the way you stepped in front of me and cut me off from that customer. It was my turn, you know.
>
> **Cade:** I did no such thing. You're totally wrong. Why are you being such a jerk today?
>
> **Jake:** Wow, I'm just saying we have a system here. I'm not happy when you don't follow it.

Cade: No, you're just trying to one-up me. You need to stop that, or I'll talk to our supervisor.

Jake: What? How obnoxious can you get? You know better than to complain to him; he'd jump on both of us, you moron!

Cade: Get out of my space, Jake. I'm tired of your constant complaining. You're no friend of mine!

Hmm, not such a great outcome, was it? Who was right, Cade or Jake? Do you really know? Probably not, given the way that dialogue went. Here's the same start with a different outcome when Cade uses defusing:

Jake: So, Cade, I'm not so sure I appreciate the way you stepped in front of me and cut me off from that customer. It was my turn, you know.

Cade: I can see where it might have seemed like it was your turn (defusing), but that was actually my customer from a few years ago.

Jake: I don't care; it was still my turn.

Cade: In a sense, that's true (defusing), but haven't we usually let each other keep our old clients?

Jake: Not always; you remember my old client, Carl? You took that one, and I agreed because I'd had a good string of really high-dollar jobs at the time.

Cade: You do have a point there (defusing). I had forgotten about that. Still, neither one of us has had a run like that lately; and we *usually* have kept our old clients, haven't we?

Jake: Well, maybe so. But I guess I'd feel better if we discussed the issue before running over to the client.

Cade: That works for me. I'm glad we talked it out.

Perhaps you can see that Cade and Jake both had good points. Neither one knew all of what was going on. Because Cade kept his ego on the shelf and searched for slivers of truth in Jake's concerns, they resolved the conflict without rancor.

To use the defusing approach effectively, it helps a lot to have some defusing phrases at your disposal. Read the following list and imagine yourself using words like these in a conflict you may have had in the past. Then try to pull them up when someone disagrees with you instead of responding with thoughtless aggression:

» "You may have a point."

» "Sometimes what you're saying is probably true."

>> "I can see how you could look at it that way."

>> "Maybe I did mess up a little here."

>> "I do agree about at least one thing you're saying."

TIP

Defusing and buffering (in the following section) are best thought of as actual philosophies rather than merely techniques. It's important to truly grapple with the idea that it's rather rare for anyone to be 100 percent correct and have access to 100 percent of the information about a topic under discussion.

REMEMBER

Defusing doesn't mean you completely agree with another person's view, and it doesn't mean that you must collapse and capitulate. Notice in the preceding story that Cade still ended up with his client, but he agreed that they would be better off talking about who takes whom ahead of time.

Buffering your own complaints

In addition to understanding the sliver (or more) of truth in other people's complaints, it helps to see that your point of view has flaws as well. Buffering involves disagreeing with yourself! Well, not exactly, but this strategy does call for you to explicitly state that you realize your own argument *may* contain inaccuracies. You point out that you could be wrong (it's always possible, you know).

Engaging in buffering helps increase the chances that other people *actually hear what you're trying to say*. That's because judicious use of buffering helps others avoid their own defensive, angry responses.

But wait, you say, "I'm right; I'm not wrong." Indeed, you may be right. But ask yourself what you want to accomplish. What's your goal? Is it to be *right* or to be *heard*?

TIP

Few people can be 100 percent right about anything. Acknowledging that fact helps others listen.

Take a look at what happens when Sandy confronts her sister Leah. First, she does so *without* using buffering.

Sandy: "Leah, every time you come to my house with your kids, you allow them to plunder my pantry and eat every snack I've got. Get control over your kids, okay?"

Leah: "They hardly eat everything. Sometimes they're coming from swimming, and they're hungry for gosh sake. What's wrong with you?"

Sandy: "They do, too, eat everything! Last week, there was absolutely nothing left in there."

Leah: "That's not true. I remember popcorn and a couple of granola bars still on the shelf, and that's just what I can remember; I'm sure there was more."

Sandy: "No, I'm right about this. Your kids are out-of-control monsters, and that's all there is to it."

Once again, not such a great outcome. Both sisters end up angry and resentful with the other. And their kids pick up on the raging conflict — not exactly a good thing, either.

Here's the same concern expressed with buffering and a bit of defusing (see previous section) along with it.

Sandy: "I could be making a little too much out of this (buffering), but I've noticed when your kids come over here, they seem to eat everything they can get their hands on."

Leah: "Well, they do come right after swimming sometimes, and they're pretty hungry. What's the problem?"

Sandy: "Well, that's true about swimming (defusing), but it makes it hard for me to shop when I don't know when they're coming or how much they'll scarf up."

Leah: "Well, how about I bring over a box or two of granola bars for them every now and then? Would that help?"

Sandy: "Sure, that would help a lot. Thanks."

Notice how just a bit of Sandy acknowledging that she "could" be making too much of a big deal about the problem and admitting that Leah had a point about swimming leads to a calmer atmosphere and opens up the possibility of effective problem solving.

Here are a few buffering phrases to consider working into your communication style when you need to confront someone about a concern you have:

>> "I could be off base . . ."

>> "Maybe I'm making too much out of this . . ."

>> "Maybe I'm looking at this wrong . . ."

REMEMBER

Just because you acknowledge that you *may* not own the entire truth of your own viewpoint doesn't mean you have to give in or give up your point of view. You can and should persist if you feel you're "essentially" right but show willingness to see another point of view.

Preventing Venting

Have you ever called a friend and said, "I just have to vent"? Venting is airing out stored-up emotion, but that's the best-case scenario. At worst, it's like one of the dictionary definitions of venting: "the discharging of volcanic products." Rage, disdain, contempt, and scorn are volcanic products.

REMEMBER

But doesn't it help to release all that pent-up lava and soot and ash? Isn't venting a good thing? Contrary to what most people think, *venting anger doesn't work.*

Venting doesn't provide the emotional relief you expect, nor does it resolve the real-life problems that trigger your anger in the first place. What it *does* do, unfortunately, is just the opposite: It makes angry people angrier and aggressive people more aggressive.

TIP

If you're feeling chronically angry, your best bet is to talk to a counselor about your emotions so you can get to the bottom of them and figure out how to move on. But if you're experiencing an isolated episode of anger, you're better off either counting to ten or thinking about what's making you angry quietly than you are venting to a friend.

WHAT WAS FREUD THINKING ANYWAY?

Sigmund Freud believed in a "hydraulic" model of human emotion. As he saw it, emotions (including anger) are a natural byproduct of everyday life, but they tend to build up over time just like steam does in a teakettle (or lava does in a volcano). As emotions build up, they create bodily tension that eventually seeks it own discharge. Freud thought that people remained healthy as long as they could freely and openly express their feelings. If you couldn't express emotion in some acceptable, adaptive way as you experienced it, then your health would be adversely affected by the mounting tension within your body.

Freud's term for helping clients discharge their residual anger was *catharsis,* which actually means "a dramatic freeing up of deep-seated anger from the past." Some experts believe that Freud had a point — it's just that most people (including lots of anger-management specialists!) misunderstood his concept of catharsis. Freud's notion of cathartic treatment was intended to be a therapist-guided, structured re-experiencing of anger. Freud never had his patients pound mattresses with a tennis racket, beat on inflated lifelike dolls, rip up telephone books, scream to their hearts' content, or engage in mortal combat with foam bats and swords, which are all forms of past approaches to anger-management therapy. Luckily, most therapists today have read a little of the past 40 years' of research showing that the popular view of catharsis doesn't work and no longer engage in the practice of venting.

Expressing Your Anger Effectively

If you can't articulate your anger (clearly express how you're feeling through language), you're more likely to act it out through some form of physical aggression. When a guy smashes his fist into a wall or, worse yet, into the face of another person, what exactly does that communicate other than the obvious fact that he's mad as hell?

How does that punching benefit him? It doesn't. Does that punch improve his relationship with the person he hits? Nope. Is the angry person calm after he's hauled off and slugged someone (or hit a wall)? Absolutely not. Expressing anger through physical violence has no upside — zip, zero, zilch.

So then is it better to yell and scream out your anger than hit something or someone? If that's the only choice you give yourself at the time, yes. But then again, verbal violence really doesn't get you anywhere, either. No one feels better after she's given someone a good tongue-lashing, no matter what she says. And the person on the receiving end of all that yelling and screaming certainly isn't a happy camper, either.

So what's left? *Talking*, or using the gift of language to express your emotions (in this case, anger) in a constructive way. Consider this example:

> **Eddie** is just finding how to talk about his anger. Ever since he was a child, he's always kept a tight lid on his anger — withdrawing into himself as soon as he starts to get irritated, until he can't hold in all that anger anymore, and then, predictably, he erupts with volcanic rage. Just recently, that rage caused Eddie to physically assault his wife, which has understandably left her terrified and put the future of their marriage in serious doubt. The following conversation between Eddie and his therapist illustrates why Eddie needs anger management.
>
> **Therapist:** You said there was an incident this past week where you lost your temper. Tell me about it.
>
> **Eddie:** Yeah, I got irritated with my wife right before we left the house to go visit some friends. And when we got to our friends' house, I ended up being an ass to everyone the whole time we were there.
>
> **Therapist:** What did you do between the time you left home and the time you arrived at your friends' house?
>
> **Eddie:** Nothing. I didn't say anything to my wife. She tried to get me to talk, but I wouldn't. She finally gave up, and we were both silent until we got there.
>
> **Therapist:** How far a drive is it to your friends' house?
>
> **Eddie:** Over an hour.

Therapist: You drove for over an hour without saying a word to your wife?

Eddie: Right.

Therapist: What were you doing instead?

Eddie: I was thinking about how angry I was and all kinds of crazy stuff about my wife.

Therapist: And did that make you more angry or less so?

Eddie: Oh, it definitely made me angrier. By the time we got to their house, I was really upset — tense and ready to explode. I never did relax the whole time we were there, and I know it ruined the evening for all of us.

Therapist: What do you imagine would have happened if you had talked to your wife about how you felt during that hour-long drive?

Eddie: It probably would have helped, but I don't know how to do that — I don't know what to say. So I just stay quiet, and it builds and builds. I've always been like that, and I don't know why.

The next time you get so angry you feel like hitting something (or someone), fol-low these steps:

1. Come up with a label to identify the intensity of your anger.

For example, are you annoyed, irritated, mad, irate, or in a rage? Start by saying, "I feel. . . ." Don't say, "I think. . . ." What you're going for here is your feeling, not your thoughts about how obnoxious the other person was.

2. Identify the thing that triggered your anger.

For example, "Every time I come home, she's on the phone with her mother. We never have any time to ourselves." Continue your conversation by saying, "I feel *[insert the word you came up with in Step 1]* because. . . ."

3. Ask yourself what it would take to help you return to a non-angry state.

For example, "I would appreciate it if she would save her phone calls to her mother for earlier in the day so that when I get home, we can have some one-on-one time."

When you're able to go through these three steps inside your head, see whether you can actually have that conversation with the person you're angry with.

Hitting a spouse or any other person constitutes a criminal act. You need to realize that engaging in battery puts you at high risk for not only losing your relationship but also losing your freedom. You should seek immediate help if you *ever* engage even in a single incident of domestic or interpersonal violence. You can't assume that you'll just "get over it."

Walking away and still having your say

Anger evolved as a means for responding to danger. People, and animals for that matter, become angry and stand up and fight or run away. The old fight-or-flight response is built into your nervous system. Unfortunately, these choices don't result in effective resolutions of whatever underlies the emotional response.

TIP

You can express your anger immediately in some hostile, aggressive manner, or you can simply walk (or stomp!) off without a word. *Or* you can choose a middle-of-the-road response: Walk off until you cool down and then return later to the source of your anger and verbalize exactly why you feel the way you do.

Try the following exercise:

1. **Think of some recent situation where you felt you were treated unfairly or unjustly but didn't say how you felt at the time.**

2. **Write out, or dictate into your favorite device, the situation in as much detail as possible.**

3. **Read what you've written or dictated.**

4. **Write down (or dictate) how you felt about the situation — not what you thought or what you did, but how you *felt* (your emotions).**

   It's okay to list more than one emotion, such as, for example, "I was angry and hurt."

5. **Record the situation that preceded your feelings.**

   For example, "She made an unkind remark about my weight."

6. **Describe what you want to say to the person with whom you were angry.**

   Be sure to start with an *I* statement, starting with a feeling, and then describe the situation that set you off. Avoid using inflammatory language (swear words).

7. **Now, ask yourself how do you feel — better, relieved?**

8. **Reinforce what you've done here with a positive self-statement: "Good for me! Couldn't happen to a nicer guy!"**

Make this a weekly exercise until you get better at expressing your feelings on a day-to-day basis.

Writing: A great way to start

Assertion doesn't always require you to express out loud what you're concerned about. That's because sometimes there's not a whole lot you can do to solve or resolve some situations; they remain out of your control. When you can't find an easy way to communicate about your anger, consider writing about the problem, your feelings, and possible resolutions. There simply may not be any solutions, but writing about your frustrations may be the best option.

TIP

If a situation is either unsolvable or if you're not ready to tackle it head-on, consider writing as a first step.

Leaving out four-letter words

Four-letter words are, by definition, incendiary. They add gasoline to the fire and only heighten emotions and increase the probability of some type of verbal or physical aggression. They're meant to hurt, not educate. And they cause the person to whom they're directed to defend herself — either by withdrawing (tuning out what you're saying) or engaging in similar behavior. So now you have two people swearing at each other, which, to quote William Shakespeare, amounts to "sound and fury, signifying nothing."

TIP

Distance yourself from anger-laced profanity by starting with the word *I* rather than *you:* "I'm furious" rather than "You're a damn idiot!" Better yet, enlarge your emotional vocabulary to include other words synonymous with anger such as these: *irritated, incensed, exasperated, annoyed, displeased, enraged, outraged, disgusted, riled, vexed,* or *piqued.* In fact, with all these words, consider softening them up with phrases like, "a bit," "somewhat," or "a little."

TIP

Put yourself in the other person's shoes and ask yourself how you'd feel if someone called you a nasty name. If he were angry with you, what would you want him to say instead?

Staying on topic

When you start speaking out in anger, you may lose sight of the issue, problem, or circumstance that initially provoked you. Your anger heads off on a tangent, jumping from one grievance to another midstream. What starts out as, "I asked you to stop at the store for me, and you forgot," suddenly devolves into, "You never help out around here. You don't listen to me. You don't care about me at all. I don't know why I married you in the first place!"

You'd be surprised at how many anger-management clients describe some horrific incident involving anger, but then when asked what started the angry exchange they say, "Beats me. All I know is that one minute we were having a civil conversation and the next minute I was yelling and pounding my fist into the wall."

REMEMBER

The more intense your anger, the more likely the emotion itself will distract you from the issue at hand. Rage is so unfocused that after you calm down, most likely you won't remember details about what you said or did. One way to remain in control of your anger is to stay focused on what you're angry about. Keep your eye on the ball, and things are less likely to get out of control.

Taking turns

Constructive anger expression should be a give-and-take proposition. You express your feelings and let others take in their meaning. The best way to lose your audience — and ensure that your message is *not* heard — is to go on and on and on . . . ranting. By all means, speak out assertively, but keep it short.

Neurological sciences tell us that human beings can only digest (and remember) so much information at a time. That's why telephone numbers are limited to seven digits and an area code. Too much information at once overwhelms people.

Speaking out in anger for five minutes is like asking someone to remember a 50-digit number. It can't be done (at least by most people)! No wonder kids never remember what their parents tell them when their parents are angry. (And you thought they just weren't listening.)

Our advice is to speak assertively one minute, or preferably, much less at a time. Then take a breath and let the other person respond. That will also keep the intensity of your feelings from accelerating, which is what you want, right? If the person you're upset or angry with reacts defensively, let her have her say, don't interrupt, and then resume expressing how you feel for another minute (at most) and take another breath.

Keeping your voice tone low and slow

The louder you speak, the *less* people hear what you have to say. Your message gets lost in your overheated dialogue. What you actually say in anger isn't the only problem; it's the *tone* in which you say it. If you can keep a civil tone to your conversation, you'll find that actively listening to the person with whom you're angry is easier. It's also easier to get your message across to that person. Moderate anger can be an effective means of communication, but if you want to be heard, you have to pay attention to two aspects of your speech:

>> **Volume:** The power and fullness of your words. The angrier you are, the louder you sound. You don't have to be a rocket scientist to tell the difference between a person who is irritated versus someone who is in a full-blown rage.

>> **Pace:** The speed or velocity with which you speak. As your anger accelerates, you find yourself speaking faster and faster. There is a pressured quality to what you're saying — as if the angry words can't get out fast enough. Pauses help accentuate and highlight what you want to say, so don't be afraid of them.

TIP

Start paying more attention to *how* you speak when you get angry. If you hear yourself getting too loud, talking too rapidly, and/or sounding shrill, adjust your speech accordingly. Think of this as an effort on your part to literally fine-tune how you speak out in anger.

Being Civil Doesn't Always Mean Being Nice

Being civil simply means being a good citizen: someone who operates within the social rules of a society. It means acting toward others in ways that show mutual respect. It means not being rude, insensitive, thoughtless, or purposely antagonistic.

On the other hand, civility doesn't mean that you're always nice, tolerant, or accepting of whatever mistreatment comes your way. It doesn't require that you be passive, someone's doormat, or the proverbial pushover. And it doesn't mean that you don't ever experience or express reasonable levels of anger.

Civil people get irritated and angry, but they express it constructively. They *respond* to their angry feelings instead of *reacting* in some mindless, shoot-from-the-hip kind of way. And they speak out in ways that inform and educate those within hearing distance about the issues that underlie their anger.

Stop saying "I'm fine" when you're not

You may have found how to avoid taking responsibility for your anger by always saying "I'm fine!" even in circumstances where that's far from the truth. This response is an example of what politicians call a *non-response response*. It's a polite way of saying, "I'm not going to tell you how I feel. Maybe I don't trust whether you'll accept my feelings. Maybe you'll get mad because I'm mad. Or maybe I don't trust my feelings myself — should I really feel that irritated?"

The next time someone asks you how you feel about something, choose an emotional label that fits the situation — for example, happy, sad, mad, or glad. Being honest about how you're doing reduces your tension and helps keep you from getting irritated or angry.

Women and assertiveness

Despite the political, economic, and social advances women have made worldwide, some remnants of the old world order, in which different standards exist for acceptable emotional behavior among men and women, remain. Even today, women who show signs of anger and who express themselves assertively are likely to be labeled as aggressive for doing so.

No such reference is usually applied to men who do exactly the same thing. Many women feel understandably sensitive to this double standard and hesitate to be completely honest about their feelings unless those feelings are positive or nonaggressive. (The reverse is true when it comes to feelings such as grief, fear, and depression. Men who openly acknowledge such feelings tend to be viewed — by themselves and others — as weak and effeminate.)

If being assertive means you admit it when you're irritated or even angry, if it means setting limits on the bad behavior of others, or if it means addressing discrimination directly, be assertive even if you're labeled as aggressive. Be proud, articulate, passionate, self-assured, and charismatic, and hold your head up high and look your adversary in the eye. Then let that be the other person's problem.

CRITICISM IN THE WORKPLACE

Kieran Snyder reported on a study she conducted for *Fortune* magazine. She looked at 248 performance reviews at a wide variety of businesses. She found striking differences between the reviews provided to men versus women. Specifically, in contrast to men, women's personality characteristics were more often commented on with terms such as *emotional, bossy, aggressive, abrasive,* and *strident.* Reviews for men contained concrete suggestions about their work performance and provided clear guidance on desired changes for them to make.

Interestingly, out of the 105 reviews of men, only 3 included the word *aggressive.* Two of those actually advised the men to increase their aggressiveness. The bottom line is that women in the workforce appear to receive far more critical, negative feedback than men. No wonder women worry about criticism more than men: They have good reason to!

Chapter **9**

Mindfully Managing Anger

The right turn at the end of my road is at a 45-degree angle. This angle causes problems. People over- or undershoot the turn — in all directions. Because of that, there are frequent near misses and minor accidents, and the road has significantly eroded in places. A couple of years back, sitting at that intersection waiting to turn left, I was rear-ended by an inattentive driver.

Our neighborhood has one of those community email lists. You can only imagine the anger and frustration people express about that intersection. The comments come like waves of rage, increasing in intensity, and then generally calm down after a couple of weeks. Complaints have reached various mayors, city council members, and the department of public works, and still, after 20 years, nothing has been done.

So those of us who live on the road have two choices: Approach each turn with anger at the inaction of our local government would mean every day starting out every day feeling frustrated and annoyed. Or accept that life is full of inconveniences, and in the overall scheme of things, this one is pretty small stuff. It's really about personal choice: acceptance versus anger. Practicing acceptance is a large part of the practice of mindfulness.

This chapter shows you how to look at the world with mindful awareness and acceptance to manage difficult feelings. First, consider how acceptance of anger as a normal emotional reaction helps you become less overwhelmed by those feelings. You experience your emotions in a nonjudgmental way and thus become more self-compassionate. Next, see how living in the present can support your journey to becoming less angry. A few techniques will encourage your pathway to a more peaceful life.

Accepting Anger

Anger is a natural reaction to frustration, and there are plenty of things to get frustrated about in modern life. Here are just a few:

>> Tailgating drivers

>> People who let their dogs poop on your lawn or the sidewalk

>> Corrupt politicians

>> Polluters

>> Liars

>> Telemarketers

>> Litterers

>> Rude people

Anger is an emotion that can be adaptive in some situations (and I cover some examples in Chapter 2). But in most instances, anger does not stop rude people from being rude, tailgaters from tailgating, corrupt politicians from being corrupt, or telemarketers from telemarketing. You get the point.

REMEMBER

Nevertheless, to be human is to feel anger. That statement is true, and the more you try to deny that truth, the more anger you will feel. Accept that you will feel anger. Do not judge yourself harshly for your anger. Embrace your anger, and your anger will decrease.

Becoming aware of your anger

Anger awareness helps you catch it before it goes out of control and consumes you. It's easy to identify anger when it's intense. You may strike out verbally or physically. For example, if someone cuts you off while driving, you might slam the steering wheel, give someone the finger, or shout obscenities. But consider those times when anger is seething, covert, and undercover. Those times are harder to detect. They may occur when you sense that something is unfair, unjust, or dishonest.

Take the time to discover how your body feels anger. When you experience anger, take note of the thoughts that run through your mind. And pay attention to how you express anger. There are techniques throughout Part 2 to help you develop that awareness. But for now, simply observe your anger without judgement. Sit with your anger for a moment.

Breaking the automatic anger reaction

Awareness of anger is the first step in a mindful practice. The next step is to reflect, not react. Most people who experience trouble with anger feel anger and reflexively react. If you are angry that someone is attacking your daughter and you reflexively jump in to save her, that's fine. However, when you have an instant response to a less dangerous situation, an anger reflex does not usually help. For example, if you choose the slowest checkout line at the grocery store, reacting with anger is unlikely to get you to the front of the line.

Instead, connect with your anger, look beyond the initial feelings and tune into what is happening right now. Ask yourself the following questions:

» Is anger an appropriate response to what is happening?

» Will anger help me make good decisions?

» Will anger get me what I want?

» Are there other ways for me to get my needs met?

Take your time. You are not your anger. Feel your feelings. Anger will pass. Let it go.

Stepping aside and letting anger fly by

When anger is directed at you, again pay attention to how you are feeling. Stop and consider where in your body you feel that anger. Are you getting angry too? Or scared?

Pause with reflection, not with reaction. Consider what you might do if someone is literally flying at you in rage and you step aside. Let it be. That angry person might just whiz by harmlessly without you as the obvious target.

Every aggression aimed at you does not have to be reacted to with aggression. You need not be passive, just present. Ask yourself the following questions:

>> What is happening right now?

>> How do I protect myself?

>> Will becoming angry help me make a better decision?

>> Will it cause me harm by escalating the situation?

>> Are there *other* ways to get what I need?

REMEMBER

You do not have to be victimized by someone else's anger. In some cases, it's best to step aside or walk away. In other cases, you need to react forcefully, setting appropriate boundaries.

TIP

You have choices when anger is directed at you. See Chapter 8 on how to be compassionately assertive. Also, see Chapter 11 for a discussion about moral issues and anger.

Finding a wise mind

A common concept in psychology about how the mind thinks and makes decisions involves two brain circuits. The first circuit, thought to be primitive, makes quick instinctual decisions based on safety, survival, and need. The other circuit is more thoughtful and takes longer to make decisions. That circuit uses past experiences, ponders future possible consequences, and considers a wide range of responses. Anger often originates in the first, more primitive circuit.

A common method of describing this way of thinking is by comparing your mind to an elephant and an elephant trainer. A well trained elephant usually does what the trainer wants. But when suddenly frightened or angry, the elephant will do whatever it needs to stay safe. It may charge, bolt, or run away. The trainer only has so much control. A wise trainer will observe the elephant, realize what's going on, and help the elephant calm down.

Think of anger as coming from your mind's elephant, not your mind's wise trainer. Your wise mind can observe what is causing you to become angry and figure out what to do. No one blames the elephant for getting frightened or you for getting mad. The key is to use your skills and find the best solution.

Mindfully Living in the Present

What are you angry about right now? Probably nothing if you are reading this book. Look around. All around. Look up and down, side to side. Where are you sitting? Are you comfortable? Feel your feet on the ground, your body on the seat. Notice the position of your arms and hands.

What sounds do you hear? Can you hear traffic, noises from heating or air conditioning? Are there dogs barking, papers shuffling, others talking, or is it quiet?

Are there smells or other noticeable sensations? Is the temperature cool, warm, or just right?

Take a few deep breaths and feel the present. Stay focused on what is happening without judgment.

Most of what makes people angry, really angry, has already happened. It is in the past. That which will make you angry in the future has not happened. By focusing on the present, you are more likely to remain at peace.

Mindful practice

Mindfulness takes practice and patience. Don't expect to experience the benefits of mindfulness immediately. Mindfulness brings peace to an angry mind. By staying focused on the present, you change the way you look at the world. You become less judgmental and more accepting of reality. You don't give up righteous anger; you become less reactive and more productive.

REMEMBER

Being mindful does not take away what happened in the past. However, it takes away the ability of past anger to stay in your body and mind. Holding on to anger from the past only ruins the present. (See Chapters 16 and 17 on letting go and forgiving.)

Staying focused on the present does not prevent you from looking at the future. Plan for your future by taking reasonable care of yourself, your finances, your family, and friends. However, life is full of uncertainty. Know that you do the best you can and accept that you cannot control the future.

Mindful meditation

At the core, meditation involves focused attention for a period of time. Various forms of meditation have been around for thousands of years. However, in recent decades, the practice has been studied by scientists interested in how meditation works and whether or not it can be used to improve health and well-being. Hundreds of studies support the benefits of meditation in the following areas:

>> **Stress:** Regular meditation has been found to reduce stress for those who practice it. It appears to improve the ability to cope with stress.

>> **Anxiety:** It makes sense that reducing stress is also likely to reduce anxiety. Indeed, studies of anxious people learning to meditate have shown decreases in anxiety.

>> **Depression:** Meditation for people who have suffered depression is especially helpful in preventing relapses.

>> **Physical health:** There are numerous benefits from the practice of meditation on physical health, such as decreasing blood pressure, reducing inflammatory responses, and improving digestive health.

>> **Chronic pain:** Multiple studies have supported the conclusion that regular meditation practice can improve coping with chronic pain.

>> **Memory, thinking, and sleep:** Meditation helps people fall asleep and go back to sleep after awakening. It improves attention and decreases a tendency to have disturbing, repetitive thoughts. In addition, some recent research has linked meditation to possible benefits in memory and coping with dementia.

But what about anger? You can use logic to assume that many angry people are, at their core, stressed out. Therefore, a reduction in stress is likely to decrease anger. In addition, people with depression, anxiety, problems sleeping, chronic pain, or poor health tend to be more irritable.

There have been some studies that find meditation lessens the physical reactions to anger. For example, people were asked to recall a time in which they became very angry. Heart rate, breathing rate, and blood pressure were measured. All increased with the recollection of the angry response. However, after a meditation session, those same recollections did not raise blood pressure, heart rate, or breathing rate.

A regular meditation practice is good for all of the above reasons. Meditation generally makes people less reactive to stress, whether related to anger or other frustrations.

Other studies have found that after learning meditation and mindfulness techniques, participants become less emotionally reactive. Overall, the expanding literature supports the use of meditation for helping people manage difficult emotions, including anger.

MEDITATION FOR DEMENTIA-RELATED ANGER

Dementia is a disorder that causes problems with memory, thinking, attention, communication, reasoning, emotional regulation, and decision-making. More than 5 million Americans suffer from the ravages of dementia, and Alzheimer's Disease is the most common form. Unfortunately, a minority of people with dementia become irritable and, occasionally, physically aggressive. Controlling that aggression is often difficult to do, especially since some of the medications that help with those behaviors lead to dangerous and sometimes deadly side effects.

One pilot study had a unique way of handling aggression. Three patients with moderate Alzheimer's were able to learn a meditation technique called Soles of the Feet (SoF). This intervention involves standing or sitting in a comfortable manner. Patients were asked to breathe naturally and do nothing. Then they were instructed to recall an incident that caused them to feel anger. They were encouraged to stay focused on that incident, feel their anger, and then change their focus to the soles of their feet. While focusing on their feet, they were asked to notice any and all sensations, including texture, temperature, and pressure. When calm, they were told to walk away with a smile because they controlled their anger.

This intervention was practiced regularly over four weeks. All participants and their caregivers reported significant decreases in anger and aggression over time. This was a very small study, so results need to be replicated with larger sample sizes and randomized controlled groups. But the intervention was easy to implement, inexpensive, and worthy of further investigation.

Meditation guidelines

When I first learned to meditate, I sat on a pillow cross-legged and uncomfortable. I was told to maintain that position in spite of discomfort. I was instructed to make deep noises that made me feel self-conscious. My voice did not resonate and sounded squeaky. Overall, it wasn't a particularly pleasant experience.

Many years later with much more training, I meditate sitting in a comfortable chair with my feet firmly on the ground. The following are some general guidelines for meditation. However, unlike what most people assume, there are no absolute rules for meditation.

>> **Space:** Most people enjoy meditating in a quiet setting. Be sure to disconnect your devices. Don't be surprised at random noises. Sirens race by, dogs bark, kids interrupt. That's okay. Let them pass and return to your meditation. Lots

of people even meditate in public areas such as subway platforms or in public parks. It's often recommended that you practice meditation in a quiet space first. Then as your experience grows, you can meditate anywhere more easily.

» **Discomfort:** If you feel the need to scratch your nose, go ahead and do it. Or you may choose to focus on the sensation of the itch and see if it goes away. If your back hurts, don't be shy about shifting position. Some practitioners of meditation have rules about this, but don't think you must follow them to benefit from meditation. Make your own choices.

» **Thoughts:** During meditation, random thoughts will inevitably go through your mind. That's perfectly normal. Sometimes angry or disturbing thoughts will seize control of your attention. Do not judge those thoughts. Simply bring your attention back to the meditation. Thoughts will come and go.

» **Judgment:** All meditation is an act of present awareness. There is no such thing as having a good or bad meditation. Sometimes meditation is quiet and peaceful, other times your mind fills with turmoil. Your experience with meditation will change over time. There is no evaluation or report card on the quality of any meditation.

TIP

If you decide to meditate, try to find a time that fits your schedule and do it most days. That may seem overly burdensome, but you only need five or ten minutes. Most people can find those minutes. You will discover that as you practice, the time you spend meditating will make you more productive, less stressed, and more content throughout the rest of your day.

Types of meditation

Meditation takes on many forms. A common component of meditation is *focused attention*. However, what you focus on varies depending on the type of meditation you are engaging in.

TIP

Try out different styles of meditation to find one that fits you. Some people need more structure in order to focus attention. You can find free or inexpensive apps that are easy to use. Many are highly rated. There are also meditation descriptions and scripts easily accessed on the internet.

The following are the most common forms of meditation:

» **Breathing meditation:** This meditation involves focusing on the breath. Usually done sitting in a quiet place, with eyes closed, you simply breathe in and out. During this meditation, it can be useful to count the breaths or concentrate on the feeling of air moving in and out. Thoughts will come and go, but gently bring attention back to your breath.

>> **Body scan meditation:** This type of meditation is especially useful for people with chronic pain. It also helps focus attention more easily for beginners. It consists of shifting attention and awareness slowly through your body — either toes to head or head to toes.

>> **Loving-kindness meditation:** This form of meditation focuses on gently sending kind thoughts to yourself and to others. It may be especially useful for people with anger issues because it involves sending love to others as well as self-care. Research into loving-kindness meditation has indicated that it increases empathy, compassion, and social connection.

>> **Sound-focused meditation:** This form of meditation involves listening to different sounds. Ocean waves, forest noises, rain, tones, or bells are used to help focus attention.

>> **Walking meditation:** This meditation focuses attention on each individual step. Mindful awareness of placing each heel on the ground, rolling to the toe, lifting each foot, and repeating forms the essence of walking meditation. You can practice walking meditation almost anywhere, but don't forget to keep an eye on where you're headed at the same time!

>> **Mantra-based meditation:** Mantras are simple sounds and phrases that you repeat throughout your meditation session. Some mantras have spiritual meanings attached. However, you need not adhere to any particular spiritual or religious practice in order to benefit from using mantras. Other mantras have no spiritual or religious implications whatsoever. They vary from mere sounds to actual words and phrases. Here are few common examples of mantras: "omm," "nnnn," "aaah," "my heart is open," "Hare Krishna," "I am," "My mind is peaceful," "I am not afraid." You can easily develop your own mantra.

>> **Movement-based meditation:** The two most common forms of movement meditation are yoga and Tai Chi. You need to learn these practices from a teacher. Classes can easily be found at recreation centers, studios, gyms, or through adult education. You can also learn from videos. When possible, having an in-person teacher is useful to help develop proper form.

You can experiment with meditation on your own for free or relatively little money. You can learn on your own or with a bit of coaching. The benefits of meditation for emotional and physical health have been proven by many research studies. Try it out.

WARNING

There are a few meditation programs that can become cult-like. They tend to overpromise life changes, encourage time-consuming training, and require ever-increasing financial commitments. These programs offer exclusive membership and usually have special leaders. Buyer beware.

Anger-specific meditation

The following meditation may be especially helpful for those with anger issues. It is a combination of breathing and mantra-based meditation. You can tailor this exercise to your own issues. Choose pairs of words from Table 9-1 that fit your situation or come up with your own.

Plan on spending five or ten minutes daily on this meditation:

1. **Find a quiet spot and sit comfortably.**

2. **Take a few deep breaths.**

3. **Close your eyes.**

4. **Now breathe in on a positive word and out on a negative word. Add the words "I breathe in . . ." and "I breathe out . . ." to your mantra.**

TABLE 9-1   ## Mantra-Based Breathing Meditation

I Breath In . . .	I Breath Out . . .
Acceptance	Judgment
Stillness	Tightness
Serenity	Agitation
Tranquility	Turmoil
Love	Hate
Composure	Conflict
Relaxation	Rigidity
Calmness	Tension
Peace	Anger
Hope	Despair

Chapter **10**

Practicing Non-Angry Responses

Y ou've probably heard the expression, "I lost control," in reference to anger. In this chapter, you learn how to take back control of your anger. Instead of anger driving you to lose your cool, you a get a brand new license that puts you back in the driver's seat.

The first stop on your road trip is an exploration of brooding. Take a look at the costs of brooding and get some tips on how to delay or disengage from rumination. Then get some useful tips on practicing self-control. The goal is to be able to accept anger into your life, stay in charge, and keep your eye on the road.

Defining Brooding

Brooding, or rumination, is the human equivalent of a cow chewing on its cud. In other words, it's like chewing food already swallowed and then regurgitated. Gross.

When you continue to rethink, reconsider, relive, and rehash some incident that provoked your anger well beyond the point of where and when it happened, you're ruminating or brooding. And brooding invariably intensifies the emotion. At first you may just be irritated, but the more you think and talk about it, the madder you become. You can't let go of the thoughts, so you can't let go of the feelings. Essentially, you're stuck!

Brooding leads to, well, more brooding. The mind keeps rattling on about the same thing over and over. You mull, complain, grumble, whine, and whimper. The following example takes a look at one course of rumination and the likely outcome.

> **Craig** works as a personal trainer. He comes from a very well-to-do family. Although his father is disappointed in Craig's choice of a profession, he wants his son to look successful. Craig is thrilled when his father gives him the money to build his own state-of-the art fitness center. He believes he deserves to take the lead in the fitness profession because he is a special, unusually talented trainer.
>
> Craig's new building is called the Fitness Institute of America and has generous space for a staff of 16 trainers, physical therapists, massage therapists, and nutrition counselors. Craig recruits some of the best trainers and therapists in town. But trouble brews within a few months of the Institute's grand opening. Craig's narcissistic, dismissive style offends many of the experienced staff, and they start leaving one by one. Craig finds himself almost unable to recruit qualified applicants. When he persuades professionals to join his Institute, they end up quickly disillusioned and leave for other opportunities.
>
> Craig broods for hours every day about his problem. He complains to his current staff members about those who have left, "The last three people who worked here gave me firm two-year commitments. They all left, even though I paid for them to obtain extra certification from the National Body Mind Academy. They couldn't be more ungrateful after everything I did for them. People just lie, cheat, and take advantage of my generosity all the time."
>
> Craig spends so much time complaining and obsessively ruminating about former staff that current staff feel considerable discomfort. They realize that Craig will probably turn on them someday. His current staff start to look at other options. Craig broods entirely on what others have unfairly done to him and never looks at his own behavior of acting dismissive and self-centered as a possible part of the problem.

TIP

Rumination and brooding almost never lead to problem solving. Instead, they make the problem worse and keep the focus away from possible solutions.

If rumination doesn't lead to problem solving, why do so many people ruminate? People brood because they believe that brooding is helpful. And frankly, sometimes it feels good to ruminate about someone or something that has angered or wronged you. You can probably think about someone in your life that you dislike and for whom brooding about for a while might feel satisfying. However, that satisfaction is fleeting and soon replaced by negative emotions.

If you're stuck in an anger/brooding cycle, consider asking yourself some of the following questions:

>> Has my brooding ever really led to solid solutions and answers?

>> Do I think ruminating helps people solve problems?

>> Do I think that ruminating keeps me from getting into future problems?

>> When I ruminate, do I feel better or worse?

If you're like most people, when you honestly analyze your answers to the preceding questions, you'll realize that brooding and rumination simply don't help. That obsessive thinking style doesn't *solve* anything, and it usually causes you to feel worse than before you started.

People who ruminate have been found to have *more*, not fewer, problems than those who don't brood. And ruminating has never been shown to prevent future harm or catastrophes. Granted, obsessing may *feel* like it will help, but it doesn't.

Brooding, ruminating, and obsessing cost you more than they benefit you. Here are just a few costs of brooding:

>> Increases bad moods

>> Disrupts concentration

>> Intensifies anger

>> Raises blood pressure

>> Leads people to overeat, use drugs, or drink too much

>> Decreases motivation to exercise

>> Interferes with accomplishing positive things

ANGER, AGGRESSION, AND RUMINATION

Rumination takes many forms. Some people ruminate about their former boyfriends, girlfriends, or spouses. Others ruminate about future worries. Still others have repetitive thoughts with themes of injustice, revenge, and unfairness. That's called anger rumination or brooding.

A study looked at 200 college students taking a class in psychology. They were asked to complete a series of questionnaires. The purpose of the study was to see whether people who tend to ruminate when angry engaged in more physical aggression, verbal aggression, hostility, and increased frequency of angry episodes.

Researchers found that, indeed, angry ruminators had more instances of hostile, physical, and verbal aggression. Somewhat surprisingly, angry ruminators experienced anger just as often as non-ruminators, but the ruminators' anger came out in more intense ways.

Practicing Delayed Brooding

Many people who brood report wasting hours per day focused on whatever has angered them. *Delayed brooding* is an interesting strategy that contains your ruminating to a very limited amount of time. Limiting brooding helps you take control of your obsessive thoughts rather than allowing those thoughts to control your life. Delayed brooding involves a few basic steps:

1. **Either jot down on paper or dictate into a device anything that irritates, upsets, or angers you.**

2. **Set aside a very specific time of day (avoid doing this three hours or less before bedtime) to ruminate about your list.**

3. **Give yourself 15 minutes to ruminate, and then stop and do something distracting.**

4. **If after 5 minutes, you feel like you're done, go over your items again until the full 15 minutes are used up.**

5. **If you don't feel like ruminating at your selected time, do it anyway!**

6. **Repeat this process daily for at least a week.**

TIP

Very occasionally, people discover some partial solution or answer to their issue during delayed brooding. If you happen to come up with something productive, great. Make a note of it and act on it — in a reasonable, calm manner. However, solutions won't likely come to you very often.

The following example shows you how Layla ruminates about her former husband. She eventually sees how much brooding costs her and uses delayed brooding to get herself to a better place.

> **Layla** remains furious with her ex after a bitter, contested divorce. She had spent most of her retirement savings, lost her house, and declared bankruptcy to pay for attorney fees related to child custody disputes. Her mind constantly reviews the lies he told in court, the false charges he made, and the manipulative ways he tried to turn the kids against her.
>
> Layla ends up with joint (50/50) custody, and the court battles are over. Her life is on a regular schedule and she's worked out ways of exchanging the kids without horrible fights with her ex. Nevertheless, she finds her days consumed with ruminative thoughts about what she's lost financially, the unfairness of everything, and even the revenge she'd like to get but knows she can't.
>
> When her ex starts dating, Layla's obsessions intensify. She can't get him out of her mind. One day, her 7-year-old son asks her why she's so mad all the time. His question serves as a wake-up call for Layla. She decides to seek therapy because of her constant ruminative rage. Her therapist suggests using delayed brooding. Layla is open to the suggestion because she wants her life to focus on what's important now instead of dwelling on the past.
>
> Layla is quite surprised to find that delayed brooding works. Merely dictating her angry thoughts allows her to let go for a while. After all, she realizes she will take a look at the thoughts later. After a few days, she even sees the futility of bitter rumination and rarely wants to engage in it at the designated time. That's when her therapist tells her she can quit the practice of delayed brooding.

TIP

Brooding consumes a lot of precious time and depletes much of your emotional resources. As good as it sometimes feels in the short run, brooding hurts in the long run. Just think of all the time you save and use more productively with limited, delayed brooding.

Disengaging from Brooding

One of human beings' greatest strengths is the ability to think. However, many times, they take their thoughts far too seriously, which leads to lots of trouble. People think that because a thought crosses their minds, the thought must represent reality. For example, right now, it's a gorgeous day, sunny, 72 degrees with a slight cool, breeze. But I'm stuck here in my office having to write. I'm utterly miserable. How could I possibly be stupid enough to have signed a contract for yet another book? What am I, masochistic?

Wow! If I let myself get into those thoughts, I might stop and walk away (which is not to say that I didn't have those thoughts — I did — but I also know that my moods and thoughts will likely change in a few minutes). In fact, my thoughts are changing right now because writing at this moment is amusing me! Sometimes I think I'm pretty funny. So maybe this gig isn't such a bad way to spend a nice day. Besides, I can take breaks anytime I want. Who has a job like that? Aren't I lucky? Yes!

Great. You see, thoughts are just thoughts. They come and go. They can take all kinds of interesting directions. It's even sort of fun to watch thoughts move from one place to another.

This section explores some techniques for dealing with angry or disturbing thoughts, all of which help you disengage or distance yourself from your thoughts. For more ways to reexamine thoughts, check out Chapter 6.

Looking at clouds

You can think about clouds in much the same way as thoughts. How's that? Well, you can look at them and work yourself up into a tizzy, or you can dispassionately watch them float by. Here's what Louise did with the first strategy:

> **Louise** looks out her office window that has a nice view of the horizon. She sees a few clouds gathering, and her thoughts go off to the races. "Oh my gosh, clouds are starting to roll in and clump together. I didn't bring an umbrella with me today. How stupid! I'm so angry with myself. I can't believe I make the same mistakes all the time. I just know those clouds are going to turn into a downpour. I can already see a hint of gray in them, and they're sure to turn black and ugly. We had a tornado last year; maybe we'll get hit again. Or lightening. That almost killed a family in another nearby city six years ago. That's just great. I never prepare like I should. I hate myself!"

You can see that Louise let her thoughts get the better of her. Are those thoughts real? Well, they're real in the sense that they went through her head, but they don't mean much about what's likely to happen.

Now take a look at how Claude dealt with those same clouds:

> **Claude** sits at his desk and wistfully looks out the window. He thinks to himself, "Oh gosh, those clouds are so interesting. You can never tell what they'll do. Maybe they'll just float by. Or maybe they'll gather into a storm, in which case, I'll deal with it."

Same clouds, different way of dealing with them. Whereas Louise engaged with the clouds and ruminated over possible catastrophes and self-hate, Claude merely steps back and observes the clouds, realizing he can deal with them if and when he must.

The next time your mind fills with angry, irritable, or negative thoughts, try putting them on a cloud. Watch the thoughts but avoid active engagement with them. Just observe. Give them time, and they're likely to slowly float away.

Thoughts are just thoughts. They don't require you to interact with them or do anything at all other than notice them.

Stepping back from thoughts and refusing to "engage" with them is far different from "suppressing" thoughts. When people suppress thoughts, they actively try not to think about a troubling issue at all. However, that tactic simply doesn't work. In fact, it usually makes things worse. When you try not to think about something, as often as not, that's all you can think about.

Dropping the rope

Have you ever been in an argument with someone who just doesn't quit? It goes back and forth, back and forth, again and again, with no resolution. Here's an example of a couple who has some issues to illustrate the process:

> **He:** Why didn't you pay that credit card bill on time?
>
> **She:** Why is it supposed to always be my responsibility? You never keep track of anything around here!
>
> **He:** What are you talking about? I do everything.
>
> **She:** Everything? What are you talking about? I do everything?
>
> **He:** You're crazy. You do nothing around here.
>
> **She:** You're calling me a nothing? You're less than nothing.
>
> **He:** That's all the appreciation I get from you? You call me names? How dare you!
>
> **She:** I didn't call you a name. I called you a nothing. No, less than nothing.
>
> **He:** Well, your family is less than nothing too. Take that.
>
> **She:** My family. How about your family?! They are trash.

Okay. You get the point. Back and forth, no resolution in sight. This example may seem like an exaggeration, but people get into these types of arguments a lot more often than you'd think. The words may be a bit more sophisticated, but the content is just as silly.

So how do you get out of that kind of power struggle? Imagine you're standing on one side of the Grand Canyon. You've been given a thick rope to hold that's strung across to the other side. Your friend has challenged you to a tug of war, and you gladly accept. But then you see that your friend has tied the rope to a huge tow truck. As you stand there, the tow truck slowly begins to drive away. The rope you're holding is stretching, and you stagger forward a bit. What do you do? How can you win this game? After all, you don't have a tow truck on your side.

There's only one solution: Drop your end of the rope! And that's what I often recommend to people engaged in pointless, unwinnable conflicts. See how dropping the rope works for the preceding "he" and "she" couple. First, see how "he" drops the rope.

> **He:** Why didn't you pay that credit card bill on time?
>
> **She:** Why is it supposed to always be my responsibility? You never keep track of anything around here!
>
> **He:** Well, I don't think this is worth fighting over. I'll just go online and pay it. [See how he drops the rope?]
>
> **She:** Okay, that would be great. Thanks.

As you can see, when he drops his end of the rope, she's able to let go as well. There are no rules chiseled in granite that you have to "win" every imaginable battle, even if you're right.

Letting go of what might happen

Angry people typically assume that the world is full of threats: threats to their self-esteem, sense of fairness, and safety. They imagine that other people are untrustworthy and dishonest. Therefore, they become hypervigilant and on the lookout for hazards, menaces, and risks.

There's just one problem with this strategy. Although bad things absolutely will and do happen, no one can readily predict which ones, where, or when they'll occur. Consider Figure 10-1, which shows you a small sample of the possible perils that all humans face in everyday life.

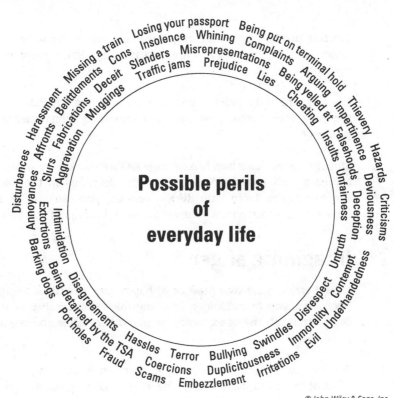

FIGURE 10-1:
Possible perils of everyday life.

© John Wiley & Sons, Inc.

No doubt many, if not most, of these possible perils have happened to you. Probably many times over. Who hasn't been cheated, put on hold, yelled at, insulted, and criticized? Assume that you know that *three* of the perils in Figure 10-1 will happen to you in the next two weeks. You still can't know which ones, where they'll occur, or how they'll play out. So if you walk around in a state of paranoid hypervigilance all the time, you're going to make yourself miserable, and you'll be primed for anger. Accept the inevitable. Respond to bad things when they happen, but not before.

Exposing Yourself to Tough Situations

Understanding techniques of disengaging from anger, irritability, and brooding is one thing. But that's not enough. You need to be able to disengage when you're under fire. The only way you can do that is by practicing the art of stepping back and disengaging when confronting difficult situations.

Exposure involves practicing anger-management skills in response to realistic, anger-arousing events. Exposure increases confidence and slowly reduces anger over time.

Like any other skill, practice improves performance. The following sections show you three ways to accomplish the goal of remaining calm regardless of what comes your way.

TIP

This chapter explains how to disengage and step back from anger. You can use this approach with anger-arousing exposures described in the following sections. However, when faced with difficult events, you can also practice rethinking (Chapter 6), assertiveness (Chapter 8), and mindfulness (Chapter 9).

Imagining anger

A great way to start your practice with exposure is to think about a situation that often leads you to feel angry. By doing this exposure in your imagination, you don't run much risk of exploding around other people and creating unnecessary problems.

You can start by writing down a scene on paper or dictating into a device. Include loads of details to make your scene as realistic as possible. Take the scene in a logical, step-by-step order. But as you do, imagine your non-angry response: Perhaps you see yourself disengaged, using relaxation, or replying in a calm and assertive way.

In the following story, **Andy** has a problem with anger management and imagines a common scenario with his wife, Brittany. Brittany starts out with her typical complaint about Andy's lack of help around the house.

I'm sitting on the couch, watching a great football game. Brittany calls out from the kitchen and asks one of her usual questions about things I haven't done, such as whether I've taken out the trash, fixed the doorknob, or picked up the dog poop in the backyard. All I want to do is watch my game, so I tell her, "I'll do this later!"

I already feel the anger rising. Usually, this sort of thing starts a fight that just gets worse and worse. But today is different; I'm going to bring things down a notch for a change. I need to step back and disengage from my ruminative angry thoughts. Here's what I'm going to do instead:

1. I'm going to take a couple of slow, deep breaths.

2. I can record this game and come back to it because it's not worth letting this thing get out of hand. I can do what she's asking in less than a half hour and save a huge, typical fight where I wouldn't see the game anyway.

3. *I say to myself, "My marriage is worth more than a football game, and she has been asking for these things for a while. This is really small stuff."*

4. *After the game, I will develop a to-do list and work through an item or two each day.*

Andy caught himself and stepped back (disengaged) from his anger just as it started. He regained control. Therefore, he found it possible to come up with several good strategies to get through the situation. This situation would have inevitably led to an explosive argument in the past. He ran this scenario in his imagination a dozen times, and just three weeks later, the event actually occurred. Andy got through with flying colors.

TIP

Write or dictate as many scenarios like Andy's as you can think of. Imagine a variety of situations that have led you into anger traps in the past. Practice disengaging and using non-angry responses over and over in your mind.

Watching the news

Most people "love to hate" certain news and/or talk radio shows, regardless of their political persuasion. If you have anger problems, these shows can serve quite well as exposure opportunities. Try listening to one of the shows you hate the most while practicing disengagement and stepping back from anger. Imagine the words are simply floating over your head. Refuse to talk back or respond in anger to what you hear. Say to yourself, "Words are just words; thoughts are just thoughts."

When you've mastered disengagement, lean in and listen carefully again. Feel your anger starting to rise. Come on, how dare they say such vicious nonsense? How can they be so stupid? Where do you feel the anger in your body? Now, step back again. Take a few deep breaths. Disengage. Rinse and repeat.

WARNING

A few folks find this exercise too difficult. If you try this exercise three times straight and just can't disengage from your anger, stop using this technique! If you're in therapy, you may want to discuss this struggle with your therapist.

Practicing with others: Bringing it on

Another important exposure technique utilizes *verbal provocations*. Verbal provocations consist of remarks by other people that you find offensive and/or anger arousing. You practice listening to these provocative statements over and over again while practicing disengagement and calmness.

You can carry out this exposure by reading written statements, listening to a recording of the statements (which you make), or having a highly trusted (as in really, really trusted) friend or therapist or coach hurl the statements your way with gusto. Even better, try starting with written statements, move up to listening to a recording, and cap it off with a real person.

WARNING

Only practice with real people if you feel ready and feel truly safe with whomever you've chosen to practice with. It's also a good idea to have first mastered responding to written statements and recordings.

Everyone has different anger buttons. The list that follows simply gives you some provocative statements that many people would have trouble hearing. Feel free to develop your own, creative list.

>> You just don't get it, do you?

>> Do you ever think about anyone other than yourself?

>> You're worthless.

>> How did you ever graduate from grade school?

>> Where did you learn to drive?

>> Watch where you're going already!

>> Can't you see that I'm busy?

>> You haven't done anything to deserve a raise.

>> Your house looks like a pigsty.

>> You're the messiest person I know.

>> What in the heck did you do with your hair? Put your finger in a light socket?

>> I find people like you offensive.

>> How entitled can you get?

>> The entire world isn't about you, you know.

>> I don't have time to deal with your stuff.

>> You make me sick to my stomach.

>> Get out of my space.

>> Are you guys ever going to vacate this table?

>> I don't have all day, you know.

>> I was here first; are you blind?

>> What's wrong with you anyway?

>> I don't think you could be any more annoying if you tried.

>> Don't bring a baby to a restaurant if you can't keep it quiet!

>> Are you deaf? Didn't you listen to what I asked for?

>> I can't stand being in the same room with you.

>> You never pull your own weight around here.

>> This paper is the worst I've ever read. Are you stupid?

Please don't be offended by some of the preceding offensive statements! They're designed to arouse anger and feel insulting. Choose some of them for exposure practice or make your own list.

REMEMBER

Just because an insult or demeaning statement comes your way doesn't mean that you should or must respond to it. You end up looking surprisingly strong if you remain calm and cool. Just take a deep breath and walk away. Who is the fool in that case?

Anger sometimes feels good because it gets you what you want — in the very short run. For example, when you angrily confront an employee of yours, she may do exactly what you want. But in the long run, you're setting the scene for increasing resentment and hostility. Anger almost always costs you more than it gives you over the long haul.

4
Managing Anger Hotspots

Chapter **11**

When You Are Morally Outraged

Right now, it seems like there is more divisiveness in the world than ever before. But when you look back in history, for gosh sake, there were a couple of world-wide wars just in the last century as well as frequent smaller wars, with the accompanying loss of life, violence, hatred. And ancient times were no picnic either. There was plenty to fight about. From family violence to tribal violence to violence against neighboring countries, the world has always been a pretty angry place.

What makes this current time seem like anger is exploding everywhere? People feel angry about the pandemic, politics, civil unrest, police brutality, economic inequalities, immigration, and climate. Perhaps it's because of the constant barrage of instant news. All day and night, phones buzz with notifications. And the news does not report on how many people manage to get along without hatred or how many people live safe, relatively happy lives. The news reports on death, disease, destruction, divisiveness, deception, and despair. Finally, the very essence of truth has come into question with every political group claiming that the opposition is delivering fake news.

This chapter takes a delicate delve into some of the hot topics of our times. Politics have ripped apart life-long friendships and split families. It has created unbearable tensions in the workplace and at social gatherings. Issues such as climate change, inequality, the pandemic, race, guns, and gender have led to arguments, protests, and violence.

The purpose of this chapter is not to take any particular stand on these issues, but to present ideas on how to improve communication among people who have different points of view. By emphasizing common human values, families, and neighborhoods, the world may be able to find some relief from the current state of fury.

WARNING

If you have a short fuse, these topics may be particularly difficult. However, it's hard to avoid having to face current controversies whether it's at work or at a family gathering. Some might find it easier to stay quiet in the midst of turmoil. That's okay; the strategies that follow may still help you understand and become more comfortable when you are struggling with a challenging situation.

Responding to Injustice

People respond to perceived injustice with anger. That anger is often thought of as morally based. Moral outrage is defined as frustration and justifiable anger toward an institution, group, or individual who violates ethical standards or values and harms others.

Moral outrage sometimes helps right wrongs. It potentially inspires and brings people together to help each other, to take action, and make changes. Most people know right from wrong. They believe that people should be kind to each other and that killing, stealing, cheating, lying, and hurting others are wrong. Morality involves being brave, fair, loving, respectful, and helpful.

However, morality is not always that simple. "Do no harm" has different meanings in different contexts and among different people. Therefore, moral outrage also breeds contempt, conflict, and intensified anger. Take for example the following situations:

> **Andrea** is a mother of two young children. She recently lost a low-paying job in a manufacturing plant. Her *Chicago* neighborhood is crime ridden. Each night, she hears gunshots and fears for her life and the lives of her children. She only leaves home to wait in food lines and complete necessary errands because of the threat of violence. She dreams of somehow leaving the area in order to improve her opportunities and to provide her children a safe and secure place to live. She is thrilled when her aunt in El Paso, Texas invites Andrea to move in with her until she can get established in a job in the much safer city.

Who could blame Andrea for wanting a better environment for her children? Isn't she lucky that her family wants to help? Most people agree that it is a moral value that parents try to keep their children safe. And that extended families help each other when they can. Now, let's change one detail in the example. Read it again.

> **Andrea** is a mother of two young children. She recently lost a low paying job in manufacturing plant. Her *Ciudad de Guatamala* neighborhood is crime ridden. Each night she hears gunshots and fears for her life and the lives of her children. She only leaves home to wait in food lines and complete necessary errands because of the threat of violence. She dreams of somehow leaving the area in order to improve her opportunities and to provide her children a safe and secure place to live. She is thrilled when her aunt in El Paso, Texas invites Andrea to move in with her until she can get established in a job in the much safer city.

Same situation, right? Still a mother looking out for her children with a family member offering to help. A considerable number of people would view both situations as equivalent: Mothers and families both looking for a better life.

Others would view the first scenario as justified; Andrea wants out of a bad neighborhood in Chicago. But if Andrea is moving from Guatemala to the United States, that would be wrong. Those people believe that illegal immigration to the United States is morally wrong. This is the problem with moral outrage.

You can see the struggle. Those who believe that illegal immigration is threatening to the United States have a point. If the U.S. opened the borders to every human on earth who wants a better life, the country would likely be overwhelmed. There are no simple answers. Yet those who simply want to help a mother and her children survive a horrible situation have strong, valid moral reasons.

So the problem with moral outrage is that rarely are overly rigid moral standards adequate to address the complexity of most world issues. Keeping that in mind, begin to see that most good people have similar morals, and they believe in the value of doing no harm. However, the world is complex, people view things from different moral perspectives, and balance is difficult to achieve.

TIP

You can see how a discussion about immigration can easily devolve into an argument. Try to see how different perspectives on moral values lie behind these different positions. It's hard to really say which "moral" stance is correct. This understanding can lead to less anger and perhaps productive discussions rather than shouting matches.

Polarizing Politics

Political divides have never been sharper. Everything from healthcare to gun control to childcare has a political flavor. And the political parties have rarely seemed more acrimonious. A large study from the Pew Research Center supports this contention. An extensive nationwide poll in the U.S. asked Democrats and Republicans about how they viewed members of the other party. Many of the findings are quite astounding.

>> Both parties agree that divisions between parties are getting bigger (85 percent Republicans and 78 percent Democrats). They are also worried and concerned about increasing partisanship.

>> In the past, most Democrats and Republicans would say that they agree on factual information about present problems but disagree on policies. Today, 77 percent of Republicans and 72 percent of Democrats declare that they don't agree on a *basic set of facts*.

>> Members of both parties lack confidence in the other party's ability to govern. Over 80 percent of Democrats and Republicans believe that the other party has few or almost no good ideas on governing.

>> Republicans view Democrats as unpatriotic (63 percent), immoral (55 percent), close-minded (64 percent), and lazy (46 percent).

>> Democrats view Republicans as close-minded (75 percent), immoral (47 percent), and unintelligent (38 percent).

>> Both Democrats and Republicans believe that members in the opposing party do not share nonpolitical values either. Republicans believe that 61 percent of Democrats do not share their goals or values. And 54 percent of Democrats believe that Republicans do not share their basic values.

Researchers found that people who closely watch and actively participate in their party's politics tend to have more extreme views about the other party than those who were less involved. However, even those who described themselves as independents yet leaning toward one party or the other expressed similar views to those who profess strong adherence to either party.

The Pew study also asked participants how warm or cold they feel about members of the other party. Scores were divided between warm, neutral, and cold. Democrats (79 percent) felt somewhat to very cold about Republicans. Republicans (83 percent) felt somewhat to very cold about Democrats. Ouch.

ONLINE DATING AND POLITICS

About a third of today's romantic relationships start online in the U.S. That number has been growing each year since the practice started in the mid-1990s. A couple of researchers from Yale and Stanford Universities were interested in whether or not politics influences the choices of potential social relationships online. They developed two strategies to study this question.

In the first study, researchers randomized political characteristics on profiles that were then presented to participants. As expected, participants were more interested in meeting people with profiles that were consistent with their own political views.

The second study was larger in scope. It used real-life data from a national online dating site. The study looked at three variables. First, it tracked political identity such as party affiliation or the overall label the individual used to describe their ideology (for example, liberal, conservative, socialist, authoritarian, communist). Then researchers looked at individual issues that participants identified with, such as pro-life or pro-choice or stands on immigration. Finally, they examined the amount of participation and interest suggested by dating profiles.

What they found was people looking for relationships using online dating apps are choosing potential dates that share political identities, issues, and degree of participation in politics. With couples sharing similar political ideology, there is not much chance for diversity of thoughts or opinions. Not surprisingly, this choice can lead to more divisiveness and polarization of our population.

With this much animosity, where do we go from here? We don't like each other, can't agree on reality, and have seemingly very different values. Yet it's dangerous to give up and give in to the present level of discord and mistrust. The next two sections offer potential strategies that may point the way to quelling the frustration of divisiveness and tame tempers.

Finding common ground

Despite political differences, people all around the world have basic needs. Those needs include food, shelter, air, water, and the ability to live in a safe environment. In addition, most people want to feel secure, cared for, well liked, respected, purposeful, and connected to others. When dialoging with people who do not share similar political views, it is important to find ways to communicate and connect to those common needs and desires.

Why bother? There are some who think staying out of the fracas is the sanest thing to do. Let each camp believe what they want, stay away from each other, and quit talking. Well, we have mutual problems to solve, and without cooperation and compromise, little can be done. Without better communication between opposing parties, stagnation happens. Diverse viewpoints provide a source of possible ideas for finding solutions for complex problems.

Finding agreed upon issues

It's not that surprising that when Americans are asked specifically about everyday issues without invoking a particular political party, there are many concerns that most people agree on. Several large current studies have found that rank-and-file Republicans and Democrats see more or less eye to eye on many policy positions. Here are a few:

>> Fix roads and bridges. Everyone agrees that our highways, roads, transportation systems, airports, and bridges need to be updated and repaired.

>> Improve access to higher education and increase job training for unemployed or underemployed. There is little disagreement among the public that higher education has become too expensive.

>> Do something about poverty. Most people believe that homelessness is a growing problem and that we should feed the hungry.

>> Do something to help reduce addiction and decrease crime.

>> Protect social security. That includes, for the very wealthy, decreasing benefits and increasing taxes.

TIP

So if you are attempting to have a conversation with someone from another political party, find some small issue to talk about that you can both agree on. Start with a policy or a worn-out bridge. Remember that, at the core, you are both likely to share at least some similarities.

Communicating effectively

The first rule of effective communication is to *listen* more than you talk. Too many conversations become independent lectures. One person states a position, there is little or no interaction, and the other person states another position. That is not a conversation. A conversation involves listening. How do you listen?

>> **Ask questions.** Don't start with "How in the world can you believe?" which really sounds like, "How can you be so stupid to believe?" Instead ask, "Tell me a little about your position."

>> **Be curious.** Ask for more details and show sincere interest. Think like a scientist attempting to discover the truth.

>> **Be attentive.** Don't dismiss what you hear simply because you don't agree. Again, the more you can learn, the better you can understand. Stay focused on the person you are listening to.

>> **Maintain eye contact.** Don't look around or at your phone.

>> **Stay in tune with nonverbal communication.** Watch your posture and facial expression. Avoid negative body language.

>> **Delay expressing disagreement.** Most likely, the person you are talking to already knows your views. No sense in bringing it up here. Your point is to communicate and start *relating rather than arguing*.

>> **When you don't understand, ask more questions.** It's perfectly fine to admit that you don't understand something. Ask for clarification.

>> **Repeat back what the person is saying to make sure that you understand.** For example, "Am I right in understanding that you think that immigrants are taking over Americans' jobs? And you worry about your own children getting jobs?"

>> **Make every attempt you can to stand in the other person's shoes.** While you listen, consider the life experiences of the other person, look at background, education, family, and finances. Sometimes an understanding of a person's history can help you understand a political stance.

>> **Remember your shared values.** Perhaps you both have a love for nature or animals. You care about your families and worry about the future for your children and grandchildren. You both respect liberty and freedom. The relationship may matter more than agreement or disagreement about a particular issue.

Don't try to change someone's mind. You are not acting as a trial lawyer here. You are attempting to find common ground or at least learn how to hold a civil discourse. A single-minded focus on winning ends up losing.

TIP

Communication skills need to be practiced for mastery. Try out the preceding advice on someone you agree with before trying them with someone who does not share your views. You are likely to find these skills help improve friendships, relationships with colleagues, and intimate relationships. Eventually, you may even shift someone's perspective.

REMEMBER

Sophisticated, non-angry communication requires considerably greater effort than simple, reflexive, anger-based interactions. The effort is worth making.

Stepping away from conflict

There are many times that walking away from conflict is the best choice. There are three situations that stand out:

>> When the cost of expressing anger is higher than the benefit.

>> When there is no chance of winning.

>> When either you or the other person is likely to lose control.

Counting costs and benefits

In some instances, looking at the balance of costs versus benefits will inform you on when to give up. For example, if you spend time arguing on the phone with a call-center employee about a minor issue, such as a $1.50 overcharge on your phone bill, you're likely to be disappointed by the results. Rarely does even asking to speak with a supervisor get you much further than another explanation of a company policy. You may spend hours making useless phone calls that leave you frustrated with little benefit. The costs to you of lost time, frustration, and anger usually don't balance the feeling that you were really able to express your distress on the phone. Even if you win the argument, were the hours of time worth the benefit of $1.50?

On the other hand, if staying on the phone for hours gets you a richly deserved refund on a defective product or a cancelled reservation, perhaps that decision was correct. The key is to stay calm, firm, and focused (and have something else to do while waiting on hold).

> **Anton** and his partner were looking forward to their cruise to Viet Nam in the fall of 2020. When the pandemic hit, they still had hope that by autumn, the disease would be under control. However, that summer, the cruise line informed them that all cruises were cancelled. Anton called the cruise line's customer service number and asked for a refund. He was on hold for over an hour. A harried representative said that they were overwhelmed, but he could expect a check in a couple of weeks. Three weeks passed without a check. Over the course of the next month, Anton called dozens of times. Customer service personnel were struggling with high volumes, working from home, and experiencing poor communication because of the chaos of the pandemic. Rather than getting mad, Anton was polite but *persistent*. He asked that each call be documented in his record. He routinely had his phone on speaker while he worked on other projects during hold times. Anton was able to take the perspective of the poor employees who were trying to do the best they could in trying times. He was finally able to get his refund — without once losing his temper.

For Anton, clearly the benefits of not walking away were well worth his efforts. However, he was able to understand the stress of those poor call center workers who had not caused the current conditions. This realization helped lead him to manage his own frustration in a productive manner.

Losing is the only option

There are some situations that are hopeless. Nothing you say or do will change the outcome. For example, when someone gets a diagnosis of a fatal disease, anger may be one of many feelings, but rarely (or never) will anger change that diagnosis. There are other times when you just have to accept that winning will not happen, such as arguing with a relative who has had stubborn views for decades. At those times, walking away is usually the best option.

WARNING

There are some things worth fighting for, even when the odds of winning are slim. Perhaps there is an injustice that leads you to protest, despite feeling like change will never come. However, decades later, those protests might pay off. So rather than walking away from all seemingly winless battles, pick and choose based on your own moral values as well as costs and benefits.

When intense conflict is likely to explode

If you are on a battlefield or protecting yourself or a loved one from attack, go ahead and scream, yell, swear, and fight like hell. However, if you are at a dinner table or in an office cubicle, those same behaviors are not likely to result in a good ending. There are some situations that get out of hand. When that happens, it's almost always best to walk away.

Chapter 10, in the section "Dropping the rope," describes a technique that is so valuable that it is worth mentioning again. When there is a battle that you cannot possibly win (think playing tug of war with the strongest human on earth), the only way to win the game is to drop the rope.

REMEMBER

Walking away is not losing. It can be a smart strategy in a potentially explosive situation. Intense conflicts usually end up with two losers instead of one.

Looking at Inequities

Studies of children as young 3 years old through adulthood show that most people believe that resources should be distributed equally. Research in which participants are asked to divide items among other participants find that they almost always divide them in equal measures. These studies show the same result among multiple populations across the world. They support the idea that people think highly of equality. Equality means that everyone should be treated the same.

In addition to a common human value of equality, there is also a desire for fairness. There is a subtle difference between the concept of fairness and the concept of equality. Fairness means giving people the same chances, of being unbiased, and following rules. Being fair does not necessarily mean being equal.

These two values often conflict. For example, is it *fair* for someone who does not work very hard to get paid equally to someone who works extremely hard? On the other hand, is it *fair* for someone who works as hard as another in the same position to receive less (unequal) pay?

With the caveat in mind that morality is a complex and intricate subject, the following sections take a look at some difficult issues that involve fairness and equality.

Mad about money

Income inequality has never been this extreme in most of the world. The very rich keep getting richer, and the poor get poorer. The middle class keeps shrinking. This makes people mad. It taps into both the concepts of fairness and equality. It seems unfair that middle class people pay more taxes than the very rich, and some of the largest corporations avoid taxes entirely.

The American dream of working hard and getting ahead has become a nightmare for many. People work full time or more and still cannot make a decent living. The tragic landscape of food lines and homeless camps causes many people to feel angry. News stories about parents paying hundreds of thousands of dollars to buy their privileged children places in good colleges adds fuel to the fire.

Public schools don't appear to be the great equalizer anymore. Even a college degree does not guarantee a middle-class life. Wages for the working and middle class remain stagnant while stockholders and the top 1 percent continue to reap staggering wealth.

TIP

If you are angry about income inequality, use your anger productively. Become active in local and national politics. Vote for people who support living wages, basic healthcare, fair housing, and improved educational opportunities.

Health disparities

Poor people and minorities have suffered greater losses during the pandemic. The rates of hospitalizations and deaths have been greater for Black, Hispanic, American Indian, and Asian patients than for White patients. Minority people are more likely to be essential workers, live in crowded homes, and have less access to healthcare. In addition, they are more likely to have underlying health conditions that increase the risk of getting serious illness or dying from COVID-19.

It's no wonder that people with limited access to healthcare feel angry about their situation. Inequality of healthcare has deadly consequences. People who are angry about an unfair social situation can work productively by participating in politics, protests, and charity.

Fearing the "Other"

People with chronic anger often identify the "other" as a cause of their anger. The "other" may refer to someone who is different in some way from them. These differences include the following:

>> **Race:** Studies of genes in the late 20th century have disproven the assumption that there are differences in the genetic structures among different races. Therefore, "race" is a culturally defined word that describes people largely based on outward appearance, culture, and developmental experiences. For example, U.S. Vice President Kamala Harris was born of parents from India and Jamaica. She chooses to identify as Black due to her upbringing and other factors.

>> **Gender:** Sex is the physical set of reproductive organs, sex chromosomes, hormones, and secondary sex characteristics that a person is born with but that can change over time with medical care. Gender identity is the personal way that individuals see themselves. Some people's gender identity departs from their original, biologically determined sex. Indeed, some people switch their gender identification based on behavioral and/or biological changes that express the identity they feel themselves as most closely aligned with.

>> **Ethnicity:** Ethnicity includes culture, nationality, and/or religion. People may describe themselves in multiple ways and often self-identify. For example, an immigrant from Mexico can identify as primarily Mexican, Hispanic, Latinix, or American. However, ethnicity may also be imposed on someone from the outside. For example, some people may consider legal immigrants never completely American.

>> **Religion:** Religion can be described as a certain set of beliefs usually involving worship of a supreme being. It helps people answer important questions about the meaning of life and death. Religion usually offers guidelines for how to live a life. Religion can be self-defined and can change over time.

Identities give people meaning. They may offer inclusion into groups, support, and camaraderie. However, too often people are judged by their identity, discriminated by their identity, or even killed because of their identity. Here are a few examples of people harmed because of their identity:

>> Jewish people during the Holocaust

>> Black men by police officers

>> Transgender or non-gender people murdered in hate crimes

>> Armenian genocide in Turkey

>> Native Americans murdered, dislocated, and discriminated against

Fear of the unknown is a natural, evolved emotional reaction designed to enhance survival. In prehistoric times, an unknown person or tribe was deemed potentially dangerous. That's because strangers were likely seeking food, shelter, or other provisions. One way of dealing with possible danger is to attack the threat. Anger fuels an aggressive, fierce response. That angry response may have saved lives in prehistoric times but doesn't serve us as well today.

Thus, anger over differences in appearance, religion, nationality, lifestyle, or political affiliation today is not necessarily evolutionarily beneficial. In fact, those angry responses now often cause harm (wars, fights, riots, and discrimination). These feelings of distrust and anger likely have deep biological roots. Grounded in fear of the "other," people tend to quickly reject those seen as different from themselves.

REMEMBER

Much of the suffering in the world reflects conflicts over different identities. However, human similarities are greater than their differences. The answer lies not in discarding the notion of valued identities but to look back to the concepts of equality and fairness and treat all people in ways that reflect those values, which is, admittedly, not an easy task.

Chapter **12**

Dealing with Anger at Work

This chapter highlights the role that anger management plays at work, the place where most people spend the majority of their time away from home. Before diving in, consider these questions:

» While you're at work, do you find yourself scrolling online rather than doing your job?

» Have you ever come to work late without permission?

» Have you ever made fun of a co-worker's personal life?

» Have you ever told someone outside work what a lousy employer you have?

» Have you ever done something at work to make a fellow employee look bad?

If you answered yes to any of these questions — and, don't worry, these situations are common — then you're engaging in what occupational psychologists call *counterproductive work behavior* (CWB). CWB is any behavior by an employee that results in harm to the organization or its members; it ranges from idle workplace gossip to acts of physical violence.

The cost of CWB to industry: billions of dollars. Direct theft by employees alone costs more than $15 billion. Then there's inefficiency, errors, absenteeism, damage to property, retribution, interpersonal conflict, sabotage, lawsuits, and employee turnover. Those costs run into the 100s of billions of dollars annually. The number-one cause of CWB? You guessed it: anger!

This chapter describes how CWB plays itself out in the workplace and which types of personalities are most prone to CWB. It shows how you can be competitive at work without being counterproductive and how you can be civil in your dealings with co-workers — by being a *mostly* anger-free employee.

TECHNICAL STUFF

A few studies have found that anger occasionally can be a useful tool during negotiations. People do best when they express anger verbally and intensely, especially when they hold positions of power and their argument is strong. Though the argument of the moment might be won by the one in power, there may be longer-term costs such as lowered morale, resentment, and increased CWB.

Identifying Counterproductive Work Behavior

TIP

Recognizing counterproductive work behavior (CWB) — in yourself and in others — can be tough. In part, that's because much of it seems "normal" at-work behavior like coming to work late or taking a longer break than you're allowed to. In addition, the majority of CWB is passive and nonviolent in nature. Here are some typical examples:

>> Failing to report a problem and allowing it to get worse

>> Ignoring someone at work

>> Withholding needed information from a colleague

>> Staying home and saying you're sick when you aren't

>> Trying to look busy when you aren't

>> Refusing to help a co-worker

>> Intentionally coming late to a meeting

>> Working slowly when things need to be done fast

>> Refusing to accept an assignment

>> Leaving work earlier than you're allowed to

>> Avoiding returning an email or phone call to someone you should

>> Purposely failing to follow instructions

Less often, CWB constitutes more active destructive or injurious behaviors, such as

>> Purposely damaging a piece of equipment

>> Stealing something belonging to your employer

>> Insulting a co-worker's work performance

>> Starting an argument with a co-worker

>> Making an obscene gesture to a co-worker

>> Threatening another employee with violence

>> Hitting or pushing someone at work

>> Purposely wasting supplies/materials

>> Intentionally doing your work incorrectly

>> Starting a harmful rumor about another employee

>> Cyberbullying a co-worker

>> Playing a mean prank on someone at work

>> Acting nasty or rude to a customer or client

TIP

Look at the lists of counterproductive work behaviors and make note of which ones you've engaged in lately — say, the last three weeks. Do you engage in any of these behaviors on a fairly regular basis, or once or twice a week? Pick one of these and tell yourself, "I'm not going to express my anger this way anymore." Then use some of the anger-management strategies outlined later in this chapter instead.

The global pandemic has changed the workplace. For those working from home, increasing feelings of isolation and lack of cohesion with other workers may be taking place. Those employees who work in manufacturing, warehouses, restaurants, or stores may be socially distanced, masked, and have other restrictions of normal activities in place.

On the other hand, some people enjoy working from home. There may be less potential for interpersonal conflict on video conferencing than at conference tables. However, some people may find Zoom meetings irritating. Perhaps some new CWBs will include the mute button sticking, pretending to have a poor internet connection, playing online games, checking email, or feigning being constantly cut off.

Frustrating, anger-producing commutes are eliminated when workers stay home. These benefits, however, are not shared equally. Essential workers, healthcare workers, and others still face the same frustrations of commuting plus the additional frustrations of the restrictions.

It's premature to know the long-term results of isolation, working from home, and social distancing. However, these new stressors are likely to change and possibly increase worker dissatisfaction as well as CWB.

Avoidance versus aggression

CWB is an employee coping strategy. It's one of the ways of dealing with work stress. The motivation behind CWB is almost always retaliation, which makes sense because the number-one cause of this kind of behavior is anger.

When someone makes you mad at work, CWB is your way of leveling the playing field. And each time you make someone else angry, you're giving that person a reason to engage in CWB. The cycle continues.

REMEMBER

Most CWB is the result of interpersonal conflict between co-workers, supervisors, and employees. The more conflict there is, the more counterproductive behavior you can expect. Conflict resolution and CWB go hand in hand.

Employees typically adopt one of two response styles when they engage in CWB: avoidance or aggression. Avoidance means you *disengage* in a variety of ways from getting the job done such as coming in late or ignoring someone. Aggression means you *attack* the source of your anger by, say, bullying a subordinate or insulting a customer. It's that old fight-or-flight pattern, common with angry responses, showing up at work.

Person versus organization

Employees also differ in terms of where they direct their CWB. About 50 percent of the time, people are apt to retaliate against a *person:* insulting a fellow worker about their performance, gossiping, or getting that person in trouble. The other 50 percent of the time, people take their anger out on the *organization:* cutting down on productivity, stealing, destroying property, or calling in sick. Either way, it disrupts the workplace and takes away from the bottom line.

TECHNICAL
STUFF

Aggressive employees are three times more likely to retaliate against people with whom they work, whereas avoidant employees are more likely to satisfy their anger by engaging in CWB directed toward their place of employment.

TIP

Which of these profiles do you fit? Do some self-examination and ask yourself why: "Why do I always attack my team members when I get frustrated or irritated?" or "Why do I always run away from my anger and the issues that underlie it?" Avoidance usually results from fear. What are you afraid of: losing your job, losing control of your temper after you get started, what? Attack typically implies that you're dealing with an enemy. Are your co-workers really your enemies? Is this work or is it war? Is it because you have a combative personality and, thus, everything inevitably becomes a war?

Knowing Who Is Doing What to Whom

Not everyone is susceptible to counterproductive work behavior (CWB). Clearly, if you're experiencing chronic anger at work, you're a prime candidate. Industry estimates that more than 50 percent of employees have engaged in petty theft, sabotage, or bullying others. CWB is obviously a significant problem!

The disgruntled employee

Employees likely to engage in CWB often exhibit one or more of the following signs of disguised anger:

- » They seem disinterested in their work.
- » They're generally disagreeable at work.
- » They show clear signs of distress.
- » They're discouraged about how their careers are progressing.
- » They keep their distance from other team members.
- » They're highly distrustful of their superiors.
- » They frequently appear distracted while completing a task.
- » They show disrespect to those higher up in the organization.
- » They're disenchanted about the mission of the organization.
- » They verbalize disappointment about issues of salary and promotion.
- » They're pretty much disgruntled, disgusted, and disheartened by everything that goes on during the workday.

Most people don't go around telling everyone within earshot that they're angry, irritated, or even annoyed. Most people express their anger in more subtle, politically correct terminology, but it's anger nevertheless.

Aaron, a 58-year-old urban planner, was definitely a disgruntled employee, and he made no bones about it. For 22 years, he had worked at a job he thoroughly enjoyed and that consistently rewarded him for his efforts. Then he decided to accept a preretirement package. For a long time, Aaron had wanted to move his family to a warmer climate and phase himself into full retirement.

At first, his plan seemed to be working. He moved south and took a job with a salary comparable to what he had previously. But then, after two years, the company unexpectedly reorganized and laid off a large number of employees — including Aaron. Despite all efforts, the only job he could find in that location that fit his résumé paid him much less than he felt he was worth. He took the job, hoping that if he worked hard and gave his employer his usual 120 percent, he would eventually receive a substantial increase in compensation. But, as it turned out, that wasn't in the cards because company policy took into consideration years of work as well as merit for raises.

He was at odds with company policy. Given his age, he couldn't afford to just quit, and he didn't want to move his family again. Aaron was stuck! All he could do was spend his time complaining about everything no matter how insignificant. His complaining, as you can imagine, didn't sit well with his employer, who finally advised him to either stop complaining or leave.

Aaron was at a crossroads. He needed help immediately — not five years of on-the-couch therapy. So his psychologist suggested that he develop an action plan and that he do the following to manage his anger (and you can do the same in *your* life):

» **Accept the reality of the situation.** To a large extent, Aaron was disgruntled because he refused to accept that he was dealing with an "immovable" object: company policy. Complaining was his way of trying to pry his employer loose from that policy, to make an exception in his case.

» **Stop personalizing the situation.** Aaron was angry because he believed the policy was directed at him. His psychologist asked him, "Do all the other employees have to abide by this policy?" His answer, without hesitation, was yes. So his psychologist reminded him, "This really isn't about you at all. It's just the way they do business." He agreed.

» **Write down your feelings.** To defuse some of the anger that Aaron was carrying around, which was leaking out in the form of complaints, his psychologist recommended that he take 20 minutes a day to write about his anger.

>> **Pull back on your efforts.** Aaron needed to stop giving 120 percent to his employer by working overtime without pay. His only rationale for this was that it was a means to an end — the end being a pay raise. His employer wasn't exploiting him; he was exploiting himself, and that's not healthy.

>> **Engage in some positive thinking.** Aaron's anger was also the result of the fact that this whole situation was constantly on his mind. The psychological term for that process is *rumination*. Because Aaron admitted he had little success in distracting himself from this problem, his psychologist suggested that he simply find something else — something positive and something that he had some control over — to ruminate about or, better yet, to disengage or delay brooding.

>> **Find some benefit in what you do.** Aaron needs to think about his current job and come up with something positive. In other words, "What are you not complaining about? Salary aside, what works for you?" Aaron needed a more balanced view of his employment situation to ease away some of his angry feelings.

>> **Get some exercise.** Regular exercise is a good way of "exorcising," not only physical toxins in the body but also emotional toxins like anger. Forty-five minutes in a gym three days a week can do wonders for your disposition.

>> **Forgive, forgive, forgive.** Aaron was carrying around *yesterday's anger,* and it was becoming burdensome both to him and his employer. The only way to unload this burden is forgiveness (see Chapter 17). Aaron needed to forgive himself for taking early retirement only to find himself in this mess, and he needed to forgive his employer for having what he considered an archaic promotion policy.

By following these suggestions, Aaron got "unstuck," not from the financial realities of his job but from the negative emotion — anger — that accompanied it. He still had to watch his pennies, but he was no longer a disgruntled man.

The self-centered employee

It's no surprise that entitled, self-centered employees have a short fuse. Chapter 7 discusses the role of inflated self-esteem and anger. Here, I show you how this problem affects the workplace.

TECHNICAL STUFF

Dr. Lisa Penny at the University of South Florida has studied the relationship between big egos (the technical term for this is *narcissism*), anger, and counterproductive work behavior. As it turns out, the bigger your ego (that is, the more self-centered you are), the more easily angered you are at work and, in turn, the more likely you are to engage in CWB. Although no one likes to be constrained at work — interrupted by others, inadequately trained, lacking the resources you need to complete the job satisfactorily — self-centered employees take these constraints *personally* (Why are you doing this to *me?*) and react with anger.

TIP

How do you know if you fall into this category? Here are some clues:

>> **You seem self-absorbed in what you're doing and unaware of (and unconcerned about) what your colleagues are doing.** You aren't a team player.

>> **You have a clear sense of entitlement.** For example, you may say things like, "You *owe* me respect" and "I have a *right* to that raise or promotion."

>> **You can't put yourself in the other guy's shoes whenever there's a conflict of some sort or difference of opinion.** You just keep reiterating what *you* want, how *you* see things, and why *your* solution is the right one.

>> **You tend to be grandiose, feeling as though you're somehow special when it comes to working with others or completing a project.** You expect your co-workers to defer to you because of your power, brilliant ideas, and charismatic personality.

>> **You tend to exploit others at work — that is, always use others to meet your agenda regardless of the cost to your fellow employees.** And, to add insult to injury, you get angry if your co-workers don't *appreciate* the fact that you chose them to exploit!

>> **You *self-reference* a lot.** The words *I, me,* and *mine* seem to permeate your speech no matter what the topic.

TIP

What if you're tired of being so self-centered? What do you do to change? Here are a couple of strategies:

>> When you find yourself thinking like a self-centered employee ("Why are these people in *my* way?"), counteract that by thinking instead, "I'm sure these folks have important things to do, just like I do. The problem is, we're both trying to do them at the exact same time. Maybe if I help them, they'll help me."

>> Stop *demanding* that your co-workers do what you want, which goes along with a sense of entitlement, and instead *request* that they do what you want. You'll be surprised at how much more receptive they are!

>> Spend more time trying to look at things from other people's perspective. Become more attuned to the people around you — to what they're thinking and feeling.

>> Remember that life is a two-way street. The more understanding and sympathetic you are to those you work with, the more they respond that way to you. Not a bad deal, huh?

>> Just as your mother taught you, always say "please" and "thank you" with every exchange during the workday. It's the glue of a civilized workforce.

Enhancing Your Negotiating Skills

Most of what you do when you get to work each day involves some type of negotiating. Negotiation is nothing more than an effort between two or more employees aimed at resolving a conflict of interests. Many companies seem to think that it's normal for their employees to be like-minded and are often surprised (and sometimes downright angry) when this isn't the case.

Negotiations always involve emotions because the negotiators are human beings. But that's only a problem if the emotions in play are negative. If negotiators are in a positive emotional state (excited, optimistic), they tend to be cooperative and conciliatory. This more often leads to a win-win solution, where both parties come away feeling like they've gotten something they wanted. If either or both negotiators, however, are in a negative emotional state (angry, pessimistic), things tend to be much more competitive and neither party is comfortable making concessions. If no one concedes, you're at an impasse. No one walks away a winner!

TIP

Negotiators respond to their opponent's emotions. The best way to ensure a positive outcome is to start with a smile. That, believe it or not, sets the tone for everything that follows. Start with a look of irritation on your face and you'll have a hard row to hoe.

Begin the negotiations by emphasizing some point of possible agreement (hard to do if you're angry but worth the effort); doing so sets a positive tone before getting down to differences of opinion. Remind yourself that, even though the other parties are your opponents, *they are not the enemy.* And if you must be angry when you enter into some type of negotiation, try to express your anger constructively. Keep your voice calm, slow the pace, and express yourself assertively (which I talk about in Chapter 8).

WORKING DURING A PANDEMIC

Arguments, threats, and violence have resulted from prevention and mandatory practices being enforced at various workplaces. The Centers for Disease Control and Prevention (CDC) reported that violence most often occurred in stores, restaurants, or other retail businesses. In fact, store clerks have been assaulted for telling customers to wear masks. The CDC suggests the following tips to help decrease and prevent violence:

- Provide options such as curbside pickup, delivery, and extended shopping hours.

- Post highly visible signs with policies and procedures.

- Assign more than one employee to enforce and encourage compliance.

- Plan on how to evacuate or isolate when threatened.

- Train employees on threat recognition, de-escalation, and other nonviolent responses

- Make sure businesses have adequate security systems and that employees know how to use them.

Unfortunately, nurses, who have been on the front line of the pandemic since it started are often the recipients of verbal as well as physical abuse. In fact, surveys before the pandemic started indicated that 50 percent of nurses were verbally abused during a 12-month period, and about 20 percent of nurses had been physically assaulted. Patients and their loved ones suffer incredible stress, especially during a pandemic. However, healthcare workers are our lifelines. More must be done to protect them.

Developing a Positive Work Environment

Anger at work isn't isolated to one particular employee, one specific exchange or circumstance, or one identifiable issue like, for example, work overload. Individual emotions originate within the general context of the overall work environment. And that context (or climate) varies considerably from one work setting to another.

Walk into any work situation — from a factory or fulfillment center floor to a corporate boardroom — and after about five minutes observing people at work, you can tell whether the climate is hostile (people at each other's throats), sad (too many lost opportunities, too much turnover in personnel), tense (lots of uncertainty), or cordial ("We love it here!"). You don't have to be a rocket scientist — it's that easy.

Dr. Barbara Fredrickson at the University of Michigan and her colleague Dr. Marcial Losada of the Universidade Catholica de Brasilia, Brazil, have come up with a fascinating theory about how workplace emotions affect employee productivity. Instead of concentrating on one specific emotion (anger), they look at the positive and negative nature of emotions and, much more important, the relationship between the two, which they refer to as the *positivity ratio*. So far, they've found that

>> For employees to flourish in their work, the ratio of emotions expressed in the workforce overall must be approximately three-to-one in favor of positive feelings.

>> If that three-to-one ratio isn't reached, workers flounder, describing their work lives as empty and unsatisfying.

>> Too much positivity, on the other hand, can also be a problem. A minimal amount of *negativity* is necessary to avoid work patterns from becoming inflexible, stagnant, boring, and overly routine (which in turn can lead to irritability among employees). But having enough negativity isn't something that most companies need to worry about!

>> The negativity must be appropriate (that is, employees may not express contempt for one another or act out in rage) for it to be beneficial.

>> The expression of positive emotions must be genuine rather than forced. In other words, you wouldn't want to send a memo to all employees: "From now on, every one of you will have a smile on your face at all times!"

Table 12-1 lists a number of emotions that you may have observed where you work. As you read the table, do the following:

1. **Circle ten emotions that you feel most accurately describe the emotional climate of your work situation *in the past week*.**

   It doesn't matter which column you circle from. You choose ten emotions total.

2. **Count the number of positive emotions.**

3. **Count the number of negative emotions.**

4. **Calculate the positivity ratio by dividing the number of positive emotions by the number of negative emotions.**

   For example, if you have three words circled in the *Positive Emotions* column and seven words circled in the *Negative Emotions* column, you do this simple calculation: 3 divided by 7 equals 0.43.

   Is your positivity ratio above or below 2.9? If the ratio is 2.9 or below, you — and everyone else you work with — are much more likely to get angry at work. If the ratio is at least 3.0 (but less than 11.0, which is an example of too much positivity), your workplace has a healthier environment.

TABLE 12-1 ## Positive and Negative Emotions at Work

Positive Emotions	Negative Emotions
Amazed	Afraid
Amused	Agitated
Appreciative	Alarmed
Cheerful	Angry
Content	Anxious
Curious	Ashamed
Delighted	Bitter
Enthusiastic	Bored
Excited	Depressed
Generous	Frustrated
Grateful	Guilty
Happy	Irritated
Hopeful	Petrified
Joyful	Regretful
Kind	Resentful
Loving	Sad
Optimistic	Sorrowful
Satisfied	Unhappy
Thrilled	Worried

TIP

If you're an employer, here are some tips on how to create a more positive work setting:

>> Recognize an "Employee of the Month" based not on productivity but rather on how positively the person relates to customers, clients, and co-workers.

>> Offer small rewards for displaying a positive attitude at work: tickets for the family to attend a theme park, a gift certificate to a restaurant, or tickets to a local comedy club.

>> Celebrate workers' performance in a short, posted newsletter.

>> Instead of observing dress-down Friday, have "lighten-up" Fridays where everyone at work is on their most positive behavior.

TIP

If you're an employee, try to do the following to make your work environment more positive:

>> Begin each workday by greeting your fellow employees with "Have a great day!"

>> Interject some humor into the workplace dialogue. Laughter communicates to your co-workers that you mean no harm.

>> Always apologize when you do something that you know offends a fellow employee. You will not only feel better but also defuse the tension in the other person and make it harder for her to hold a grudge.

>> Make a friend at work. Surveys show that having a friend at work, particularly if it's your best friend, greatly increases the odds that you'll enjoy going to work and be more satisfied with what goes on there.

Making Civility the Norm

At work, niceness counts. Treating your fellow employees in a civil manner — fair, respectful, courteous, pleasant — improves the odds that you'll be treated with civility yourself. The reverse is also true: Be rude and hostile to others and they will, in turn, act that way to you, or go out of their way to avoid you.

Anger is often the byproduct of being on the receiving end of incivility. And incivility typically leads to some form of counterproductive work behavior.

TECHNICAL STUFF

How big a problem is workplace incivility? Huge! Approximately 90 percent of all working people believe a lack of civility at work is a serious problem even though it doesn't rise to the level of workplace (physical) violence. Incivility is a major reason for turnover, with approximately half of the employees who have been targeted for uncivil treatment contemplating looking for another job and one in eight actually quitting.

TIP

If you're an employer and you want to ensure that civility is the norm, follow these suggestions:

>> Make it clear — from the top down — that uncivil behavior won't be tolerated (no matter what was allowed in the past) and that no exceptions will be made in terms of job status.

>> Introduce training in civility as an integral part of recruitment and orientation.

>> Have written policies on what constitutes civil and uncivil behavior and what consequences are attached to the latter. Invite input from all employees.

>> Make civility counseling a vital part of the human resources program.

>> Survey employees periodically on the status of civility in your workplace.

>> Institute a peer-review system for recognizing and sanctioning uncivil behavior.

>> Emphasize *constructive* criticism, *constructive* anger expression, and *constructive* competition.

TIP

If you're an employee and you want to make civility the norm where you work, do the following:

>> Make "Do unto others as you would have them do unto you" your personal mantra at work.

>> Be constructive in your criticism of fellow employees. Tell them how to do what they do better.

>> If you think your workplace is too uncivil, initiate some positive change. Don't wait on the other guy.

>> Make it clear to all those you work with that you expect to be treated in a civil manner at all times and do not be afraid to provide corrective feedback when it's called for.

>> Remind yourself and others at work that civility isn't about who's in charge or who's right. It's about mutual respect.

>> Always allow your fellow employee to save face by addressing any problems or criticisms in private. It's less intimidating and leaves him less embarrassed.

>> Be optimistic and always assume the best when it comes to the efforts of those with whom you work. Give them the benefit of the doubt until you have proof to the contrary.

>> If you have to be critical of a fellow employee, show them the courtesy of saying what you have to say face to face. And if you can't say it to their face, don't say it at all.

Speaking Up, Not Out

Anger always speaks out — if not in actual words, then through efforts on your part to "act out" what you're feeling. Acting out feelings is what counterproductive work behavior is all about.

Better than speaking *out* is speaking *up*, which means saying what's on your mind and in your heart. Psychologists refer to this as *assertiveness*. The assertive employee provides face-to-face, one-on-one feedback that affirms his needs ("I'd like to be treated with more civility"), authenticates his emotions ("Yes, I'm annoyed and I think I have a reason to feel that way"), acknowledges the positives as well as the negatives of the situation ("You know I like working here, but . . ."), and assumes a positive outcome — all without being in the least bit aggressive.

Assertiveness is more about action than attitude. On the contrary, if you rarely stand up for yourself, you end up being perceived by those you work with and for as weak and someone not to be respected or taken seriously, which invites others to treat you badly. Rarely do you hear someone at work say, "Boy, I really admire her. She's such a mouse!"

TIP

So how exactly are you supposed to speak out in an assertive manner? Follow these tips (and see Chapter 8 for more information):

>> **Take ownership, and always start with the word *I*.** For example: "I need to talk to you about something that is bothering me." "I need to give you some personal feedback about this morning's meeting." "I may not have been clear about where I was coming from so let me explain."

>> **Open with a positive statement.** For example: "I think you know how much I like working here, and at the same time, ..." "I think it's fair to say that you've always been fair with me in the past, and . . . ."

>> **Stop bobbing and weaving and get to the point.** Be specific about what it is that is bothering you and making you angry. Don't just say "I'm angry!" Tell the other person exactly why.

>> **Appeal to the other person's empathy.** For example: "I'm not sure you appreciate the impact your words earlier had on me." "I want to think you weren't intentionally trying to make me mad, yet it sort of seemed like. . . ." "I may have heard you incorrectly because it felt like what you said was a little rude."

>> **Avoid four-letter words.** No one likes to be sworn at, not even the person who swears at you. Besides, the message gets lost when surrounded by expletives.

>> **Be persistent.** Don't expect one assertive act on your part to change the world. Change the dialogue first, and the world will follow.

IN THIS CHAPTER

» **Understanding how anger begins**

» **Figuring out when anger hurts**

» **Looking at parenting and anger**

» **Conversing with your kids**

» **Fostering adaptive anger management for kids**

Chapter **13**

Understanding and Helping Angry Children and Teens

ave you ever had a meal ruined by a 3-year-old throwing a tantrum in a restaurant? Or witnessed a screaming match between a parent and child in a store? How about a young child kicking the back of your seat on an airplane while his parent frantically whispers for him to stop?

From screaming toddlers in the grocery store to sullen teens refusing to do what they are told, kids get angry. No child goes through life without expressing anger. Angry children can be very frustrating to those around them. Children use anger, just like adults, as a method of communication.

Anger is a perfectly natural emotion in children and teens. Like adulthood, childhood presents plenty of opportunities in which to get frustrated. This chapter takes a look at the origins of anger through childhood. It helps identify when anger is normal and when it becomes a more serious problem. The bulk of the chapter gives family caregivers and concerned others a blueprint for handling anger and helping children develop more adaptive ways of managing frustration.

The final section of this chapter spells out when anger is out of control and professional help is needed. It tells you what to look for in a therapist and how to get help.

The Origins of Anger

Like adults, children experience anger in their bodies. There is a rush of stress hormones, a quickening of the breath, a flushing face, and a need for action. Babies and toddlers cry out in anger. Older children may lash out verbally or physically.

Challenges in development

In babies and very young children, the most common cause of anger is simply not getting what they want — immediately. Common reasons for anger include

>> I want my toy.

>> I want my bottle.

>> I want my mother.

As children develop, they still get angry when they don't get what they want, but they also get angry when they are restricted from doing something they want to do (think of a fidgety toddler in a car seat). Toddlers want to explore their environment. They start resisting nap time and bedtime. They grab their spoons and try to feed themselves. When they don't get their way, they scream or fuss.

A developmental challenge in the preschool years is learning how to share. Preschoolers need to share toys. In addition, they must learn to share the attention of their primary caregiver. Both of these tasks cause frustration and anger. Not only can it frustrate the child, but the caregiver as well. If you've ever had a toddler in your care, think about all of the interrupted times when attempting to talk on the phone or paying attention to something or someone else.

When they enter school, children must also learn to wait their turn, perform tasks that might not be entertaining, and navigate their relationships with peers and adults. All of these developmental steps require the ability to delay gratification and to regulate emotions. Childhood is the best time to learn these skills, and parents, teachers, and other caregivers have the responsibility to develop and nurture emotional regulation.

The ability of children to master emotional regulation is determined in part by their genetic makeup. That genetic makeup is then influenced by the environment that the child is exposed to. Both genes and learning effect how children learn to express and aggression and learn self-control.

Nature

Humans are genetically programed to respond to danger by fighting or fleeing. The ability to fight off threats helped our ancestors survive. There are some interesting biological reasons that everyone has the capacity to become angry. For example, aggressive cavemen survived longer and had more children: survival of the fittest.

Like many other personality traits, aggressiveness is thought to be about 50 percent genetically determined. This finding has been confirmed by studying identical and fraternal twins living apart. The genetic tendency to become aggressive does not necessarily result in an aggressive personality. People with this tendency may be raised in such a way that their self-control overrides their aggressive nature.

Temperament may be one way that aggressive genetics is expressed. Babies show their temperaments early in their lives. Most research has identified three types of baby temperaments:

>> **Easy:** Babies with easy going styles tend to eat well, sleep with a regular schedule, cry only when hungry, tired, or uncomfortable, and are easily soothed. They adapt to new situations and people easily.

>> **Difficult:** When you have a baby with a difficult temperament, prepare for a lot of sleepless nights. These babies are hard to soothe and do not follow any regular schedule of eating and sleeping. These babies do not adjust easily to changes and may show early signs of frustration.

>> **Slow to warm up:** Babies who are slow to warm up are a bit shy and withdrawn. These are the babies that seem quiet, but once a situation becomes familiar, they are comfortable. They do not adjust quickly to changes, especially change of caregivers.

Not all babies fit neatly into the categories. They may bounce around day to day. However, for most babies, these categories are reasonably consistent. So what does temperament have to do with anger?

Although more long-term research is needed, there are a few studies that suggest difficult babies have more problems regulating their emotions. Therefore, they react more strongly to small stressors than easy babies. One of those unregulated emotions, of course, is anger.

Learning

If aggression is 50 percent biologically determined, then the environment makes up the rest. Imagine a difficult baby in a home with a caregiver who has a hot temper. When that baby cries, the caregiver gets angry. Not a good fit, unfortunately for the baby.

On the other hand, imagine a difficult baby with an even-tempered caregiver who responds with calmness and empathy. That baby may become less difficult over time and eventually learn sufficient emotional regulation so that any genetic predisposition to aggression is basically snuffed out.

Trauma resulting from natural disasters, emotional or physical abuse, or accidents can also cause anger to erupt in children.

BUT JUDGE, I WAS BORN THIS WAY

Just because someone is born with a tendency toward aggression does not excuse their behavior. However, genetics may explain why some people are inherently at risk for losing their temper. There have been studies on a particular gene that appears to be related to aggression: monoamine or MAOA. Men appear to have either a high-functioning version of this gene or a low-functioning version. Those men who have a low-functioning type tend to be more likely violent, especially if they were traumatized in childhood.

Researchers studied nonviolent college students to determine if that tendency was apparent in an experimental situation. They identified a sample of male students with high-functioning and low-functioning MAOA genes. While scanning their brains, each subject was insulted. Those with low-functioning MAOA genes showed greater reactivity in regions of the brain related to emotion and emotional regulation than those with high-functioning MAOA genes. More research is needed; however, this finding does suggest that provocation of people with low-functioning MAOA genes is, well, more provoking. Note that a bit over a third of all males have that low-functioning gene, which may explain why most violent behavior is conducted by males. However, the vast majority of males with those low-functioning genes never engage in violent behavior.

Knowing When Anger Is Unhealthy

Anger is not a bad emotion. Like all emotions, it is a response to a situation that needs attention. Children should not be told that anger is bad or that they are bad to be angry. Children need to learn how to express their anger in acceptable ways. They also need to be taught how to tolerate frustration and manage difficult emotions.

Anger becomes a problem when it interferes with functioning in the home, with friends, and at school. Anger is also a concern when it masks or accompanies depression. Anger in children is often a sign that something else is amiss. Chronic anger should be investigated by concerned caregivers.

Family discord

Every family has a disagreement from time to time. That's perfectly normal. Anger occurs in families when members are competing for power or control. Rarely is anger a constructive response to a family situation. Anger becomes a problem when it is the most common response to the multiple challenges of people living in one household. The following are a few typical examples of power struggles that often result in anger in families:

>> **Chores:** Families fight over chores. Parents tell their children to perform a task. The dishes don't get done or they come out dirty. Anger results.

>> **Curfews:** Parents and children disagree about bedtimes and curfews. Both get angry.

>> **Screen time:** How much and when is a common battle between parents and kids. Other battles involve social media use and video game choices.

>> **Food fights:** Parents feel responsible for making sure that their children eat a reasonable diet. Kids like ice cream and chips, not broccoli and lima beans, which results in conflict.

>> **Time:** These conflicts arise when kids don't respond to parental demands. They take too long to get dressed, get ready for school, or fail to turn off their devices.

>> **Homework:** Getting kids to complete homework ends up in conflict in too many families.

Most of the conflict listed above reflect parents trying to control the behavior of their children. Anger escalates when children do not meet parental expectations. When parents react with anger, children have a role model to copy. The anger cycle begins. See the section "Managing Anger from the Top Down" for strategies on handling conflict in your family.

Conflicts with friends

Conflict teaches children how to get along. Disagreements, arguments, and fights are common childhood occurrences. Small children often disagree about who gets to play with a certain toy. Among preschoolers, it's not unusual to see a push or shove over a prized possession. Older children fight about who gets to choose what to do: "I want to play with blocks." "No, let's play store."

As children begin elementary school, there are many more opportunities for conflict. These conflicts may revolve around being part of a group or excluded from a group. Betrayal and competitiveness emerge as themes.

WARNING

Anger and conflict among children are normal unless they cause physical harm or lasting emotional distress. School-age children should rarely be involved in physical conflict with others because most have the skills to solve problems with verbal negotiations. If a child is regularly involved in physical altercations, causes such as developmental delays, abuse, bullying, or emotional disorders should be investigated. See the upcoming section "Knowing When to Get Help for Angry Kids" for more information.

Defiance at school

It's a rare child who doesn't have an occasional problem at school. Some of the natural exuberance of kids leads to discipline by teachers. Or occasionally a student and teacher just have a personality clash. But a few kids are regularly defiant, angry, and aggressive. They ignore directions, refuse to complete assignments, and are chronically disrespectful.

These behaviors are signs that definitely should alarm a parent, teacher, or caregiver. Kids who display such defiance are screaming for attention. Children may have underlying learning, emotional, or attention problems. They may be experiencing abuse, neglect, or severe bullying. Definitely do not ignore chronic defiance at school.

Depression and anger

Like adults, when children are depressed, they have trouble concentrating. Their sadness makes them apathetic. Irritability is also a common symptom of depression. Not surprisingly, school performance may be negatively impacted by depression.

DIAGNOSES OF CHILDHOOD ANGER

The Diagnostic and Statistical Manual of Mental Disorders Fifth Edition (DSM-5) is a book published by the American Psychiatric Association. It classifies various adult and childhood mental disorders and is used widely throughout the world. Several diagnostic patterns in children include anger as one of many symptoms.

- **Oppositional Defiant Disorder (ODD)** is a pattern of behavior that includes angry, irritable moods, frequent arguments, refusal to comply with adults, and vindictiveness.

- **Conduct Disorder (CD)** involves even more anger and aggression. Kids with conduct disorder are cruel and aggressive to people and animals. They destroy property, engage in lying and theft, and violate rules or laws.

- **Disruptive Mood Dysregulation Disorder (DMDD)** consists of regular, severe temper outbursts that are not consistent with the developmental level of the child. For example, a 2-year-old might have a tantrum in the store when denied candy. However, an 11-year-old should know better. In addition to temper outbursts, kids with DMDD are usually irritable or angry most days.

In addition to the above disorders, kids with Attention Deficit/Hyperactivity Disorder (ADHD) are often subject to impulsive, angry outbursts. However, being angry is not part of the diagnostic criteria of ADHD. Quite a few children with ADHD are impulsive but not particularly angry.

Children or teens with depression have trouble paying attention and get into conflicts with teachers about following through on assignments or arguments with parents about not completing daily tasks. Their irritability easily converts to anger. Depressed kids are often angry about things that happened in the past, current events, and their perceived future.

Managing Anger from the Top Down

REMEMBER

Family members — parents and children alike — learn by example. If children see their parents rant and rave, cuss, and hit one another in anger, they'll learn to handle anger poorly themselves. Similarly, if parents allow their children to throw angry tantrums every time they don't get their way, and fail to set limits, their children learn that tantrums work, which is not such a great strategy.

Parents are the ones who set the tone for the home environment, and they need to take primary responsibility for ensuring that anger is expressed in a civil and constructive way. (You may be able to hold your kids responsible for cleaning their rooms, but you can't hold them responsible for the anger in your household.)

The home environment is a learning laboratory, a classroom where all the important lessons of life, and survival, are taught. Chief among these is the lesson on how to survive — and even benefit from — conflict between family members. Conflict is inherent in all families. The home is also the place where kids learn how to manage conflict with friends, at school, and in the community.

Simply put, family members have different interests, personalities, temperaments, values, wants, likes, dislikes, and anxieties. These differences have to be negotiated if the family is to operate in relative harmony. The major distinction between healthy and unhealthy families is how they choose to resolve these conflicts, not whether they have the conflicts in the first place.

TIP

So if you're the parent, how do you set a healthy tone for your family? Here are some tips for managing the anger that results from family conflict:

>> **Be accepting of conflict and anger.** Don't disapprove of or dismiss conflicts between family members or try to distract people's attention away from problems.

>> **Talk about anger comfortably.** Don't make anger a taboo topic that becomes yet one more "elephant in the living room" — something everyone knows is there but no one talks about.

>> **Distinguish between different levels of anger and conflict.** You want to help your family differentiate between being irritated, being "just plain mad," and being in a rage. The first two are okay; the third is not.

>> **Keep your cool.** You don't help children keep their cool by losing yours! You're the adult, so even if you don't feel like you have much ability to keep your cool, you can bet that you're better able to keep your cool than your kids are able to keep theirs.

>> **View anger and conflict as an opportunity for new learning.** Step back, look at each other, and find out something about the other person. The result is a greater sense of intimacy (sharing of one's real self).

>> **Don't punish. Instead, problem-solve.** Instead of fussing at each other for being angry, ask each other two simple questions:

- What are you angry about?

- What would you like to do about it?

The first question defines the problem; the second question defines the solution. If the other person knows what the problem is but doesn't have a solution, help her find one — one that doesn't involve acting out her anger in some hateful and vengeful way.

>> **Seek win-win solutions.** No one likes to lose, certainly not someone who's already angry. She just gets angrier! What you want is to find a solution to family anger that leaves everyone feeling that they got something positive out of the exchange, even if only the fact that they were actually *heard* for a change. Here's where a non-aggressive approach works best. Try an approach that isn't competitive ("I win; you lose!") or confrontational and where one person in the family doesn't try to dominate the others.

REMEMBER

Anger is a signal that something is wrong and needs to be resolved. You *want* those signals, and if you didn't have them or didn't heed them, the anger would only grow.

Helping Kids Manage Anger

Kids learn how to deal with emotions, both positive and negative, largely from the adults in their lives. Parents, teachers, neighbors, friends, and relatives all influence how children respond to events. Teaching children to appropriately manage anger and frustration is particularly important. Life is guaranteed to be frustrating at times, and how children handle those frustrations can either improve or damage their well-being.

Talking with kids

Quite a few kids and their parents spend much of their time with faces focused on phones. Even the youngest toddler screams for a device while grocery shopping with mom or dad. You see families at restaurants, phones in hand, texting or scrolling between bites. As a psychologist, I worry about what all of this screen time will do to connections between others, especially between parents and their children.

This section begins with a rather obvious but extremely important statement: *Please talk to children.* Introduce them to the art of conversation. You need to find time to listen to them ramble on about school, friends, clothes, teachers, troubles, and whatever they want to talk about. Turn off the electronics in the car. That's a great time to have family conversations. Spend a few minutes before bedtime; eat together without devices; take a walk and talk. Ask questions, but don't push. Leave room for silence, and be attentive.

If you can't talk to your kids about their days, distance grows. And distance stands in the way of talking about more difficult subjects, which, if left unaddressed, creates resentment, hostility, and anger.

Finding consistency

Kids do better when they know what's happening, what to expect, and what the rules are in all the situations they find themselves in. If you think about it, kids have to adjust to a lot of changes throughout their childhoods.

>> **Home:** Multiple adults can have different rules, and some kids (when parents are separated) have more than one home, each with different expectations.

>> **School:** Teachers' rules will also vary some from what parents expect. And when you have multiple teachers in a day, each classroom varies a bit.

>> **After-school activities:** Kids have sports and coaches, daycare, and clubs, all with variable policies.

>> **Religious activities:** Kids who attend church, synagogue, or mosques are exposed to different conventions.

>> **Home of relatives:** Aunts, uncles, and grandparents probably have different values and guidelines.

Therefore, it's beneficial if major caregivers can agree on a short set of *general* rules that can be applied consistently across most settings. The rules can be rather broad and widely applicable. For example:

>> Be respectful to people and their possessions.

>> Be polite and nice to others.

>> Act safely.

>> Take care of your possessions and person.

>> Be responsible (for school, family chores, and so forth).

That may be enough. *Being respectful* could include not farting at the dinner table, not talking back, and doing what is asked by parents or teachers. *Being polite* could include no hitting, and *nice* might mean not teasing a sibling.

Acting safely includes putting on seat belts, riding bikes with helmets, and not going out without permission. *Taking care of possessions and person* comes into play when kids are asked to pick up, clean up, brush teeth, comb hair, or bathe. *Being responsible* means to do schoolwork (including homework), help out with chores, follow through, use good judgment, and be trustworthy. The general concepts of being respectful, acting safely, and taking care of possessions remain the same, but rules should be adjusted as children grow older.

REMEMBER

Childhood is a time of learning. Kids make mistakes; they test the rules to see whether parents or caregivers actually mean what they say. Look at intentional rule breaking or unintentional mistakes as opportunities to learn.

TIP

Life isn't always consistent (or fair). Many kids live in more than one situation. Sometimes teachers, coaches, or other caregivers have different rules and expectations. But part of growing up is learning to adjust to the realities of life. Kids can learn to adapt to different sets of rules, but you want to be as consistent as possible on your part of the equation.

Keeping cool

Part of any anger-management program is learning to keep your voice low and slow. In working with families, therapists often emphasize *emotional neutrality*. Emotional neutrality means keeping your cool. When you give directions to children, do so with a matter-of-fact, calm demeanor. Here are a few tips:

>> **Make sure that children are paying attention before you speak.** If a child is engrossed in something else, stop the activity, have the child look directly at you, and give short, simple, one-step directions.

>> **Ask for understanding.** Have the children repeat back to you what you requested.

>> **Give a time limit for completing the task**. Now, in five minutes, today — whatever is appropriate.

>> **Thank children for listening and give positive feedback when they complete the task.**

REMEMBER

Children watch and learn from the people around them. If you want your children to have an anger problem, all you need to do is show them how angry you can be. On the other hand, if you want them to learn self-control, be a *model of self-control* for your children.

Setting limits

It would be very nice if children followed rules, listened to parents and teachers, were polite, and generally behaved like little, well-behaved adults. Well, not really. Part of the fun of raising a child is watching the stages and changes of development. Kids don't come into the world knowing the rules.

Setting limits with children is a necessary part of parenting. One principle that many people have great difficulty with is to *mean what you say*. Take the following example:

> Five-year-old **Daniel** watches his older sister at swim practice. Although **Maria,** his mother, brings toys for him to play with, he gets bored and impatient after a while. Right now, he's throwing his action figures up and down the stairs of the bleachers where families sit to watch the practice.
>
> Daniel almost hits people in the stands with his toys, and a couple of people are looking at Maria for her response. "Daniel, stop throwing those things close to people, or I'll take them away."
>
> Daniel takes his toys and moves farther away from his mother. She goes back to scrolling through her phone. In about 30 seconds, Daniel is back to throwing the figures up and down the stairs. Maria looks up when she hears someone say, "Hey, kid, stop that!"
>
> "Daniel," Maria yells, "I mean that. Get over here this minute and play by me, or I'll take those toys away."

I could go on and on with the story, but by now you know what Maria probably will do next. She will give poor Daniel another chance and maybe even another. Then most likely, she'll explode, and Daniel will end up pouting or in tears. What did Maria teach Daniel? That he can misbehave and not listen to his mother for at least two or three times. Not a very good lesson for a child.

With very young children, it's okay to give *one* chance or warning. That's the way they learn. But once your child knows the rules, no more chances. Otherwise, you're saying, "It's okay to misbehave, at least until I get really, really mad."

Designing rewards and costs (and then following through)

Behavior modification is a method of parenting that involves increasing positive behaviors and decreasing negative behaviors. Behavior modification is commonly used when training animals, in classrooms, and by parents. In most cases, it is the easiest and kindest approach to changing challenging behaviors as well as teaching positive behavior.

Rewarding the good

The most important principle of behavior modification is called *positive reinforcement*. Basically, that means when a child does something that is good, offer a reward. In the beginning of training, rewards should be delivered immediately following a desired behavior. What positive reinforcement does is increase the likelihood that a behavior will be repeated.

Rewards do not have to be big to work. In fact, simple praise usually works fine. Here are a few examples of typical rewards for kids:

>> Give a high five.

>> "Good job!"

>> "Way to go!"

>> A hug.

>> A sticker.

>> A quarter.

>> Staying up late or another special privilege.

As the desired behavior increases, rewards should not be given every single time. In fact, research suggests that a schedule of rewards that is somewhat unpredictable works better than constantly rewarding all positive behavior.

TIP

Compliments are great ways to provide rewards. Compliment kids regularly when they do something you want them to continue to do. Here are some examples:

>> "Thanks for taking your dishes to the sink without me reminding you."

>> "Wow, you finished your homework on your own."

>> "I love to see you and your sister get along. Great job."

Catching almost good behavior

One scientifically based strategy for changing behavior is known as *shaping*. Shaping involves giving positive reinforcement when a behavior is moving toward the desired behavior but not quite there. Here is an example of someone shaping the behavior of an aggressive child:

Sebastian is a first-grader who gets physically aggressive with other children. During the fist week of school, he has several fights on the playground. His teacher makes it a point to watch him carefully the next recess. She can see that he gets frustrated when other children are not paying attention to him. Before he actually pushes anybody, she approaches him and says, "Good job for keeping your cool today and not pushing, Sebastian."

During subsequent recesses, his teacher continues to monitor his behavior and praise him for not getting aggressive. She also teaches him alternative ways to communicate and get the other kids to play with him. Because she spends time catching Sebastian being good, his behavior improves quickly.

TIP

Shaping involves catching the child doing something in the direction of what you want and offering praise or another reward. Shaping should result in gradual improvement. The end result will be regular performance of the desired behavior.

Penalizing the bad

There are three ways to respond to undesirable behavior that is consistent with the principles of behavior modification. Depending on the circumstance, all three are valuable tools for parents and caregivers to use.

>> **Ignore the behavior.** This response is ideal if a child is trying to get your attention through bad behavior. By ignoring, you are not giving into these attempts. If you give in, you are rewarding the behavior. For example, if a temper tantrum occurs at home, that's a wonderful time to ignore. However, if the temper tantrum is in a busy store or restaurant, ignoring would be quite annoying to the other patrons.

>> **Take a time out.** This technique has been used by parents and teachers for decades. It is also misused. To be effective, time out has to involve time away from what the child wants to do. Sending a kid who has misbehaved to his room for a time out where he then plays video games is hardly an effective strategy. Time out can be conducted almost anywhere. Supervise young children during time outs. Don't interact; just watch. Time out is most effective for preschoolers through early elementary grades.

>> **Response cost:** This is probably the most effective measure for children in the upper elementary grades through adolescence. Like a fine for a traffic ticket, response cost involves taking something valued away for a specified period of time. Here are some examples: "You came home past curfew, so you lose the car keys for the weekend." "You didn't pick up the toys after I told you to, so they are going into the garage for a day." "I asked you to take out the garbage, but had to do it myself, so you lose a dollar of your weekly allowance."

TIP

Knowing these simple methods of changing behavior — reinforcing good behavior, shaping, and making bad behavior cost something — usually improves even the most challenging behaviors over time. The key is consistent use of these strategies and not giving into children's protests.

Staying away from reassurance

Lots of people (and that goes for kids, too) get angry when life seems unfair. If you're one of those people who believes that life is fair, you're likely to feel frustrated and irritated much of the time simply because life really isn't fair.

And if your kids complain about life's unfairness, it's tempting to reassure them that things will work out and that fairness will prevail. Many times, things do, but you set them up for anger if you lead them to think that bad things either won't or shouldn't ever happen. Kids need to deal with reality.

Handling tantrums

Almost all kids have temper tantrums here and there. Interestingly, kids rarely tantrum without an audience! That's because tantrums have a purpose: getting what the kiddo wants. Whenever a parent gives into a tantrum, the message is "If you want something, just pitch a fit and make me miserable. Then I'll cave in to your desires."

Obviously, it's never a good idea to give in to tantrums. Instead, swoop in, stay cool (that is, *emotionally neutral*), and move your child to another location. Thus, if you're in a store or restaurant, you need to be prepared to swiftly take the child outside even if it inconveniences you.

TIP

Take *consistent* action when your child is young, and a terrible habit will be avoided. However, the same strategies can work with older kids; it just takes considerably more patience and time.

Positive Anger Management for Kids

Whether a child is born with a difficult temperament, has experienced trauma, or simply seems angry all of the time, if a child has a problem with anger, there are strategies to help. Children with anger issues do not have to become adults with anger issues. Positive anger management are strategies to help children and teens accept and express their feelings in ways that will allow them to be heard.

REMEMBER

One chapter in a book cannot fully address all of the strategies for helping kids with anger issues. However, many of the strategies throughout this book regarding adult anger management can be easily adapted to help kids manage their angry feelings more effectively.

Accepting negative feelings

All feelings are acceptable, even anger. This is an especially important message to give to children and teens. Once the feeling is accepted, help the child to do the following:

>> Understand the good consequences of expressing anger.

>> Learn to express anger without harming someone or something.

>> Know what situations call for expressing anger.

>> Understand any potential negative consequences of expressing anger.

>> Understand other ways of dealing with a problem.

Help children see that they are not their anger. Anger is a brief emotion that comes and goes. Sometimes anger leads them to act in ways that hurt others or gets them in trouble. So learning skills for expressing anger appropriately will help them get through tough situations more effectively.

TIP

Be clear that feelings and behaviors are different. For example, it's perfectly okay to be angry when your brother breaks your toy, but it's not okay to throw the broken toy at your brother.

Keeping active

Boredom can lead to kids bickering and eventually getting angry. Busy children are happy children. Every child should have frequent opportunities for about an hour of rigorous physical activity. Such exercise should occur on most days of the week. Physical activity is one important tool in quelling feelings of frustration.

Regular exercise for kids is a challenge because of the changing nature of neighborhoods and schools. The days of letting kids out to play until the streetlights go on are long gone for most families. In addition, schools watching their budgets have cut out many of their afterschool sports programs. It's really up to caregivers to make sure that critical activity happens.

TIP

Jogging or hiking is a free activity that can become a family affair. If anger lives in your house, regular exercise might also decrease tension in the whole family.

Teaching frustration tolerance

Angry kids have trouble handling frustration. Even small frustrations lead to anger and sometimes aggression. Easily frustrated children tend to blame others and make excuses for their behavior. Improving frustration tolerance serves children well throughout their lives.

Parents and caregivers can do much to help kids increase their ability to handle frustration by modeling patience whenever possible. The following suggestions provide guidance on possible ways for caregivers or parents to model frustration tolerance:

» I am frustrated today because I was interrupted when I wanted to work on this project, but I realize that I have plenty of time to finish later.

» Sometimes it gets annoying to wait in a long line. I like to amuse myself by looking at other people and imagining what their lives must look like.

» When someone cuts me off in traffic, I get angry, but then I calm down, realizing that they might be driving someone to the hospital or have some other important reason for being in a hurry.

» When I can't follow the directions on how to put something together, I feel upset and want to just quit. But then I think that if I slow down, I might get it. If all else fails, I can ask for help.

Try to talk to children when you actually are frustrated and describe the reason. Then explain how you manage to calm yourself down. Talk slowly and be specific. After you describe your situation, ask if the child has ever felt something like that and what happened.

In addition to modeling, let the children you care for struggle with difficult tasks. Don't offer assistance immediately. Give the minimum help necessary, and don't expect perfection. Kids need to learn that it's okay to work hard.

Finally, use what is generally called *Grandma's rule:* First you do this and then you can do that. In other words, first eat your dinner and then you get dessert. Or first you clean your room and then you can play games. This rule teaches children that they get rewarded with desired options for completing less desirable ones. In other words, tolerating a bit of frustration usually pays off in the long run.

Giving kids tools for handling anger

First, help children discover the triggers for their anger. Be sure to do this in a setting that feels safe and private. Help them, in a nonjudgmental way, figure out any common themes:

>> Who does anger erupt with? Friends, family, teachers?

>> What happens? Screaming? Hitting? Yelling? Crying? Pouting?

>> When does it happen? Every day, once a week, in the morning, in the evening?

>> Where does it happen? At home, at school, on the playground? In public places? In the car?

>> Why did it happen? Did it happen when being told what to do? Was it an argument with a sibling or a friend? Was it because something was unfair? Was it because something was too hard?

Now problem solve. Work together to see if there are any solutions to what is happening that could decrease anger. Establish clear expectations about how to express anger. These rules should be consistently enforced whether they exist in the home or classroom. For example, it's okay to raise your voice, but you can't insult or call names. You may not throw things. You can't destroy property. You can't hit others. No slamming doors.

Give kids better options for expressing frustration and anger:

>> Count to 20 forward then backward.

>> Take slow deep breaths until they're calm.

>> Take a walk around the block or the house.

>> Do 25 jumping jacks.

>> Write about how they feel.

>> Play a game.

>> Draw a picture about their anger.

>> Talk to a parent or teacher about their feelings.

>> Listen to music.

>> Text a friend.

>> Use words to express their feelings.

Kids often have problems with anger because they lack adequate social skills. Help kids learn how to negotiate from a state of calmness. Teach them how to compromise and take turns. Demonstrate how you check out the evidence before jumping to conclusions.

Avoiding trouble spots

There are times and situations that increase the likelihood of anger. That goes for kids and adults as well. When people are getting sick, irritability often increases. Keep sick kids away from situations that might be frustrating. After the pandemic, people are much more aware of isolation as a way to protect against the spread of disease. Isolation can also sometimes decrease the spread of anger.

Tired kids make poor decisions and also become frustrated more easily. Make sure your kids and teens are getting enough sleep. Ask any parent what kids are like after a sleepover: cranky!

Hunger also increases irritability. Whether it's chronic hunger or a missed meal, a hungry child is likely to have a short fuse. Some kids get irritable after eating too much sugar or snacks. If you are a caregiver of a hungry child, give them healthy food.

Too much stimulation can also cause kids to become overly crabby. Birthday parties, large family gatherings, and crowded places are all potential trouble spots. That's especially true if the temperature is hot and there is lots of noise.

REMEMBER

Avoiding these situations is not always possible. But it's a wise caregiver that is prepared to swoop in and prevent escalations before they explode.

Knowing When to Get Help for Angry Kids

All kids get angry. When a child does not know how to talk, the only way to express anger is through crying and throwing a temper tantrum. When kids learn to talk and express more feelings, temper tantrums should start to decrease significantly. By school age, most kids stop having frequent tantrums or serious anger outbursts.

If a child continues to show these behaviors and they disrupt learning at school, normal family life, or childcare situations, then professional consultation should be considered. In fact, disruptive behavior and anger issues are particularly common reasons for kids to be seen by mental health professionals.

Getting evaluated

It's extremely important to get a full evaluation for a child with anger issues. That's because the cause of anger could stem from so many different sources. Anger could be a reaction to an undiagnosed learning disability. It could emerge from unknown bullying at school, or from abuse or neglect. Anger could also be a result of a physical or mental condition that has not yet been identified.

A full evaluation should consider the child's environment and interview caregivers as well as get information from teachers. The child should be seen by a physician to rule out medical causes. Psychological evaluations may also involve formalized testing if a learning disability or other disorder is suspected.

WARNING

Don't expect to drop your kid off at a therapist's office and expect them to be fixed. Therapy for anger issues just about always includes family members.

Exploring types of therapy

Disruptive behavior is the most common reason for the initiation of professional treatment for children and teens. Many psychological disorders have an anger component. For example, anxious kids get angry when they are forced to confront situations that increase their anxiety. Kids with attention or learning problems get angry when frustrated by challenging academic tasks.

There are two types of therapy that have been extensively studied and found to be effective for kids with anger problems:

» The first type, **parent management training (PMT),** teaches parents the methods of behavior modification, improves communication skills, and increases positive interactions between parents and children.

» The second approach focuses on the child. However, parents are usually involved as well. This approach, **cognitive behavior therapy** (the focus of much of this book), teaches specific problem-solving and emotional regulation skills, and helps develop changes in thinking, feeling, and behaving.

TIP

If you take your child to a mental health professional, be sure to ask what form of treatment they offer. Don't be afraid to ask for evidence of research that supports their treatment.

Chapter **14**

Subduing Anger in Intimate Relationships

I magine yourself at a party. You hear a couple of raised voices that sound increasingly angry. Two people apparently arguing about politics. What do you think? You're probably dumbfounded that people would be so stupid as to talk about politics at a party. How do you feel? Possibly annoyed? Maybe a little uncomfortable with the atmosphere?

But what if one of the people in the argument is your spouse or partner? Your reaction explodes. You feel extremely embarrassed, possibly angry, and even consider grabbing your partner and leaving the party. In other words, when anger and love mix, angry feelings and/or emotional distress escalate.

This chapter addresses issues of anger management within intimate relationships. Here, you discover how to avoid becoming part of an angry couple. You see how to set better boundaries as well as how to think and behave your way into healthier relationships. This chapter also exposes the mental traps that keep you in harm's way while dealing with those you love. Finally, the chapter shows how to avoid facilitating anger or being victimized by anger.

The Loving-But-Angry Relationship

When you think of domestic violence, what comes to mind? If you're like most people, you immediately conjure up an image of a couple engaged in an angry, violent exchange. This couple could be two men, two women, a husband and wife, partners, or cohabitants. What makes it domestic violence is that they live together in some sort of committed relationship.

These relationships are the most difficult ones in which to manage anger because you can't walk away from them (at least not easily) and because you probably have a different standard for what is acceptable behavior for loved ones versus strangers (in other words, you'll tolerate more from your loved ones than you will from strangers).

For example, if a stranger comes up to you and slaps you across the face, you'd probably call the police. But if your girlfriend does the same thing, you very well may just let it go or get into a rousing argument but probably not involve the authorities.

Intimate partner violence

The term *intimate partner violence* (IPV) encompasses a variety of aggressive behaviors committed by current or former partners. Victims of IPV can be either male or female. Types of IPV behaviors include the following:

>> **Physical violence:** These acts include punching, slapping, shoving, throwing objects at someone, stabbing, shooting, and any behavior intended to inflict physical injury.

>> **Intimidation:** This form of abuse bridges and overlaps with physical abuse and emotional abuse. Behaviors such as destruction of property (punching a hole in the wall), cruelty to animals, and threats to other family members are all forms of intimidation.

>> **Emotional abuse:** These behaviors include expressions of contempt, yelling, screaming, name calling, making threats to harm, humiliating, and blaming. Psychological aggression includes threats of suicide or self-harm as a means of preventing one's partner from leaving. It also includes unreasonable, controlling demands to isolate from friends and family, wear certain clothes, or engage in unwanted activities.

>> **Sexual abuse:** This type of IPV involves forcing a partner to engage in nonconsensual sexual activities of any sort. Victims of sexual abuse feel guilty, ashamed, and afraid, and they often "agree" to sex acts without physical force.

>> **Stalking:** This category of IPV refers to a series of undesired actions that individually may not always appear particularly ominous but, when seen as a pattern, clearly communicate an intention to cause fear for one's safety. Common stalking behaviors include sending repeated cards or love notes, showing up unexpectedly, transmitting unwanted texts and voice messages, delivering flowers and gifts, and breaking into homes.

WARNING

Some stalkers spend hours every day planning their crusades. A number of stalkers continue their campaign for years. If you're the victim of a stalker, call The Domestic Abuse Hotline (800-799-7233) or chat on their website www. thehotline.org for more information and advice. Stalking often leads to violence.

How does IPV affect people? According to the United States Centers for Disease Control and Prevention, victims of IPV are at heightened risk for a variety of health problems, such as

>> Heavy smoking

>> Excessive drinking

>> Drug abuse

>> Poor physical health

>> Unsafe sex (multiple partners, nonuse of condoms)

>> Panic attacks

>> Eating disorders

>> Depression

>> Suicide

Not a pretty picture.

The angry partnership

Marriage and committed partnerships are perhaps the most intimate relationships of all. Ideally, they're based on trust, mutual respect, complementary interests, shared values, and abiding love. Many marriages and partnerships, however, are far from ideal. A couple who began as blissful lovers ends up in an angry relationship.

REMEMBER

"Angry relationship" doesn't mean a couple who occasionally shares an angry moment. What couple doesn't? An angry partnership is one in which anger defines both the emotional tone of the relationship as well as the couple's *primary* style of interacting with one another.

TECHNICAL STUFF

The legal, moral, and emotional acceptance of various types of relationships other than traditional marriage has mushroomed. Therefore, the terms *spouse*, *partner*, and *marriage* to refer to all types of committed relationships. The terms *spouse* and *marriage* generally cover relationships that have been sanctioned by a legal and/or spiritual entity; the term *partners* usually involves a less formal yet still committed relationship. For this book, the terms are used interchangeably.

To test whether you and your partner qualify as an angry couple, ask yourself the following questions:

>> Do you and/or your spouse get angry at least once a day?

>> Would you rate the intensity of your anger (or that of your partner's anger) a 7 or higher on a 10-point scale, ranging from 1 (very mild) to 10 (very intense)?

>> Once provoked, does your anger (or your spouse's) last for more than a half-hour?

>> Have either you or your partner ever pushed, shoved, or hit one another when you were angry?

>> Has your anger (or your spouse's) ever left you (or your spouse) feeling anxious or depressed?

>> Would you say that you (or your partner) have become a much angrier person since you got together?

>> Do you or your partner find yourselves worrying about each other's temper?

>> Do you frequently use inflammatory language (cursing) to communicate with your spouse (or does your spouse frequently use such language to communicate with you)?

>> Have you or your partner ever treated each other with contempt — belittling, demeaning, or devaluing each other?

>> Are you (or is your spouse) beginning to question whether you love your partner?

>> Do you (or your spouse) find yourselves answering anger with anger most of the time?

>> Do you (or your partner) feel unsafe in your marriage?

>> Do you or your partner always have to have the last word in a disagreement?

>> Have you or your partner ever thought about or actually sought counseling for problems arising out of anger?

Sometimes, even if you answered yes to one of these questions, you should consider the possibility that you and your partner are an angry couple. Certainly if you responded with yes to more than two or three of these questions, a problem is evident. How do you change this situation? Take advantage of the solutions offered in the remainder of this chapter as well as throughout the book.

When You're Angry at Your Loved One

All the various anger-management strategies outlined in this book apply to you. What's *different* about anger in intimate relationships is the fact that you're dealing with loved ones rather than strangers or casual acquaintances. The fact that you're angry with the people you love can actually be an *incentive* because you have more to lose than you do if you're too angry at work. At work, you can get fired or quit, but if you're angry with your loved ones, you can lose the most important people in your life.

The following sections let you know what may happen if you let your anger continue and give you some tips if you're the angry one in your intimate relationships.

You may become the person you fear and hate

People are changed by intimate relationships — sometimes for the better, sometimes for the worse. Regrettably, in a loving-but-angry relationship, you can and often do end up acting just like the person you fear and hate. You may not start out the relationship being an angry person, but over time, you develop into one in an effort to defend yourself and level the playing field. This transformation doesn't happen overnight, but it does happen. Consider the following example:

> Amanda, a young married woman in her late 20s, finds herself experiencing fits of rage every few days. Her husband, whom she has assaulted more than once, fears her. Her family urges her to get help. Finally, she does.
>
> In one of Amanda's early therapy sessions, the counselor asks her about her parents, "What kind of people are they?"
>
> Instantly, Amanda replies, "My mom, she has a worse temper than I do." She recounts how her mother has always been overly critical and how she gets very angry when Amanda doesn't do things perfectly.

"You mean she acts just like you do with your husband," Amanda's counselor observes.

Amanda appears stunned by what the counselor said. It was obviously something she had never thought of before. Without realizing it, Amanda had become the person she loved (but also feared) the most: her mother. And she had transferred what she had learned in one intimate relationship (mother-daughter) to another (husband-wife). By making this observation, the counselor gives Amanda a choice: Repeat the cycle of intimate-partner violence, or make a change.

Two wrongs never make a right

In an intimate relationship, one angry person can be a problem, but two is a disaster! Some people think they'll feel better if they answer anger with anger, but they're wrong. An exchange between two angry people is definitely a no-win situation.

Many men end up in legal trouble because they react to an angry wife (or ex-wife) in anger. The following conversation typifies that experience:

Client: I messed up again. I got arrested and charged with assault and battery. I can't believe I was so stupid.

Psychologist: How did that happen?

Client: It was weird. I was having an enjoyable dinner with some friends when my wife (they were separated) called and wanted me to come pick up the kids right then. She sounded upset.

Psychologist: So what did you do?

Client: I excused myself and left the restaurant, even though my friends urged me not to. I went to the parking lot at the mall where my wife wanted to meet me.

Psychologist: The mall parking lot? Why there?

Client: I have no idea, but I went there anyway. As soon as I got there, my wife charged at me angry, yelling, and screaming. I told her to back off, but she just got more agitated. I took the kids and was putting them in the car when my wife got in my face, and I just got angry and pushed her away. Then I got in my car and drove off.

Psychologist: Then what happened?

Client: When I got home, the police were waiting for me. They'd gotten a complaint from my wife that I had just assaulted her. So they took me in and booked me.

Psychologist: So what's the lesson learned here — about anger, that is?

Client: I should have stayed at the restaurant and finished my dinner with my friends. Plus I should have kept my cool, even though my wife had obviously lost hers. Then I wouldn't be in all this trouble.

Psychologist: Right!

The client was reacting to his wife's anger with anger. If someone close to you hurts you, it's only natural to want to hurt them back. "You push my buttons, and I'll push yours!"

Unfortunately, that is exactly how exchanges that begin with one or both parties getting irritated end up in domestic violence. This need for emotional reciprocity accelerates the process of toxic anger. It adds fuel to the fire.

TIP

Responding in kind when someone gets angry with you is a reaction, and a reaction is any behavior that is highly predictable, mindless, impulsive, and typically leads to negative consequences. What you want to do is respond in a deliberate, thoughtful way to your loved one's anger, not impulsively *react* to it.

Healthy boundaries are essential

Boundaries are limits. They tell you when you've gone too far. They also tell you when your anger is out of bounds. One way to think about rage is that it's anger that has crossed the line, the point beyond which you can't control it. You should consider all emotional, physical, and sexual violence as entirely out of bounds.

TIP

Here are some examples of healthy boundaries surrounding anger:

>> When your anger gets too intense, stop whatever you're doing and walk away.

>> Commit yourself to the idea that physical violence is *never* acceptable.

>> Request that others respect you as much as you respect them.

>> Tone it down. The message gets lost when the volume and the pace increase.

>> If you're getting too angry, let your loved one have the last word, which effectively puts an end to your anger and hers.

>> Don't be afraid to call a timeout when you're getting too angry.

When You're on the Receiving End of a Loved One's Anger

If you're on the receiving end of the anger, the most important thing you can do is to stay out of harm's way. Your job isn't to fix your loved one's anger; that's your loved one's job (which is covered in the preceding section).

Most people who are on the wrong end of a loving-but-angry relationship have four options:

>> Hope and pray that the angry partner will change.

>> Seek professional help to undo some of the damage done by the abusive anger.

>> Make sure you do all you can to communicate effectively.

>> If all else fails, terminate the relationship altogether.

WARNING

Although the following sections give you ideas about how to respond to an angry partner, that doesn't mean you should assume that your partner's anger is "fix-able" or under your control. Know your limits and be prepared to leave if things aren't improving. Realize that emotional and physical costs occur when you remain with an angry person.

Eliminate the mental traps

If you're in a loving-but-angry relationship, you probably got stuck there through a series of mental traps, traps that have to do with two equally strong emotions: love and anger. What's in your mind — firmly held beliefs about love and anger — keeps you from achieving what matters most: a relationship that is both intimate and safe.

TIP

To counteract the mental traps in the following sections, you need to practice what psychologists call *cognitive restructuring*. That is, rewire your thinking about the relationship between love and anger. Start by challenging any of the false beliefs listed in the following sections. For instance, if your mind tells you, "If my husband loves me enough, he'll stop being so angry," then restructure that thought by saying to yourself, "My husband definitely has an anger problem. He needs help. I can't be the one to fix him; he needs to be responsible for that. What-ever is causing his anger, it's not me. The answer to his anger is inside him. And loving me can't make all that right."

The belief that you can eliminate someone else's anger

The most pervasive mental trap of all is the idea that a loving relationship will make the person you love less angry. Nothing could be farther from the truth. You can't do anything to make your loved one less angry; it's what your loved one does that counts. For example:

> **Tina** fell into this trap years ago and tries to fix her female partner's intermittent-rage disorder with love and support. As Tina says, "Living with her is like living on top of a volcano: You never know when she's going to erupt next."
>
> In the end, all Tina gets for her efforts is a trip to the emergency room, a fractured skull, a ton of medical bills, and a restraining order against her lover. Obviously, Tina's lover needs anger management.

The belief that anger is fleeting but love is forever

A second mental trap has to do with the belief that anger comes and goes but love is forever. No way. For a large and perhaps growing segment of the population, anger is anything *but* fleeting. Anger is a chronic condition — and a toxic one at that. All too often, anger holds on long after the love has gone.

The belief that when people love you, they'll change

Another myth about anger and love is that if the angry person loves you enough, he'll change. Not really. Although love for another person can be an incentive for becoming anger-free, by itself it isn't enough motivation to alter long-standing, complex emotional patterns that have a life of their own.

The belief that all you need is love

The Beatles may try to convince you otherwise, but you need a lot more than love. Many people believe that as long as two people love each other, nothing else matters. Some people still believe that even after they're released from an emergency room following an assault by the person they love.

REMEMBER

Lots of things should matter in your life in addition to love. Energy, health, your career, friendships, activities, hobbies, and neighbors come to mind as starters.

The belief that anger is just a sign of caring

The last mental trap is the one that tells you that if someone you love is angry with you, it means she actually cares. Parents or spouses sometimes engage in outrageous behavior (including violence) toward someone they supposedly love, all the while saying, "I'm doing this for your own good."

Rubbish! Angry people care about themselves — what *they* want, what *they* expect, what *they* demand, what *they* think — not you. They're expressing anger for their own good: to let off some steam, to relieve tension, or to protest what they regard as unfair treatment. If they actually cared about you, meaning your welfare, your safety, and your sanity, they would take whatever immediate action was necessary to short-circuit their anger.

Don't facilitate anger

If you can't be the solution to your loved one's anger, don't be part of the problem. Relationships are two-way streets. Your loved one's anger affects you, and your behavior in turn affects his anger. What you don't want to be is an *anger facilitator* (the person who makes it easier for the other person to move ahead with his anger beyond the point of no return).

WARNING

When someone, obviously in a state of rage, says, "I'm warning you, don't say another word," take them at their word and shut up. If a person who is well on their way to losing their cool says, "Get out of my way. I've got to get out of here," move aside, or you'll very likely get hurt. It doesn't pay to push someone who's already angry.

TIP

Here are some other ways you can keep from adding to the problem:

>> **Don't apologize for someone else's anger.** That's just another way of helping them avoid responsibility for their own emotions. Instead of saying, "I'm sorry I made you mad," tell him, "I can see you're angry about something. Do you want to talk about it?"

>> **Don't keep silent about someone else's bad behavior.** People who exhibit unreasonable anger need corrective feedback. They need to hear when they're getting too loud or acting in ways that make others afraid. If you're quiet and you let things slide, the other person may think her behavior is just fine and dandy.

>> **Don't minimize the problem.** Many people respond to intense anger by telling themselves things like, "Well, it wasn't that bad; besides, I messed up."

>> **Get a life of your own.** Too many people make their loved one's anger the centerpiece of their lives. You put everything else on hold while you try to fix the other person's anger. Instead, follow your own interests. If you have buddies you play basketball with or friends who meet to chat about the latest bestselling book, you'll have someplace to go, something to do, when your loved one flies off the hook.

>> **Don't help the other person save face.** People who have too much anger need to confront their problem directly. Stop coming up with excuses for the other person's outrage.

>> **Pretend your loved one is a stranger.** Ask yourself if you would allow a stranger to treat you the way your angry loved one does. Most people with angry partners would never tolerate that same behavior from a stranger.

Refuse to be the victim of anger

When you're confronted by a loved one's anger, clearly the anger is the major problem. But anger isn't a reason to feel like a helpless victim. To keep that from happening, try the following:

>> **Get help.** Your friends and family are great resources. But, when dealing with an angry loved one, they can't give you an objective perspective. You can get objectivity from a therapist, counselor, or psychologist.

>> **Hang on to your sense of hope.** When you're faced with an angry loved one, it's easy to fall into a trap of hopelessness. To keep hope intact, try spending some time with a supportive friend who can remind you that you're not a worthless person.

>> **Do something, anything, to avoid feeling a sense of helplessness.** For example, make an escape plan if you are afraid of violence. Know where you can go before things escalate.

>> **Use the support resources at your disposal to keep yourself safe.** If you need a "safe house," this isn't the time to be bashful. Call a friend and ask for sanctuary. Call the police, if necessary, and ask for protection. The National Domestic Violence Hotline has trained personnel at 1-800-799-7233, and their website is www.thehotline.org. You can also chat online with a counselor.

>> **Be assertive.** Find your voice and speak up for yourself. Remind yourself that you have a right to be treated with respect and restraint, and the last thing you need is to be someone else's verbal or physical punching bag! There's a big difference between telling your angry loved one, "I can't stand it when you treat me like this!" and saying, "I won't stand for that kind of behavior anymore." *Can't* has to do with ability; *won't* indicates a sense of will.

>> **Be honest with yourself and admit that you have a problem.** As long as you deny the reality of a loving-but-angry relationship, you're stuck. You have to acknowledge a problem before you can hope to solve it. This book is about solving problems associated with anger (yours and the other person's), but you can't make any progress until you face the truth.

Chapter **15**

Rage Behind the Machine

As someone who has worked in medical facilities, I've had multiple occasions to wear surgical masks. Mask wearing was usually required when a patient had a contagious disease or a compromised immune system. I found that working as a psychologist with patients in hospitals, the mask sometimes made it more difficult to communicate with people. Wearing a mask makes me feel more anonymous and less relatable. Furthermore, it makes it harder to see the full facial expression of my patient, which also makes them feel more disconnected from me. But after awhile, I got used to it. It was irritating, but certainly not enraging.

And I never thought about mask wearing as a particularly controversial requirement. It was simply best medical practice under the circumstances. That all changed during our recent pandemic when simple surgical masks became statements about truth, justice, freedom, and political party. People on both sides of the mask requirement issue expressed rage at each other. How in the world did that happen? And why?

In this chapter, you will see the connection between anger and anonymity. How did a rather innocuous piece of cloth or paper became a nationwide controversy, tearing apart families and friends? The viral content spewed in social media holds significant blame. I discuss ways to tamp down the fury on the information superhighway, which is what we used to call the internet back in the day.

Furthermore, violence erupts on our highways. Behind the wheel, anger and vengeance cause tragic results. About a third of all traffic accidents involve road rage. The carnage left behind often snares innocent victims. This chapter provides tips on taming road rage and finding calmer ways to enjoy the ride.

What's the Common Denominator?

Imagine that you are completely disguised. Your friends, family, co-workers, neighbors, or fellow citizens have no idea who you are or where you live. There is no possibility of anyone ever discovering your identity. Are there a few things you'd like to honestly express? For example, I'd like to ask my neighbor why in the world does a single man need a trailer that he never uses, a huge ugly green truck he never drives, two ratty cars, and a motorcycle? How about you? Might you want to ask . . .

>> **Your kids:** Why they can't put their dirty glasses in the sink, just once?

>> **Your family:** Why must every birthday party be celebrated with chips, pizza, cake, and ice cream when we're all supposed to be watching sugar and carbs?

>> **You boss:** Why he needs to have meetings about having meetings when there is real work to be done?

>> **You friends:** Why can't they stop telling the same boring story over and over again?

>> **Your fellow citizens:** Why they can't stop constantly complaining about what's wrong with their country and instead get involved and do something?

If you were totally disguised, really, wouldn't it be fun to be completely honest for a day or two? Innocent musings. You probably wouldn't be very popular.

So what does this have to do with internet rage and road rage? The same disguise or anonymity that would allow you to say what you mean, even if unkind, is what people feel from the comfort of their car or keyboard. The common denominator is the feeling of being anonymous, unseen, and unknown.

Warriors: Behind the keyboard or steering wheel

The belief that you won't really be seen gives rage permission. You can so easily, with little risk to yourself, cuss out the driver in the car who can't hear you, or leave insulting comments for the blogger who doesn't know who you are. You can spread rumors, tell lies, honk your horn at the driver who's too slow to start after the light turns green, or tailgate, supposedly without cost.

Interesting research on crowds backs up the idea that anonymity may be partially responsible for bad behavior both online and on the road. Social scientists have studied behavior in crowds over many decades. For example, the bystander effect suggests that when a large group of people witness a crime or other dangerous situation, the crowd is less likely to intervene and help than when a single or a couple of people witness the same event.

TECHNICAL STUFF

The bystander effect has been replicated in many studies. However, different studies suggest that multiple factors may be at play. For example, if someone is well trained in emergency response (such as a firefighter or nurse), that person would feel compelled to help even in the presence of a large crowd. Similarly, people with strong feelings of sympathy or empathy in the face of a negative event are also more likely to intervene.

When people are in a large crowd, it is hypothesized that individuals feel invisible, de-personalized, and lose their sense of identity. In other words, they become anonymous. Self-control decreases and people are easily influenced by the mentality of the crowd. Those feelings may increase the risk of dangerous, antisocial behavior. Think of mob behavior.

On the other hand, if the intentions of the group overall are benign or pro-social, research suggests that the anonymity of a group can lead to appropriate behavior. Whether good or bad, being part of a crowd increases the influence the crowd has on individuals.

Bringing this back to internet and road rage, in both cases, whether behind the wheel in your steel cage or behind the keyboard on your couch, you can feel relatively anonymous. If you are in a group of aggressive drivers on a crowded freeway, the group norm to drive aggressively may influence you to increase your speed and determination to get where you are going faster by dodging in and out of lanes. If you are in a chat group that sends barbs, insults, and threats around, those same tendencies may up your own aggression.

Intensity on the Internet

Cyberbullying uses information and communication technologies to intentionally harm or frighten someone. Examples of cyberbullying include posting humiliating pictures, threatening, making fun of someone's looks, harassing, spreading false rumors, impersonating someone, cyberstalking, or just saying mean things. These activities usually occur on social media, online games, chat rooms, message boards, or through text messaging.

Like other forms of internet rage, cyberbullies use their perceived anonymity to inflict pain on their victims. Cyberbullying has been linked to cases of adolescent suicide. Victims show higher levels of stress, depression, anxiety, physical complaints, and suicidal thoughts. Adolescent victims often suffer academically, have trouble sleeping, and may engage in drastic activities to change their looks. Cyberbullies tend to have higher rates of substance abuse, delinquent behaviors, and aggression.

Social media and the internet have changed the world. They allow us to communicate with far-flung family and friends and share pictures of our lives. They also have inspired movements, helped educate millions around the world, and given many joy. However, not all of its effects are positive.

Viral emotions and echo chambers

Online sharing and posting is an international pastime. What makes some content go viral and spread rapidly throughout social media? The answer is complicated and depends on many factors. However, simply put, emotions spark virality. An intense emotional reaction to content increases the likelihood of it being shared.

Both highly positive, awesome content (think a definitive cure for gun violence) and highly negative reactions or content (witnessing extreme acts of violence or cruelty) cause a huge increase in sharing. The more intense the emotion, the more viral the content.

A large study tracked millions of messages and looked for embedded emotions. What the research found was that although joy spawned sharing faster than sadness, rage is the quickest emotion of all to go viral. It's no wonder that angry websites are quite popular.

Rant-sites are specifically designed websites that allow people, usually anonymously, to express their rage. You can rant about whatever you want. One site had a menu of topics such as mask wearing, family, politics, religion, relationships, and more. Another site suggested that ranting was good for your mental health.

WARNING

These sites are based on an outdated concept called *catharsis*. The premise is that by venting your anger, it somehow releases it and you feel calmer. That is simply not true. Most of the time, punching pillows or venting online may provide brief but temporary relief. However, in the long run, people who practice catharsis actually experience more anger. Research specific to rant-sites found that frequent users usually had significant anger problems and were more likely to engage in both physical and verbal aggression than people who do not read or write on rant-sites.

An *echo chamber* is literally a space in which sounds reverberate and echo. On social media, it means a space in which people with similar points of view reinforce their ideas among themselves. Beliefs and opinions are confirmed, not debated. These groupings have increased anger and fear, spread online conspiracies, inspired protests, and further divided people with different opinions.

Echo chambers are formed by internet algorithms that track searches, likes, and internet usage. Similar to viral material, emotional content increases responses in echo chambers. In other words, extreme emotions such as anger and rage may increase the readership of polarized communities contributing to more societal tension.

SOCIAL MEDIA AND DEPRESSION

Correlation is the relationship between variables. For example, depression rates go up as teenagers spend more time online. As rates of murder go up in New York City, so does the sale of ice cream. So do people buy ice cream after murdering someone? Or does ice cream cause murderous rage? Neither. Just because two variables are correlated does not mean that one causes the other. It could be something else. For instance, higher temperatures are thought to contribute to both eating more ice cream and increases in violence. So we can't say for certain yet that depression is increased by social media usage. More research is needed and is being conducted.

In the middle of the last century, when doctors started noticing that the vast majority of their lung cancer patients were smokers, they started asking questions. From the start of their questioning, tobacco producers argued that there was no proof that cigarette smoking caused cancer. Since then, considerable research has concluded that smoking indeed increases the risk of cancer. Now, the relationship is well established, and people are warned that cigarette smoking leads to cancer.

Recently, psychologists note that their depressed patients, especially adolescents, appear to be heavy users of social media. In fact, multiple studies have been conducted that show the more time kids and teens spend on their devices, the more they tend to suffer depression. This research does not "prove" that social media usage causes depression, and that's the argument of some of the richest people in the world who happen to own social media companies. Just saying.

An interesting study about online echo chambers found that angry people were more likely to virulently debate online with both like-minded and opposing people. They were more likely to accept only information that confirmed their prior beliefs and dismiss contradictory information.

Protecting against and preventing cyberbullying

The most important way to prevent cyberbullying, harassment, or internet crime is to avoid posting personal information on the internet. Remember that posting is forever. Once you post, you can't really ever take it down.

Use privacy settings on all the websites you use. Adjust your settings so that only trusted friends can see your content. Recheck your privacy settings occasionally because they may change.

Never post your phone number, address, account numbers, or social security numbers. Watch out for location sharing on your smartphone because you may not want others to always know where you are. Always keep passwords private.

If you become a victim of cyberbullying, do not respond. Responding only increases the interaction. Block the bully from your phone, email, and social media accounts. Keep copies of the evidence. Report the bully to social media sites.

If the bullying becomes extreme, it may be illegal. Threats, obscene calls, child pornography, stalking, and exploitation should be reported to the police.

The very best way to prevent rage on the internet is to turn off your devices. Find other, more active, prosocial things to do. Volunteer. Read a book. Visit with friends. Consider giving up social media except to exchange pictures and information with close family and friends. Look for recipes on the internet rather than rebellion.

Reeling in Road Rage

Sitting in your steel cage, behind the wheel, music playing, a huge red pick-up truck starts to creep up too close. You purposely slow down, annoyed by the tailgating. The truck gets closer and then suddenly jumps to the next lane, whizzing by, horn blaring. You feel a surge of anger. Swearing, you start to speed up, trying to catch up with the pick-up. But calm down please. Road rage does not end well.

Just the week before I wrote this chapter, a 6-year-old boy was shot and killed on the highway while sitting in his booster seat. He was being driven to his first day of kindergarten. I'm guessing his killer did not look into the 6-year-old's face when he pulled the trigger. The perpetrator likely felt anonymous: unknown yet powerful enough to kill a 6-year-old. What a horrible, cowardly act.

The statistics are frightening. Each year in the last decade, about 30 people were murdered in road rage incidents. Road rage is responsible for about a third of all collisions, and aggressive driving is involved in over two thirds of all fatal accidents.

Think twice before engaging someone who is driving dangerously or aggressively. About one third of all road rage incidents involve guns. You don't want to get killed over someone cutting you off.

Be the other driver

Are you the person who roars past the little old man driving under the speed limit, shaking your fist and screaming for all the world to hear, "They shouldn't let old farts like you drive!" and "Get out of the way, you old fool!"?

Well, consider this for a second: One day, if you're lucky and your road rage doesn't kill you first, you'll *be* that old guy. That's right, that will be you, slumped down in the seat, white hair hardly visible above the wheel, staring straight ahead, oblivious to everything around you, and driving 35 in a 55-mile-per-hour zone. Try to visualize yourself as the other driver. Put yourself in his shoes. And then ask yourself, "How would I want other drivers to act toward me?"

TIP

Here are some anger-freeing ways to think about slow drivers:

>> "Wow, it's great that he can still drive at his age."

>> "I hope I'm still that independent and able to get around on my own when I'm that old."

>> "Maybe that's the secret to growing old gracefully: driving slowly."

>> "I bet he feels a whole lot more relaxed right now than I do."

>> "He doesn't look angry, so maybe there's a lesson here."

Take the "I" out of driver

Driving should be about *the ride*, right? Not just about *you*? Of course, road-ragers would disagree: "Get out of *my* way, damn it!" "You're holding *me* up, and *I'm* going to be late for *my* appointment." "*I* hate drivers like you." "You're not going to pass *me* — no way."

Make driving more about the other guy:

>> "I'll slide over and let *him* pass. *He's* in more of a hurry than I am."

>> "The way *she's* driving, *she* must really be enjoying her day."

>> "Wow, what an angry fellow. I wouldn't want to be in *his* shoes."

>> "I used to drive like *she* does, but thank God I don't any more."

>> "I'm sure *they* have somewhere important to go too."

Drive with humility. Be ordinary, and don't think of yourself as someone who's entitled to special consideration out there on the highway. Avoid stereotyping your fellow travelers: women drivers, old drivers, teenage drivers, Yankee drivers, redneck drivers, truckers, and so on. Don't set yourself apart from the pack. Just be an ordinary person and relax.

Look on the bright side

Every problem has a silver lining. If someone ahead of you in traffic slows you down, you end up feeling less rushed. That's good. If you tend to speed a lot and suddenly find yourself stuck behind a slower driver with no opportunity to pass, maybe he's keeping you from getting your next speeding ticket. That's good.

If you see another driver doing something that you regard as "just plain igno-rant," that makes you a smarter driver, right? That's good. If it takes you longer to get somewhere than you had planned, you end up having more time to relax and enjoy your own private thoughts along the way. That's good. You can use this kind of logic with just about every situation.

TIP

The next time you feel yourself on the verge of rage, ask yourself: "What *good* can possibly come from this?" When you come up with an answer, you can relax.

Realize that they are not the enemy

Rage is an emotion that people should reserve for their true enemies. Enemies are those folks that you believe mean to harm you deliberately and intentionally. "That S.O.B. tried to hit me just now!" He's out to get you, plain and simple. So you protect yourself with rage.

Problem is, those other drivers aren't your enemies. They don't even know you. They're strangers. Truth is, they're not thinking at all about you; they're thinking about themselves. There's no grand conspiracy operating here. Granted, they may be a nuisance sometimes, but your enemy? Nah.

Here's the litmus test: You're driving down a stretch of highway with no cars anywhere around you. Up ahead, you see a truck on the side of the road, waiting to enter the lane of traffic. Just as you get to where the truck is, the driver suddenly and without warning pulls out in front of you, causing you to hit your brakes and veer into the left lane.

Why did he endanger you (and himself) by doing that rather than waiting until you passed? Did he do that on purpose? Was he waiting for the right moment to whip out in front of you, hoping to startle you and maybe cause you to crash? If you believe this, you'll experience road rage, guaranteed.

Or is it just that he doesn't know any better. Maybe he doesn't have a clue about safe driving? Or maybe he just got distracted by something and made a stupid error. Can you honestly say that you've never done the same thing — probably more than once or twice? If you look at the situation this way, you'll be far less likely to feel enraged.

The choice about how to respond emotionally to a situation is always yours. Take a few moments to think about unexpected gaffes by other drivers. It's really not about you.

5

Handling Anger from the Past

IN THIS PART . . .

Let go of past anger and rewrite your story.

Recognize the value of forgiveness.

Look for warning signs of relapse.

Calm down and carry on.

Chapter **16**

Letting Go of Past Anger

nger is an emotion, and emotions are meant to be short-lived. Excitement, fear, sadness, surprise, and irritation are all emotions that pass through you throughout the day. But, for some people, anger persists, and through its persistence, anger causes harm, as in the following example:

> **Marilyn** is a 55-year-old married woman who continues to be angry about the mistreatment she suffered at work over 15 years ago. Marilyn was injured on the job, and, as a result, she not only had to change jobs but also had to endure continuous pain in her lower back. Marilyn found her employer to be woefully unsympathetic, which only gave her *more* reason to be angry.
>
> After several years of struggling, Marilyn's co-workers started complaining about her anger outbursts. Eventually, her employer terminated her. The resentment that Marilyn harbored over the years all but ruined her health and has taken its toll on her marriage. She isn't just a victim in the sense of having been permanently injured; she's also the victim of her own unresolved anger.

This chapter discusses some of the reasons people like Marilyn hang on to anger. They have anger that's unresolved from their past and have no idea how to get through it. I offer solutions for dropping the anger habit.

Living Without Resolution

Maybe you're the kind of person who holds on to anger until you can resolve the problem that caused it in the first place. That's a great approach if you're dealing with a solvable problem. But what if the problem can't be resolved at all, or at least not completely? What purpose does hanging on to anger serve then?

You'll encounter lots of problems, conflicts, and situations in life that, despite your best efforts, will never have a happy or satisfying outcome. These situations you have to live with — *without* resolution. Examples include the following:

- » Childhood abuse
- » Being raised in an alcoholic home
- » Sexual assault
- » Birth defects
- » Being the victim of a serious crime
- » Loss of loved ones (through death, divorce, or abandonment)
- » Chronic illness
- » Natural catastrophes (like floods, hurricanes, or tornadoes)
- » War or terrorism
- » Disfigurement
- » Serious harm to a loved one
- » Accidents
- » Serious, acute illnesses or injuries
- » Disability
- » Irreversible loss of income
- » Having an addict in the family

TIP

The next time you get angry, ask yourself these questions:

- » Can my anger correct the situation?
- » Can my anger undo what has been done?
- » Is this one of those times when "after the toothpaste is out of the tube, I can't put it back"?

If anger can't correct the situation, if it can't undo what's been done, and if it can't rewrite history, then maybe it's time to *let it go.*

Recognizing anger in post-traumatic stress disorder

Almost everyone who either experiences or witnesses extremely traumatic events feels strong emotions such as fear, terror, anger, anxiety, or panic at the time. Evidence suggests that a significant minority of these people acquire an emotional problem known as post-traumatic stress disorder (PTSD). Many of them improve on their own within a year or so following the event. At the same time, many people experience little or no improvement over time.

PTSD consists of having experienced a traumatic event followed by an enduring group of symptoms, such as the following:

>> **Intrusive thoughts or images,** such as flashbacks, nightmares, and distress when reminded of the event.

>> **Avoidance** of people, places, or things that remind the person of the traumatic event. Avoidance also encompasses attempts to avoid thinking about the event by turning to drugs or alcohol.

>> **Distressing changes in moods and thoughts,** such as feeling detached from other people; inability to experience joy; lack of interests in things; blaming self or others for the event; ongoing thoughts that are exaggerated dangers in the world; excessive dwelling on fear, shame, guilt, and feelings of anger; and problems remembering details about the actual event.

>> **Changes in reactions to the world,** such as increased irritability, aggression, self-destructive behavior, easily startled and frightened, excessive focus on imagined dangers, sleep problems, and trouble concentrating.

WARNING

You shouldn't use the preceding list of symptoms to diagnose yourself or someone else. If you think you may have PTSD, please seek professional help to diagnose and treat whatever problem you're experiencing.

PTSD is a growing concern in today's world that's filled with wars, terrorism, and constant media coverage of various horrors. In addition, those afflicted with COVID and treated in the Intensive Care Unit (ICU) often suffer symptoms of PTSD. Anger and irritability frequently pose problems for people with PTSD both interpersonally and by making treatment more difficult and less effective. Therefore, anger-management training may be a useful piece of the therapeutic approach for many people who have PTSD accompanied by anger.

FIRST RESPONDERS AND PTSD

Police officers, paramedics, nurses, firefighters, and emergency room healthcare providers encounter highly traumatic events repeatedly. All of these individuals experience grief, sadness, anxiety, and stress after exposures to trauma. Not all first responders develop PTSD, but they do have an increased risk. Sometimes they manage to successfully work with literally hundreds of traumatic cases without developing clinically diagnosable PTSD.

But, every now and then, a single, unusually disturbing event triggers a full-blown case of PTSD in someone who has years of successfully treating trauma. This happens when the trauma is particularly meaningful to the person. Examples include the death of a child, serious injury or death of a co-worker, or witnessing an overwhelming horrible event, such as the Boston Marathon bombing, 9/11, or the stress of watching people die alone during a pandemic. First responders should seek professional help if they experience PTSD symptoms that persist for more than a month following such an event or even sooner if the symptoms interfere with their life.

TIP

If you suffer from PTSD, some effective treatments are based on cognitive behavior therapy. However, if you have PTSD, find a therapist with expertise in these approaches to help you.

The anger that frequently accompanies PTSD is anger from the past that has no clear path to resolving it.

Accepting rather than suppressing anger

Ever try not to think about something? Maybe you've heard of the exercise where you try not to think about or imagine a pink *elephant* for five minutes and see what happens. The more you resist that thought, the more it persists: pink elephant, pink elephant, pink elephant! In other words, attempts to suppress thoughts usually backfire.

It's the same with emotions like anger. The more you tell yourself, "I'm not mad; I'm not hurt; it doesn't bother me," the longer you stay mad. And, after a while, that feeling begins to fester. Consider the following example:

> **Jason** had recurrent migraine headaches for most of his adult life — that is, until his wife's untimely death at the age of 60. Shortly after his wife died, Jason's headaches stopped completely. The reason: Jason no longer had to resist expressing the anger he felt toward his wife, a woman who he says, "was angry all the time about almost everything and took it out on me."

Jason's wife would explode with verbal rage and five minutes later, she was fine. But not Jason. He held on to his anger for days, sometimes weeks, expressing it through silence and pain. "When she lashed out at me, I couldn't let it be. Staying angry was my way of telling her, 'You're not going to get away with this!'"

But who was Jason really hurting by hanging on to his anger? Himself.

Isn't it time you stopped resisting both the experience and expression of anger in your life? If the answer is yes, start letting go by following these five steps:

1. **Identify the source of your anger.**

   What person, event, or circumstance provoked your anger? How long ago was this?

2. **Acknowledge your angry feelings.**

   Say aloud, "I am angry because. . . ." Then decide how angry you are. Rate the intensity of your emotion on a scale of 1 (mild) to 10 (extreme). Ratings of 1 to 3 translate into irritation, ratings of 4 to 6 suggest that you're mad or angry, and ratings of 7 to 10 imply a state of rage.

3. **Legitimize your anger.**

   Remind yourself that you have a right to experience anger, just as you have a right to feel joy or excitement. You don't really need to justify your anger.

4. **Give yourself permission to express anger if you can think of a potentially useful outcome.**

   Anger has gotten a bad rap because people all too often associate it with violence, rudeness, and incivility. But you can express anger in a lot of healthy, assertive, constructive ways (see Chapter 8 if you want some examples). And sometimes, direct verbal expression of anger won't accomplish anything. In those cases, the section "Telling Your Story Your Way," later in this chapter, gives you ways to express your anger in written form.

5. **List three or more ways in which your life is better off by *letting go* of anger.**

   For some people, letting go of anger allows them to enjoy better relationships. For others, becoming calmer decreases anxiety, stress, and pain. Still others find themselves more able to be productive. Finally, dropping the anger habit allows space for emotions like joy.

Being nice doesn't mean being powerless

If you're stuck on anger from the past, you may worry that giving up your anger will make you look weak and helpless. For example, some people think that *nice* automatically goes along with powerlessness. No doubt, you've heard the phrase, "Nice guys finish last."

The dictionary defines a nice person as someone who is pleasant, agreeable, courteous, considerate, and delightful. It doesn't say anything about being a victim of other people's bad behavior. Being nice absolutely doesn't mean that you don't stand up for yourself. It doesn't say you don't deserve to be respected, safe, and treated fairly by others.

If you associate *nice* with powerless, you'll store up feelings of anger instead of letting them go. In an effort to be seen as ultra-nice, you'll say you're "fine" when you're actually irritated, as Mark does in the following example. Those irritations will linger and, slowly but surely, accumulate into a feeling of anger.

> Publically, **Mark** was one of the nicest guys in town. He was a man in his 60s, raised in the traditions of the Old South, where a gentleman never showed his temper in public. By day, Mark was a sweet, pleasant, charming, and accommodating man. No matter how badly he was treated, he would simply respond by saying, "That's fine. Don't worry about it."
>
> But by night, Mark raged. While sleeping peacefully, he ferociously ground his teeth (he even had dreams about all those who had wronged him during the day). On one occasion, he woke up to find his bed sheet covered with blood from three of his broken teeth. His dental bills climbed. Despite his calm façade and cordial demeanor, Mark was a walking time bomb of rage.
>
> Therapy changed all of that. Mark found that he could continue to be nice without being powerless. So when a friend stood him up for a luncheon appointment that had been planned for weeks, instead of waiting patiently for an hour and ruminating about his irritation, Mark left after 15 minutes, went home, and called his friend to ask if something happened. His friend explained that he simply forgot. Mark replied, "Well, I admit I was a little worried and then frankly, annoyed. Maybe next time you can be more careful to get our lunch into your calendar. Deal?"
>
> The result: He stopped grinding his teeth at night altogether, much to the chagrin of his dentist, who remarked one day, "I don't know what's changed in your life, but it's been over a year since you've been in here with a tooth problem. If you keep this up, I'll go broke!"

If you hang on to anger from the past, it becomes yesterday's, today's, *and* tomorrow's anger.

Telling Your Story Your Way

One of the most powerful methods for letting go of unresolvable anger from the past is through writing. Consistent writing in a journal about difficult emotions helps people cope and move on with their lives. Writing in a journal, in this case about anger and other unpleasant emotions, is about telling a story — *your* story. How you construct that story, however, makes the difference between whether this exercise will help. The following guidelines show you how.

TIP

Make your anger journal a daily exercise for at least a couple of weeks. Continue it as long as you find it useful. You can turn to this strategy off and on for the rest of your life.

Make yourself the audience

In expressing the emotions that made up your day, you're both the speaker and the audience. In effect, you're entering into a private conversation that's for your eyes only. You won't share your thoughts and feelings with anyone, and your confession will end when you complete the exercise. So what you write in your journal doesn't need to impress, educate, or make someone else feel better.

REMEMBER

Your anger journal is meant to be a dialogue between you and yourself, not between you and someone else.

Use the first person

Writing in the first person (using *I*) may be the most difficult aspect of making your anger journal. Most people are so accustomed to defining and understanding their emotional experiences in terms of *other* people's actions that they feel things in the third person. To illustrate this point, think about how you and others you know talk about anger:

"My **mother** made me so angry."

"My **boss** got me so pissed off!"

"If **they** didn't push my buttons, I wouldn't get so mad."

WARNING

If you think about your emotions like this and you write this way in your journal, everything you glean will be about *those other* people and not about yourself. Writing in the first person makes *you* responsible for *your* emotions:

"**I** got so angry at my mother."

"**I** got pissed off at my boss."

"**I** get angry when they push my buttons."

If you write in the third person about your emotions, you'll feel more like a victim — a victim of the other person's behavior. And victims end up feeling *more* anger when they finish writing, not less. Feeling more upset is exactly the opposite of what you want to accomplish with this exercise.

Don't worry about grammar

You don't have to be an English major to keep an anger journal. What's important here is putting your true feelings into words. Writing gives you some immediate relief from the physical tension required to hold on to unexpressed emotion. Writing also educates you about your own emotional self.

Grammar, spelling, and punctuation are *completely irrelevant*. (So you have a few dangling participles or split infinitives? Who cares?) My advice instead is to do the following:

>> Write spontaneously.

>> Write carelessly.

>> Write with abandonment.

>> Write continuously.

>> Write without a clear sense of purpose.

>> Write with your heart, not your head.

>> Write with passion, not perspective (perspective will come later).

>> Write for no one but yourself.

>> Write as if this is the last conversation you will ever have on earth.

>> Write just for the hell of it!

>> Write first; read later.

Focus on the negative

Storing up feelings of joy and satisfaction won't make you sick, whereas storing up emotions such as anger and sadness will. So the focus of an anger journal must be on anger and other negative feelings. What you're trying to do here is to reexamine and reprocess the thoughts and feelings that can poison your life as time goes by. Think of it this way: Holding on to positive feelings leads to contentment; holding on to negative emotions ends up in resentment. The aim of an anger journal is to avoid the latter.

REMEMBER

You may confuse feelings (emotions) with thoughts and actions such that if asked about how you feel, you'll answer, "Well, I thought he was stupid!" or "I just got up and left after I realized that she forgot about our lunch meeting." Emotions are simply statements about how happy, mad, sad, or glad you are, not why you feel that way or what you're going to do about those feelings.

TIP

You may not be fluent when it comes to emotional terminology. In fact, even if you aced your SAT vocabulary words, your *emotional* vocabulary may be limited to a few general terms like *upset, bothered,* and *nervous.* Here's a list of words people often use to describe the emotion of anger. If you're at a loss for words to describe your feelings, you may want to choose some from this list. See more about feelings in Chapter 5.

>> Annoyed

>> Disappointed

>> Disgusted

>> Displeased

>> Dissatisfied

>> Enraged

>> Fuming

>> Furious

>> Incensed

>> Indignant

>> Irate

>> Irritated

>> Mad

>> Outraged

>> Pissed

>> Vexed

Establish causal connections

In carrying out this exercise, try to identify the causes of your negative feelings. In other words, as you write in your journal, you need to ask yourself exactly *why* you felt angry, sad, or hurt. Simply acknowledging uncomfortable emotions through journal writing can help change these feelings, and the tension that accompanies them, from your mind and body.

However, expressing thoughts and feelings alone won't provide the insight and understanding of *why* anger plays such a prominent role in your emotional life. The insight, which is how you eventually gain greater control over your anger, comes from giving meaning to these feelings and thoughts.

Here are some excerpts from an anger journal kept by **Carl,** a 32-year-old single dad, who was trying to understand why he stayed irritated so much of the time:

> I got really annoyed **because** the kids wouldn't stop running through the house when I told them not to.

> **Why** do I always have to get mad before anyone **understands** that I need some help getting everything done around here?

> I think I'll go crazy if one more person tells me that there's no **reason** for me to get so upset. I've got plenty of reasons!

> Being mad at the kids isn't getting me **what I really want.**

> What I **really want** is for my kids to do what I say, but I **don't know how** to get that to happen.

> I **realize** I **need help;** I just don't know where to turn.

> Maybe I'll **ask** the kids' pediatrician if he knows about any good parenting programs.

The boldface words help Carl engage in some much needed self-reflection, which will eventually lead to self-correction. In this case, what Carl is confessing to himself is that he can't deal with life's challenges without support. Then he figures out one resource (the pediatrician) to try first.

If Carl gets the message and acts on it, his situation will become much less stressful and he'll have a lot less reason to constantly be on the verge of becoming angry. However, if he doesn't hear the meaning in his writings, his emotional life will remain unchanged.

Write until time is up

Give yourself sufficient time to do the exercise in a meaningful way. Fifteen to 20 minutes should suffice. Make it easy on yourself by setting your phone (or other device) and writing until you hear the bell, which is your cue to stop. Go ahead and finish your last sentence.

Grammar and sentence construction aren't important. What is important is that you write until the time is up.

If you run out of things to write about before the end of the allotted time (not likely when you get started!), go back, read what you've already written, and find something that you can expand on. With a little prompting, you'll quickly tap back into those emotions that are just waiting for a chance to be expressed.

Don't let emotions get in the way

Most likely you'll feel relieved, content, and far less tense when you finish with your anger journal for the day. That, after all, is the goal of the exercise. But sometimes, typically when you first start journaling, you may also experience negative emotions such as sadness, irritation, apprehension, anger, and nervousness.

These feelings may be quite strong and can even feel overwhelming at the moment. Keep in mind that these feelings are natural. After all, you're confronting uncomfortable emotions that you've kept hidden away throughout the day (sometimes much longer), and they usually subside with time and practice.

If you become upset while you're writing in your journal, don't let the feelings stop you from completing your work. You can write and cry at the same time, right?

If the negative feelings you encounter after journaling are too strong for you to handle or if the feelings persist and interfere with your day-to-day life, consider stopping the exercise and talk to a therapist. Counseling provides a safe, structured, and supportive environment in which you can discuss your difficult emotions. And if you need to talk to someone, it doesn't mean that you're crazy. Everyone needs some outside help from time to time.

Suspend judgment

Human beings are, by definition, judgmental creatures. You make literally thousands of judgments each and every day of your life about one thing or another: What should you wear today? What should you have for breakfast? Which freeway should you take to work? Where should you have lunch? Which emotions should you express, and which ones should you keep to yourself?

Unfortunately, anger is one of those emotions that people tend to judge harshly. You may think of anger as one of the "bad" feelings, and you may assume that no one around you wants to hear about your anger. You probably think it's all right to tell another person you feel wonderful, happy, or blessed if they ask how you are, but you won't be as honest or candid if the answer is instead "angry, pissed off, and/or mad as hell!"

You're telling yourself that the world around you doesn't really want to hear the bad news about your emotional life and that they want only the good news. If there is no good news, then the best course of action is to keep quiet or lie: "I'm fine."

Sometimes, that probably is the best thing to do. Maybe you're right. Lots of people don't want to hear about your bad day. But it can be useful to try and find at least one trusted friend to confide in. Or express your feelings in your daily journal.

Don't be judgmental when writing in your journal. Be open, honest, and forthright. Tell it like it is!

As far as the rest of your world is concerned, you're writing in your journal with anonymity. What you write is for your eyes only. No one else is going to see what you write, so they can't judge it, and you shouldn't, either. This non-judgmental stance may be harder for you to do than you think. You may be so used to critiquing your emotions as (or before) you experience them that letting the feelings flow freely may be difficult at first. That's okay. In fact, that's also part of the goal: helping you become a less emotionally constricted person.

Stick to pen and pencil, or not

You may be wondering how and where you should record this journal. Can you make your entries on the computer, phone, or tablet? Well, of course you can.

But try both handwritten journals as well as digital entries. Some people find that writing by hand feels like a much more intimate mode of expression. For them, there's something more personal about hand-written journal entries than those that are typed into a computer. However, in today's world, many people find handwriting tediously slow. They've been brought up on keyboards. That's how they feel comfortable expressing themselves. Do whatever works for you.

If writing isn't your thing and you tend to be more fluent (and comfortable) with the spoken word, then you may want to find a recording device and use that. But don't change anything else, so talk for your ears only, speak in the first person, continue the conversation for 15 to 20 minutes, look for causes, suspend judgment, and so forth (see previous sections).

Whether you write, record, or type, be careful about protecting what you write from the peering eyes of others. Your journal is *your* journal. You can even rip up paper or totally delete files (make sure you know how to do that) when you've thoroughly processed them.

Find a quiet place

You need to find a quiet place to write in your anger journal, a place where you can be alone (and uninterrupted) with your thoughts and feelings. Journaling isn't a community activity. If you can't allow yourself any personal time until everyone else's needs are taken care of and all the chores are done, then make writing in your journal the last thing you do after everyone else has been safely put to bed.

WARNING

Sometimes people find journal writing a bit arousing and/or upsetting. If that's your reaction, don't journal within an hour or two of going to bed. See Chapter 20 for more tips about sleep, which is a common problem experienced by people with anger issues.

Another good time to journal, though sometimes a bit tricky to engineer, is right after you come home from a day at work but before you jump headfirst into the demands and challenges of the evening. In fact, if you purge the unwanted emotions of the day, you'll most assuredly enjoy better relationships with your loved ones.

If you have the kind of job where you find yourself more and more fed up as the day progresses, you may want to use your lunch break to journal. It may make the rest of the workday go a little smoother and avoid any blowups along the way.

Take time to reflect

After you feel you've expressed your anger issues about as well as you can in your journal (or device), consider adding a section about what your anger has taught you. What did you learn from your anger? How have you figured out how to move forward in a healthier way? Anger can drag you down or provide motivation for figuring out what's gone wrong in the past and how to do better in the future. Which choice do you want to make?

Chapter **17**

Finding Forgiveness

orgiveness is a complex mental process. Forgiveness involves looking forward to the future with an awareness of the past. In no way does forgiveness mean that horrible and unfair events never happened. Nor does it mean that what happened was okay. Forgiveness includes hope, confidence, and courage. Forgiveness lights the pathway out of victimhood and toward a self-empowered future. Here's an example to illustrate what happens without forgiveness:

Jack is in his 50s now. His health is poor. He's lonely. And he has little to show for his life. Jack is a broken man. Looking back, Jack has many regrets. Chief among them is the fact that he alienated himself from his family years earlier. "I know now I was wrong. My family, all they were trying to do was help me. I turned them away. I needed their help, but I turned them all away. And, for that, I feel sorry," he laments.

The one thing Jack doesn't regret, however, is his life-long anger at his mother, who had to put him in foster care for a brief time when he was very young. "She abandoned me, left me with strangers, and I'll never forgive her for that!" he explains.

Just the mention of that hurtful time elevates Jack's voice and brings tears to his eyes — 45 years after the fact. His mother came back to get him out of foster care after a year, when she was back on her feet and able to provide Jack and his brother with a stable home. Over the ensuing years, she raised Jack until he graduated from high school and joined the Army. But none of that mattered to Jack. His mother had committed an unpardonable crime and he would punish her — and himself — for the remainder of his life for that one act.

The anger toward his mother that Jack carried all through life, in the end, broke him. Anger, which on more than one occasion resulted in physical violence, cost him two marriages, a relationship with his only son, his job, and ultimately his health. Yet, even today, Jack remains unforgiving.

This chapter offers strategies for letting go of old feelings of anger and hurt that are tied to past grievances. It provides you with both a rationale and a road map for handling yesterday's anger, which may be the most difficult type of anger to manage.

Possibly the last thing in the world that angry people want to do is forgive people who have wronged them. They wonder why in the world they would want to do that. That reaction is totally understandable. However, hang in there and suspend your judgment about forgiveness until you've finished this chapter.

Forgiveness Is Never Easy

Forgiveness doesn't come easily to human beings. Anger certainly comes easily, but forgiveness? No. You were born with an instinctual capacity for anger, but forgiveness is something you have to learn. It's a skill, really, that's no different from riding a bicycle, playing soccer, or speaking a foreign language.

You may be one of those lucky people who was raised in a tradition of forgiveness. You learned to forgive by observing the forgiveness that your parents showed one another. Or you learned it through your participation in organized religion such as in church, synagogue, mosque, or temple. If so, forgiveness comes easier for you than it does for others.

Life experiences that are most difficult to forgive include physical, emotional, and sexual abuse. Betrayals, assaults, and death or injury caused by someone else's negligence or malicious intentions also pose considerable obstacles to forgiveness.

Forgiving takes time

Forgiveness is a *process*, not a thing. It's a journey, really. A magic wand is a thing. And when it comes to forgiving those who have wronged you, there is no magic wand. The longer you've held on to anger, the more time you need to reach that point of resolution called forgiveness. Is today the day you're ready to start this journey and free yourself from yesterday's anger?

Forgiving requires support

Forgiving someone takes strength, courage, and maturity. Some of that you can draw from those around you. Who do you know who can serve as your forgiveness ally? Who has already been encouraging you to let go of anger from the past? Who can serve as a positive role model, someone who has forgiven a past transgression and moved on with his life?

It's true that forgiveness is a voluntary act. No one can (or should) force you to forgive another person. Forgiveness is an *option* that you might consider in your effort to find peace of mind. But the choice is entirely yours.

TIP

Forgiveness will come to you more easily if you have support. But support can be found in many places. Some people look to great literature, historical figures, or compelling stories to find role models of forgiveness. Others turn to friends, family, or therapists.

TIP

Support is only support if you take advantage of it. Your support network is the number of people you can count on to help you deal with adversity in life. Support, on the other hand, has to do with your willingness to avail yourself of that help. Some people actually have a small network yet feel a tremendous sense of support as they struggle through life. Others have a huge network yet feel isolated and alone. The irony is that people who are full of anger and resentment, who need support the most, are the least likely to accept it.

Forgiving demands sacrifice

Now comes the hard part. To forgive someone, you have to sacrifice something. Something has to give. Finding forgiveness sometimes feels like you're "allowing" someone to have wronged you. But forgiveness is really more about giving yourself a gift: the gift of peace and serenity you had before you were wronged. To get there, you'll likely have to give up on the following:

>> Being a victim

>> The myth that "life must always be fair"

>> Your use of anger to protect yourself from emotional pain

>> Reliving the initial grievance day after day

>> This hold you're letting the other person have on you by keeping him foremost in your thoughts

>> Your "right" to revenge

>> The notion that by holding on to anger you can somehow undo the injustice that was done to you

>> The idea that you're entitled to the good life, free of stress, misfortune, pain, and injury

>> The belief that everyone, especially those closest to you, must always approve of you and treat you with consideration

>> The idea that forgiveness is a sign of personal weakness

Preparing to Forgive

Conditions need to be right before you can honestly expect to begin a journey of forgiveness. Don't start this process if you've recently encountered trauma, assault, violent crime, or other horrific event. Give yourself some time. You may need to experience and explore your anger for a while first. No set timeline works for everyone.

Staying safe

Anger does play a protective role in unsafe life circumstances, including situations where mistreatment is ongoing, where you're on guard against the potentially hurtful actions of others, and where you believe your physical or emotional survival is threatened. To ask yourself to forgive someone who is actively harming you here and now is, too much to ask. You have to be safe first. Consider the following example:

Truman is 46 years old and receives a summons to his father's deathbed. His father had been a violent alcoholic his entire life. Truman had chosen not to see him for decades. He'd never considered forgiving his father as he was simply too cruel, unrepentant, and physically intimidating.

When Truman sees his father in his hospice bed, he barely recognizes him. His father looks frail, shrunken, and fearful. Surprisingly, his father takes Truman's hand and starts to cry. He says, "I know now that I was a miserable failure as a father, husband, and human being. I'm so, so sorry. I know it's too much to ask for your forgiveness, but I am sorry."

Truman also tears up and without thinking says, "Dad, I forgive you," and his father passes that night.

When Truman goes home to his family, he feels a sense of peace that had eluded him for decades. His own struggles with anger softened. He now spends more time with his family and lets them know how much he cares about them.

When Truman's father was an imposing, violent, alcoholic, Truman made a wise decision to stay away from him. He couldn't risk having his family or himself around his father. He understandably didn't feel safe, so his anger at his father protected him. But Truman, a basically kind human being, was able to forgive when he saw his father's vulnerability.

Hopefully, you'll be able to forgive those who have wronged you before they're on their deathbed. But, when safety is an issue, you probably won't be able to forgive someone in person. Nonetheless, in those cases, you still may have the option of finding forgiveness of others within your own mind. Are you safe enough to start a process of forgiveness?

Accepting the frailty of human nature

The thing we mostly need to forgive others for is being human. Humans are actually very frail creatures, despite all the marvelous advancements in technology that we find around us each and every day. People make mistakes. People routinely hurt other people's feelings, intentionally or not. At times, people are far too selfish. They say no when they should say yes.

REMEMBER

Most people mean well. Most people do the best they can under the circumstances. But often that's not good enough. So people end up blaming each other for what? For being human.

You probably get angry with people because they don't do what you expect of them. But do you expect too much? Nobody has the absolutely perfect parent, child, boss, spouse, or friend. And if you can't forgive yourself ("I hate myself. I'm a loser. I never do anything right."), is that because you hold yourself to an unrealistic, all-or-nothing standard of performance?

Allow yourself humility and self-compassion. Do the same for others. We are all in this together, and we all make mistakes.

WARNING

Some would argue, with good reason, that certain acts are unforgivable. However, forgiveness is about you, not the perpetrator. It is a gift to yourself to let go of the always present anger that lingers in your life.

A Cost-Benefit Analysis of Forgiveness

If you're going to forgive someone, something has to be in it for you. You have to believe that it's in your self-interest to let go of yesterday's anger. Chapter 3 lays out procedures for conducting a cost-benefit analysis to help you decide whether you're ready to change your ways of dealing with anger in general. Here, the same technique is applied to deciding whether it's worth it to search for forgiveness.

The primary beneficiary of your forgiveness is *you*. Forget about the other person. Do it for yourself! Forgiveness should be about *your* anger, not *her* bad behavior. In fact, the thought that you're doing something good for a bad person can only serve as an obstacle to starting this journey.

So see what it's costing you to hang on to old anger as compared to how you may benefit if you let go. Table 17-1 shows you a sample of costs and benefits for finding forgiveness. Feel free to add your own, personal ideas.

TABLE 17-1   ## Costs and Benefits of Forgiveness

Costs of Not Forgiving	Benefits of Finding Forgiveness
You constantly relive the painful past.	Your energy is freed up for constructive use.
Old anger finds its way into your present and future relationships.	Your life is now focused on the present rather than the past.
You feel drained as a result of all that anger.	You no longer feel so vulnerable.
You lose sight of the positives in your life.	Your outlook becomes more optimistic.
You remain in a constant state of mourning.	When you forgive, others tend to forgive you.
Your health is compromised.	Your health improves.
You remain in a constant state of agitation and tension.	It becomes easier to forgive yourself for being human.
You become bitter and hostile.	You experience an inner peace that you haven't felt in a long time, if ever.
	You have a newfound sense of maturity.
	You move beyond the pain of past transgressions.

Isn't it time to let yourself off the hook? You deserve to be unencumbered by anger. But the answer to that question is really something you have to decide for yourself. If you agree, then you have to let go of the recurrent memories of past wrongs, the blame you attach to the other person's behavior, your desire for revenge — all that baggage. You see, bitterness and happiness are incompatible. If you keep one, you lose all chance for the other.

Is there some reason you feel you don't deserve a chance at happiness?

Accepting the Finality of Being Wronged

Another obstacle on the journey of forgiveness has to do with accepting the *finality* of being wronged in some way. Have you ever thought in an angry moment, "I'm going to stay angry until I get justice, until things are set right again, or until I can somehow even the score?"

Well, good luck, because that day will never come. For example:

>> What in the world can a parent do to truly even the score when his child dies at the hands of a drunk driver?

>> How does the wife of an unfaithful man get true justice?

>> How do you set right the fact that your employer went out of business, causing you to lose the best job you ever had?

>> How do you make up for parents who neglected or abused you?

TIP

To forgive someone, you have to accept that they did you wrong, not that you overlook what they did. Absolutely not. Nor do you approve of their hurtful behavior. And you don't pardon them for their sins. No need to. But you do have to *accept* what was done and move on. To forgive, you have to live in the present, not the past.

TIP

Living in the present moment is a principle part of the practice of mindfulness. Mindfulness fosters forgiveness. See Chapter 9 for ways to increase your mindfulness.

You don't have to forget the past

The truth of experience is that once something happens to you, you never totally forget it. However, your interpretation of what happened can change over time. You can move from anger to hurt to sadness then forgiveness.

Human beings don't *get over* bad things; if they're lucky (or get the right kind of help), they just move *beyond* those things. Bottom line: You'll never forget whatever it is that you have trouble forgiving. But you don't have to. The memory will linger.

TIP

Moving beyond what's happened to you means arriving at the point where you can *remember without anger*. And the only way to do that is through forgiveness.

WARNING

The harder you try to forget something (the more you try not to think about it), the more you remember it. Attempting to suppress thoughts forces you to attend to those thoughts to tamp them down. You get exactly the opposite of what you're striving for.

Choose pain over anger

Most people hang on to old anger as a way of avoiding pain. That makes perfectly good sense because anger (particularly rage) is a strong emotion that can mask even the most severe physical and emotional pain. But sooner or later, you're going to have to deal with the pain anyway.

> **Heather,** age 18, loves horseback riding. One day, her horse spooks and she falls, suffering a spinal cord injury. She is confined to a wheelchair. Heather falls into bitterness, rage, and anger. She dwells on the idea of seeking retribution from the manufacturer of the helmet she wore as well as her riding instructor. She fails to find a competent attorney willing to take her case as they all told her there was no one really to blame; her accident was tragic but not due to anyone's negligence.
>
> Heather's anger keeps her focused on the past. She feels like a victim and snaps at everyone who tries to help her. She passes up a generous college scholarship and avoids physical therapy, which could improve her functioning.

Heather has a choice to make. She can remain angry and out of touch with her grief, or she can allow herself to realize that she's using anger to cover up her emotional pain. She needs to forgive herself, her horse, her trainer, and even the helmet manufacturer.

Sometimes that's the way anger works. It can cover up other difficult emotions like grief. Frankly, anger feels better than emotional pain. But the only way to heal in the long run is by letting go of anger, thereby allowing yourself to feel any negative emotions that may emerge, and ultimately finding forgiveness.

Chapter **18**

Preventing Relapse

A ssume that you've made excellent progress on managing your anger problems. That's great. You should feel very good about your achievements so far.

But here's the bad news: Life remains unfair; injustices continue to happen; people still cut you off in traffic; and you'll no doubt encounter gross rudeness from time to time. (See Chapter 2 for more information about typical anger-inducing situations.) So your odds of never feeling angry again approach zero.

The good news: Feeling anger doesn't mean a full return to serious anger problems. You can feel angry and express your feelings constructively or even rethink the angry feelings in a way that makes you feel better. But no matter how good you get at managing your anger, you should expect to blow it once in a while.

Blowing it doesn't mean you've relapsed. In other words, a few lapses don't mean you've relapsed. Relapse implies that you've gone back to square one. That's hard to do because you'd have to forget about everything you've read and changes you've made.

This chapter explains what to expect about progress. It also discusses how to manage anger slip-ups as well as ways to keep an eye out for high-risk situations.

Anticipating Bumps

Progress always proceeds unevenly. You'll make gains, possibly more gains, and then inevitably you'll stumble. You'll walk two steps forward, one step back, three steps forward, another step or two back, and so on. Sometimes you'll stall for a while. That's just how it goes with humans. And that's the way anger management proceeds.

TIP

Mistakes and missteps have much to teach you. Look at them as opportunities to figure out what pushes your buttons or what stresses you out. Then you can be better prepared to deal with such events in the future.

You're at risk of losing your cool when you feel tired, sick, or emotionally drained. And sometimes people simply lose their cool and have no idea why. This section discusses the situations that commonly make people feel lousy and more prone to anger.

TECHNICAL STUFF

Chapter 3 reviews the stages of change, which include precontemplation (not even thinking about changing), contemplation (giving it thought), preparation (figuring out how to get started), action (working through strategies), maintenance (things are going pretty well), and termination. Success in anger management should be declared at the maintenance stage. Only a minority of people reach the last stage of *termination*, which means they have minimal or no risk of lapses or relapse. In other words, their anger management has become part of who they are. For most people, there's always some risk of slip-ups. We are human, after all.

Getting sick, injured, or hurt

The mind and body work in synchrony with each other. When one is out of whack, the other easily falls into a similar state. How do you feel when you have a nasty cold, the flu, or a stomach malady? Not so great. When your body's resources are tied up getting you well, there's little left for other endeavors like anger management.

If you're so sick that you're bedridden, you likely won't have a lot of irritating interactions with other people. In fact, you just may not even have enough energy to get angry! The actual risky times are when you're not bedridden and trying to slog through your day with whatever malady you have.

TIP

When you don't get enough sleep, it's like being a little sick. Fatigue carries a big risk of making you vulnerable to anger outbursts. Be careful if you feel tired. See Chapter 20 for ideas about how to improve your sleep.

Steeped in stress

Stress is another problem that depletes your mind and body of precious resources. But, unlike anger, stress can pop in very subtle ways. You may feel a bit pressed or a little anxious. You may have some worries about work deadlines or visiting relatives, which are everyday issues.

TIP

Be on the lookout for stress. When stress shows up, you're far more likely to experience irritation and anger. Stress is often cumulative. For example an already stressed, busy parent gets into a minor car accident and then blows up. See Chapter 19 for ways of managing stress and reducing your risks of lapses and slips.

Lingering losses

Every well-lived life piles up losses along the way. Losses appear in a wide variety of forms, including

>> Loss of loved ones

>> Financial setbacks

>> Loss of a job

>> Loss of relationships

>> Loss of innocence

>> Loss of health

>> Loss of attractiveness

>> Injury

>> Loss of youth and vitality

Almost all losses involve grief. And many people find that anger feels better than grief. Grief flat out hurts more than anger. Therefore, instead of sadness, many people resort to feeling irritable or hostility.

REMEMBER

But the downside to using anger as a cover for grief is that people need to process loss. There's something useful about feeling grief, thinking about the loss, and discovering how to live on regardless. Anger blocks that healthy process.

That's not to suggest that anger isn't a normal response following loss; it is. However, at some point, it's important to get in touch with grief and let go of the anger.

The following example of William illustrates someone who was exceptionally successful at conquering his anger problems. Nonetheless, he finds himself depleted due to various circumstances. He blows up over something minor, but, as stated earlier, a lapse is not a relapse.

> After a tumultuous adolescence filled with trouble at school, with his family, and even a couple of arrests, **William** finally was sent to a skillful therapist to work through his anger. Their efforts were very successful. Now, friends describe him as mild mannered and easygoing. He turned his life around, went back to college, and rarely even gets irritated. His mantra became, "Don't sweat the small stuff."
>
> Today, William finishes his last final exam and walks out of the engineering building. He grabs a tissue from his pocket and blows his nose; his throat is a bit scratchy. He hopes he's not getting sick. The next week, he flies out to the West coast to begin his career. He's already found an apartment close to his job and met with his new boss and colleagues. He anticipates a very busy week.
>
> William gets to his car and pulls out into traffic. He should feel excited and happy, but he simply feels overwhelmed. A traffic light up ahead turns green, but the car in front of William doesn't move. William notices the head of the driver is looking down. They're probably texting. William suddenly feels incredible rage. He slams down on the horn while shouting obscenities.

Why was William so angry? Well, he has several risky situations going on. He is feeling a bit under the weather, not sick enough to be in bed, but just enough to deplete his reserves. He's also under stress with a new job, moving, and beginning a new life. Although William is glad to finally finish school, he is giving up the role of student. William should give himself a break, realize what happened, and go on with his life.

Slipping up for no good reason

Sometimes, people slip up for absolutely no discernable reason. They aren't under unusual stress, they aren't sick, and they aren't particularly fatigued. Perhaps they encounter a situation that is unexpected yet had caused great troubles in the past. Or who knows? Humans make mistakes; it's really that simple.

When you slip up for no particular reason, just go back to what's worked for you before. Avoid the temptation of berating yourself for doing something that's inevitable. Accept the slip as a part of life.

Preparing a Relapse Plan

Because slips, backslides, and lapses are inevitable, you need to plan for them. And in the process, you can probably reduce the frequency of those setbacks by looking ahead and mentally preparing for problematic events. You may want to consider seeking professional help if you haven't done so previously.

If you've already gone to counseling, sometimes *booster sessions* work wonders. Booster sessions are where you go back to a previous therapist for a little extra work on your issues. Sometimes it really helps to review your anger management strategies, go over current stressors, and get objective input. Don't think of booster sessions as meaning that you've failed.

Rethinking slip-ups

When you slip up, and you no doubt will, pay attention to what you say to yourself. The *thoughts* you have about backslides can make things better or much worse. When you beat yourself up, you're likely to have more problems with anger. Although people often think otherwise, abusive self-criticism doesn't motivate you to do better.

Table 18-1 shows a few of the more common irrational thoughts or self-statements that frequently follow lapses. The table also gives examples of more reasonable, rational thoughts.

TABLE 18-1   **Irrational and Rational Thoughts about Anger Lapses**

Irrational Thoughts	Rational Thoughts
I have gotten nowhere.	I have improved in many ways. I've learned skills and have managed my anger in lots of situations that I didn't before.
I am horrible.	I am human.
I'll never get better.	That's simply not true. My trend has been good. It's the trend that matters, not each little slip.

Trying what worked before

Anger management involves a variety of skills, such as relaxation, rethinking anger beliefs, exposure to anger-arousing events, assertive communication, forgiveness, and disengagement from brooding. Most likely, if you've made progress, you've found one or more of these strategies especially helpful.

But maybe you stopped using that coping skill, believing you don't need it anymore. Nonsense! Go back and practice what worked before once again. You may never reach the point that you can permanently lay these skills aside. You should *expect* to pull them off the shelf, dust them off, and practice them from time to time.

Trying something different

Go through this book and look for strategies that you either haven't tried or didn't pay much attention to. Consider reexamining those strategies and give them a shot. You've got nothing to lose and much to gain. *Could I be more trite?* Probably not, but the saying really does apply.

Seeking feedback

Significant people in your life — spouses, partners, trusted friends — can become, in effect, your personal lifeguard(s). They can throw you a life preserver when you're falling into old irritability or anger habits, even when you're not aware of it. In other words, they can help you catch a regression before it gets out of hand. However, they can only do that if you ask them. So at a time when you're doing well, ask your potential lifeguards to look for times that they see you starting to feel irritable or out of sorts. Develop a word, a phrase, or a signal that they can give you in a calm, neutral manner. Here are a few examples of signals:

>> A downward hand motion

>> A reminder, "Let's breathe a bit."

>> A gentle tap on the shoulder

>> A simple question, "Are you doing okay?"

Your first reaction to seeing that signal may be to reflexively deny it. *Try not to get defensive.* Instead, tell yourself that your lifeguard probably has your best interests in mind and can see your behavior more objectively than you can. Consider the following example:

> **Elizabeth** has an anger problem, and she's made some good progress. She notices that she sometimes blows it when she's at large family gatherings. There's just so many difficult memories combined with noise and chaos. So she asks her brother, **Michael,** if he'd be willing to serve as her anger lifeguard. He says, "Absolutely! I'd be happy to help."

Elizabeth and Michael work out a plan. Michael agrees to gently squeeze Elizabeth's elbow when he sees her starting to get upset or agitated. Eighteen family members attend the next Thanksgiving dinner. Elizabeth focuses on managing the kitchen. As usual, various family members constantly interrupt her, asking where things are, wondering what they should do, and engaging in small talk.

Michael can see that Elizabeth is feeling increasingly stressed and irritated. He gently squeezes her elbow. Elizabeth jerks her elbow away and barks, "Keep your hands off me. Can't you see I'm busy?"

Elizabeth probably chose the wrong lifeguard. She and Michael had a long history of conflict throughout their childhood. She also might be a bad candidate for this kind of help because she gets very defensive, very easily.

WARNING

Some people don't have a truly suitable lifeguard available to them. Others find that sort of feedback too difficult to take. If that's you, don't use this approach.

Calming down

You don't want to or have to put your feelings in charge of your behavior. Just because you feel angry doesn't mean you have to act on it. And you are capable of turning those feelings around.

Try calming yourself down. Take a few breaths, count slowly to ten, repeat a key word or two in your mind (such as *relax, chill,* or *calm*), and remind yourself that reacting with anger, unless you're under attack, is rarely useful or productive.

Incentivizing yourself

Make a list of three reasons you no longer want to let anger dominate your life. These reasons can serve as powerful incentives for keeping anger at bay. For example, maybe you're tired of embarrassing yourself. Or perhaps you've lost friends unnecessarily. Maybe you want to be seen as a positive role model. You could probably come up with a dozen reasons. But it will be more effective to choose the top three and read the list over and over again. Pause and reflect on each reason and why it's important to you and your values.

6

Living Beyond Anger

Chapter **19**

Soothing Stress

Think about some of the times when you lose your cool. You might get irritated and say unkind things to your family, friends, or co-workers. What sets this process off? Do the following statements sound like typical triggers for your anger?

» I have too many things on my plate, I can't do it all.

» My family is coming to stay for a week and I don't have time or energy to entertain them.

» I don't know how I'm going to stretch this month's paycheck to cover my bills.

» Everyone is counting on me and I can't take it anymore.

» If I get one more complaint about why our organization doesn't do more, I think I'll explode.

If so, your problem isn't just anger. You also struggle with stress and overload. You either have too much stress or the wrong kinds of stress, but either way, you're stressed. Anger is your way of expressing it. Some people withdraw and get quiet under fire; others lash out. Unfortunately, neither strategy works well, and both strategies end up endangering your health.

This chapter shows you what to do when your plate gets too full and you see the warning signs of impending anger. You learn how to identify those stress carriers that, if you weren't feeling irritated before you encountered them, will cause you stress. The chapter also explains how to avoid stress burnout and why it's the little hassles of everyday life that do you the most harm. And, most important, you see how to thrive under stress: how to be a hardy personality. It's easier than you think.

Examining Stress and Strain

Believe it or not, your great-grandparents didn't get stressed out. Well, maybe they *felt* stress, but they didn't call it that. *Stress* and *strain* are engineering terms that were first applied to human beings in the 1930s.

Stress is a normal part of daily life. It's what fuels that built-in fight-or-flight response that you have for help in defending yourself against things — people, circumstances, events — that threaten your survival. Stress isn't a choice; it's a gift (even though it doesn't feel like one).

TECHNICAL STUFF

Here are some of the changes that occur in your body every time you feel stressed:

>> Your pupils dilate.

>> Your blood sugar rises.

>> Your blood pressure increases.

>> Your blood clots faster.

>> The muscles throughout your body tighten.

>> You breathe more rapidly.

>> Your heart rate increases.

>> Your pituitary gland is activated.

>> Your hypothalamus gland is activated.

>> Adrenaline flows freely.

>> Your palms become sweaty.

>> Your blood cortisol level rises. (*Cortisol* is a stress hormone that enhances and prolongs your body's fight-or-flight reaction.)

>> Fat is released into your bloodstream.

>> Your liver converts fat into cholesterol.

Prolonged stress causes what you can think of as *strain*. Strain is what happens to your body when you become chronically *overstressed*. Think of a bridge that has cars constantly crossing it year after year. (As noted earlier, the terms *stress* and *strain* originally came from the field of engineering.) Because of their weight, the cars stress the bridge. The more cars that pass over, the greater the stress.

Now, imagine that after a couple of decades, cracks begin to appear under the bridge that are small at first but growing larger as time goes on. These cracks threaten the integrity of the bridge, which is what's known as *structurally deficient*. The cracks represent the strain that inevitably occurs from too much stress. The bridge is you, your body, your health. And you don't want to let your body become structurally deficient. Ouch!

Now imagine the bridge creaking and groaning as it begins to show signs of strain. You can see the role that anger plays in communicating to the world just how much strain you're under. Anger is simply your way of creaking (showing your irritation) and groaning (flying into a rage).

Stress and strain have been linked to depression and cardiovascular disease. They also greatly exacerbate virtually all chronic diseases.

TIP

Caregivers have a particularly heightened risk of stress. If you take care of disabled or elderly family members, try to get respite care and take care of yourself. Consider joining a support group as well.

WORKING OUT TO REDUCE WORK STRESS

Katherine Sliter, PhD, and colleagues studied the relationship between physical activity and workplace stress. They reported their results in *The International Journal of Stress Management* (yes, there really is such a magazine). A group of 152 nurses participated in the study. They experienced stress from the usual culprits: managing difficult patients, overwork, and not having enough staff. Nurses were asked to complete questionnaires regarding their mood, physical activities outside of work, level of life satisfaction, and work commitment. The researchers hypothesized that nurses who engaged in physical activity would likely be less depressed, more engaged in work, and more satisfied with life. The responses of the nurses supported these three hypotheses.

Other research also has supported the value of working out for improving moods, increasing energy, boosting quality of life, and decreasing stress. The authors of this study wondered whether physical activity works in part because it distracts people from ruminating about stressful thoughts. In other words, physical activity may give people, in effect, time away from work-related distress. So in addition to the obvious benefits to your body, physical activities may also give you a needed break, and that's just one more reason to take your dogs for long walks or join a gym.

Some people notice that their anger fuse shortens over time, and they wonder why. Generally, they have experienced more and more stress that evolves into strain. Slowly, but surely, life begins to weigh heavily on them. Their tolerance for stress decreases and their fuse shortens. What used to be a hassle becomes unbearable. This outcome doesn't occur with normal, everyday stress; rather, it happens when stress becomes chronic and extreme.

Staying Away from Stress Carriers

Do you know someone who, when they walk into the room, seems to disrupt everything around them? Before that person arrives, people are in a good mood, laughing, talking, getting their work done, enjoying life, and this person changes all of that. The laughter stops, moods change, and tension suddenly permeates the air. That lovely person is a *stress carrier.*

You can tell a stress carrier by the following traits:

>> Tone of voice (rapid, pressured, and grating)

>> Body posture that communicates aggression or defensiveness (such as puffed up posturing or arms crossed tightly over the chest)

>> Tense facial expression (clenched jaw, frown, or narrowing around the eyes)

>> Fist clenching

>> Use of obscenities

>> Talks over other people in a conversation

>> Jarring laughter

>> Fixed, angry opinions

>> Rapid eye-blinks

>> Sighing

>> Excessive perspiration

>> Finger tapping

>> Jerky body movements

>> Tendency to walk fast

>> Eats too fast

>> Frequently checking what time it is

>> Attempts to hurry up the speech of others by interjecting comments such as "Yeah," "Uh-huh," "Right," and "I know"

>> Talking or seemingly listening to you while the person's eyes continually scan the room

TIP

Stay away from stress carriers as much as you can. Their stress is contagious, so if you're around them very long, you'll feel stressed too. If a stress carrier's stress spills over into anger, guess what will happen to you? You'll find yourself angry, and you won't know why.

WARNING

You may be a stress carrier yourself. Check the list again, and see if you have any of those stress carrier characteristics. If you're really brave, ask someone who knows you well to examine the list and tell you what he thinks. You may not be the best judge of your true self.

Recognizing the Sources of Your Stress

Stressors, which are those people, events, and circumstances that cause you stress, come in all sorts of sizes and shapes. Some are physical (noise, pollution), some social (nosey neighbors, meddling in-laws), some emotional (death of a loved one), some legal (divorce), some financial (bankruptcy), and so on. Some are even positive (such as getting a new job, getting married, graduating from college), and they excite your nervous system no less than the negative experiences do.

Psychologists tend to group stressors into two primary categories: minor irritants (or hassles) and major, critical life events.

Minor day-to-day stressors that you're likely to experience and that can eventually set the stage for anger include the following:

>> Hurrying to meet a deadline

>> Being interrupted while talking

>> Finding that someone has borrowed something without asking your permission

>> Being disturbed while taking a nap

>> Seeing that someone has cut ahead of you in line

>> Driving in heavy traffic

>> Misplacing something important

>> Caring for a sick child

- » Having unexpected company

- » Having to deal with car repairs

- » Developing a cold sore

- » Seeing that a bird has unloaded on your brand-new car

- » Having an appointment with someone who shows up late

- » Hearing a rude remark directed at you

- » Having too *much* time on your hands. (You read that right: People with too much time on their hands get bored. Scientists call it underutilization when it occurs in the workplace, and the same is true for teenagers stuck at home, especially during the pandemic). Too much unfilled time inevitably causes problems of one kind or another if it persists.)

Major stressors, which can have a much more significant impact on your life, include the following:

- » Being fired from your job

- » Being sentenced to jail

- » Having a chronic or life-threatening illness

- » Living during a pandemic

- » Experiencing the death of a close friend

- » Having the bank foreclose on your home loan

- » Separating from your spouse

- » Getting pregnant

- » Your children leaving home

- » Moving

- » Winning a big lottery prize

- » Losing your job

- » Starting a new job

- » Being promoted at work

Which type of stressors, minor or major, would you guess are the unhealthiest? If you're like most people, you said the major ones. But the reality is that you're almost as likely to be undone by the small things in life. Why? Precisely because they're small and they occur on a daily basis. People see minor stressors as so universal ("Hey, that's just part of life, right?") that they don't take them seriously, and that's a mistake.

The good news about major stressors, the ones that potentially affect your life in some critical way, is that they don't occur that frequently, and you tend to marshal all your resources to effectively deal with them. Some people even report growing in positive ways following adversity.

Looking at Types of Stress

Each person has a finite *carrying capacity* for stress — that is, the amount of stress she can accommodate without showing signs of serious strain. Even the most resilient people can find themselves overloaded from time to time. That's when you need to take stock of what's going on around you and work to restore some semblance of balance in your life.

Stress can become an addiction. If you can't remember the last time you didn't feel overwhelmed by the demands of your day, if you enjoy the adrenaline rush or high that goes along with meeting one challenge after another, if you seem to invite and sometimes create stress where there is none, and if you find yourself restless and bored when things are too quiet, consider yourself a stress addict.

If you're a stress addict, you need to start weaning yourself off stress with small steps. You can start by doing the following:

>> Set aside one otherwise busy evening a week to just hang out with a close friend who isn't competitive and who doesn't require a lot of conversation.

>> Take off your watch and turn off your phone in the evenings and for portions of your weekend.

>> Sign up for a yoga class or spend a few minutes in a hot tub three or four times a week.

>> Practice meditation through apps or a class.

>> Take regular walks outdoors.

Cumulative and chronic stress

Cumulative or *chronic stress* is stress that — you guessed it! — accumulates over time. It's one thing adding to another, and another, and another, until you can't take any more. Cumulative, chronic stress interferes with good logic and problem solving. In other words, people get irritable rather than figure out what's going on.

That's how **Henry** feels. Recently retired, Henry thought he was beginning to live out his golden years. He had a secure income and a paid-for home, and both he and his wife were in good health, or so it seemed.

Now Henry feels alarmed. His wife of many years is starting to forget where she puts things, occasionally gets disoriented, is unable to master simple tasks, and has to have things repeated over and over so she won't forget. Henry told her a week ago, for example, that he would be out one evening at a volunteer meeting. The very next morning, she asked, "When is it that you'll be going to that volunteer meeting?"

Henry told her again, giving her the benefit of the doubt. The next morning, she again asked, "And when is it that you'll be going to that meeting?"

Now clearly frustrated, Henry told her for the third time. Same thing again the next day. Finally, after six consecutive days of having to repeat himself, Henry erupted in a state of rage. He yelled; she ran to her room in tears, and both were left feeling bad afterward. Henry wasn't stressed because his wife asked when his meeting was. He felt stressed because she kept asking over and over. One or two times, fine. Six times, no.

However, yelling at his wife wasn't such a good strategy. Instead, Henry needs to take her for a medical evaluation to determine the cause of her memory problems. That action will cause Henry stress as well, but he'll likely obtain a better understanding of what's going on with his wife and a greater ability to control his anger.

Catastrophic stress

Events such as terrorist attacks, pandemics, tsunamis, or hurricanes devastate people, particularly if you're one of those most immediately affected. They represent the most horrific, life-altering kind of stress: *catastrophic stress*. Some people never recover from catastrophic stress (for example, Vietnam veterans who almost 50 years later still relive that war as part of a post-traumatic stress disorder); those who do recover from catastrophic stress usually take a long time to heal.

Multitasking stress

Today's culture seems to glorify the virtues and value of the ability to multitask. You see workers talking on phone headsets while answering email and sending text messages. Students work on their homework while watching TV, gaming, and texting.

Many of these jugglers proudly claim that they're extremely effective at multitasking and get more done than most other people because of their talent. However, research indicates otherwise. Your brain really can't focus on more than one item at a time without losing efficiency.

At Stanford University, psychologists found that self-proclaimed multitaskers performed worse on tasks that require memory and attention than participants who don't regularly engage in multitasking. Multitaskers were found to be more distractible and less efficient than one-task-at-a-time people. Bottom line: Multitasking may give you the illusion of accomplishing more, but it doesn't work. And it causes more stress.

Avoiding Burnout

Burnout is a form of strain that inevitably results from prolonged, intense, and unresolved stress. The dictionary defines *burnout* as "the point at which missile fuel is burned up and the missile enters free flight."

Guess who the missile is? You. The fuel? That's your physical and psychological energy. And, the free flight is all the disorganized, erratic, and inefficient behavior that you find yourself engaging in lately.

TIP

The best way to avoid burnout is to see it coming. How many of the following symptoms do you have? If you have more than a few on a regular basis, you could be well on your way to burnout.

>> Chronic fatigue

>> Struggling to get yourself to work

>> Loss of appetite

- » Insomnia
- » Chronic procrastination
- » Lack of interest in work
- » Headaches or muscle aches
- » Heartburn, acid stomach, or indigestion
- » Anxiety
- » Slipping job performance or evaluations
- » Cynicism
- » Hopelessness
- » Feeling bored and unmotivated
- » Abusing alcohol
- » Missing work
- » Hostility, irritability, and resentment
- » Agitation
- » Frequently critical at work
- » Spontaneously crying
- » Sudden bursts of temper
- » Loss of passion for your work or life in general
- » Feeling just as tired on Monday morning as you did on Friday night
- » Poor concentration
- » Confusion about routine things both at work and at home

If you do have a variety of burnout symptoms, take them seriously. Try to step back and ask yourself where they're coming from. Review your options. Don't just sink into despair.

Take **Michelle,** for instance. She's a bright young woman, who had a great head start on a promising career in marketing before the corporation she worked for went into major reorganization. Michelle found herself with no immediate superior, a doubled workload (with no additional compensation), and too few resources to meet the demands of her job. Worst of all, she no longer had time to devote to the activities she did best.

Normally, Michelle was an energetic, positive, dynamic personality, but since her company's reorganization, she found herself exhausted all the time, dreading going to work, irritable, and suffering from migraine headaches and stomach pains. Michelle's life was out of her control, and she was experiencing burnout.

TIP

Michelle needs to find a solution for her burnout. She just may need a new job. But before she starts applying for jobs, she should explore all other options, such as talking to a higher level manager, her human resources department, or her co-workers for ideas. Michelle may also benefit from becoming more assertive with her communication style (which is covered in Chapter 8). One of the best ways to avoid burnout is to take a proactive stance toward troubling issues.

TIP

If you want to avoid burnout, be realistic about what you can expect from the situation you find yourself in as well as your own abilities. Burnout usually occurs when there's too big a discrepancy between those two. Forget how things "should" be and deal with them as they really are. And quit demanding more of yourself than is reasonable.

Whatever your job is, it's not to save the world (or the company you work for) single-handedly. Do as much as you realistically can about your work problems. But at some point, you may need to back off a little and set some limits to protect yourself.

Discovering How to Be Hardy

In the mid-1970s, researchers, led by Dr. Salvador Maddi, began to follow a large group of people who worked for a major phone company. The company had large layoffs and major changes in their corporate structure. About two-thirds of the people working at the company showed significant health or emotional problems largely due to the increased, ongoing stress. These problems included heart attacks, substance abuse, strokes, and mood disorders.

Remarkably, the other third of the employees demonstrated great resilience. Despite hardship and stress, these workers sailed through the storm without negative effects. The researchers discovered that the people who coped well had three qualities in common:

>> **Control:** A sense of having power and influence over their own destinies

>> **Commitment:** Being involved, curious, and interested in events

>> **Challenge:** An ability to view negative events as normal and as providing opportunities for growth

Truly hardy people face daunting challenges with strength, resolve, and endurance. They refuse to buckle. When terrible things happen, they rarely complain. The following example demonstrates this process.

Lillian was a hardy soul. She grew up in an orphanage after her parents both died suddenly in a flu epidemic. Vivacious and athletic, she was almost killed in a head-on collision with a drunk driver in her early 20s. The accident left her with a mangled knee and stiff leg for the remainder of her life.

An attractive woman, she had few suitors due to her injury, and she ended up marrying a much older man. She wanted children but couldn't have any, so she became the patron aunt of a host of nieces and nephews. She worked full time for all her adult life, long before women were liberated from the confines of home.

She and her husband managed a modest living, although money was always a concern. Following a severe stroke, she spent the last ten years of her life in a nursing home, paralyzed on one side of her body and strapped to a wheelchair. She died quietly in her sleep at age 88.

The remarkable thing was that Lillian never complained about life being unfair or about her physical limitations. She refused to adopt the role of a disabled individual. She rarely displayed anger toward anyone, even if the person deserved it. Instead, she was legendary for her forbearance, her good humor, her forgiving ways, and her optimistic, anything-is-possible outlook.

Hardy personalities are more likely to utilize *transformational coping strategies* (transforming a situation into an opportunity for personal growth and societal benefit) when faced with stress. They're also less likely to try to deny, avoid, or escape the difficulties at hand.

People who lack hardiness tend to feel alienated from the world around them. They don't have the support and feeling of being socially connected that their hardy counterparts enjoy, and that connectedness goes a long way toward minimizing the impact of stress in their daily lives. Because their lives are devoid of value and purpose, they have no real incentive to solve their problems, so it's just easier to be mad.

There appears to be no gene for hardiness; it's a style of dealing with stressful life circumstances that is a byproduct of life experience. In other words, it's learned, and if you haven't learned it already, it's not too late.

Be the master of your own destiny

To have the kind of hardy personality that helps you cope with stress, you need to believe in your own ability to deal with adversity. Call it self-esteem, self-confidence, self-efficacy, or whatever you want, it comes down to being the master of your own destiny.

What do you do when you're on the wrong end of some major stress? Do you run and hide? Do you avoid even thinking about the problem or how you can resolve it? Do you distract yourself with a cigarette, a beer, or some serious online shopping? Or do you ask yourself, "What can I do to make things better for myself?" and then act accordingly.

TIP

Practice thinking like a hardy personality by repeating to yourself statements such as the following:

>> If I act in a respectful way, I'll likely get respect back from others.

>> Good grades in school are no accident. They're the result of hard work.

>> Luck has little effect on how life turns out.

>> Capable people become leaders because they take advantage of opportunities that come their way.

>> What happens to me is mostly my own doing.

>> People only take advantage of me if I let them.

Be a player, not a spectator

Hardy people have a deep sense of involvement and purpose in their lives, which is the commitment component of a hardy personality. In the game of life, you have to decide whether you want to be a player or spectator.

TIP

While non-hardy folks wait idly by for life to improve (that is, become less stressful), hardy personalities do the following:

>> Vote at all levels of government: local, state, federal

>> Join civic groups that have a mission to help people

>> Run marathons

>> Beautify roadways and public spaces

>> Volunteer for community service

>> Tackle projects at work that nobody else wants

>> Find meaning in the smallest things

>> Have a willingness to make mistakes to develop new skills

> » Assume leadership positions

> » Pray actively for themselves and others

> » Take classes to better themselves (or just for the fun of it!)

> » Become totally involved in family activities

> » Get regular health checkups

> » Seek out new relationships

> » Find something interesting in everyone they meet

Transform catastrophes into challenges

Life forever changes. Sometimes these changes are in your favor; other times they're not. Either way, they're stressful. What matters is whether you see these changes as catastrophes or challenges. People respond actively to a challenge and retreat from catastrophes.

Two people unexpectedly lose their jobs. One thinks of this as the end of the world as he knows it. He goes home, gets drunk, loses his temper with his family, and spends the next two weeks sleeping and watching TV. The other man tells himself, "Great, now I can look for an opportunity in something that has more security and pays better," and then he develops a plan (with his family's support) for what to do next.

When you're hit with some major stress in your life, which person are you?

LAUGHTER EASES THE PAIN

Before being subjected to pressure-induced pain in an experimental setting, men and women were allowed to listen to one of three audio tracks: one that made them laugh, one that relaxed them, and one that was on an educational topic. Pain tolerance, it turns out, was greatest in those who shared a good laugh. The next time you're feeling pained (challenged) by some stressful event or circumstance, find someone or something to make you laugh. It's good medicine!

Laughter changes your body because it increases your intake of oxygen, raises levels of endorphins (naturally produced pain killers), and stimulates circulation and muscle relaxation. Pretty good stuff.

TIP

The next time you have to deal with a major stress, and you start thinking it's the end of the world and want to retreat, try taking these steps:

1. **Clearly define the problem.**

   Did you lose your job? Did your youngest just leave home, leaving you with an empty nest? Is your spouse gravely ill?

2. **Ask yourself: What is the challenge?**

   If you've lost your job, you have to go find another one. If your house is soon to be empty of children, you'll have to find other things you're passionate about. If a loved one has just been diagnosed with a fatal disease, you'll have to prepare to grieve over that loss and to handle life more on your own in the future.

3. **Determine whether you have enough support to meet the challenge.**

   Support is all-important in dealing with major challenges in life. Figure out how much support you have on your side. Ask yourself: "Who can I count on to help? How can they help? Can they give moral support, lend a hand, tell me I'm okay? Is their support up close and personal or long-distance? Do I need to find new sources of support like, for example, legal assistance or counseling?"

4. **Develop an action plan.**

   Ask yourself: "What specific steps do I need to take to meet this challenge? Where do I start? Where do I want to end up? What's my goal? How will I know when I've met the challenge?" Set some timelines for each of the individual steps. Reward yourself along the way as you complete each step. Celebrate when you've completely met the challenge and your life becomes less stressful.

These steps work whether you've experienced a true catastrophe (a hurricane has destroyed everything you own, you lost a loved one in a pandemic) or you're facing something more common. What matters isn't whether the event was a true catastrophe; what matters is that it *feels* like a catastrophe to you, and you can transform the catastrophe into a meaningful challenge. The more traumatic the event, the more help you'll need in facing the challenge. But you *can* get through it, no matter what it is.

Coping with Stress: What Works and What Doesn't

Everything you do to get through the day — every thought, every deed — is an act of coping with stress. Going to work, paying off debts, laughing, crying: All are acts of coping. Some ways of coping with stress are aimed directly at the source of stress; other ways of coping have more to do with the strain that is produced by this stress.

Here are some examples of coping strategies that feel good and provide some *temporary* relief from stress but that *don't* resolve the problems that do you the most harm:

>> **Avoiding:** Avoidance basically means dealing with stress by *not* dealing with it (for example, by eating, smoking, or getting high).

>> **Blaming:** If you cope with stress by assigning blame, you either point the finger at other people or you beat up on yourself.

>> **Wishing:** Some people sit around and try to imagine their problems away.

>> **Acting on impulse:** When in doubt, some people shoot from the hip. They don't think; they just act.

Here are some *effective* coping strategies for dealing with stress:

>> Try to find out more about the situation.

>> Talk with a spouse, relative, or friend about what's bothering you.

>> Take things one step at a time.

>> Pray for guidance or strength.

>> Draw on past experiences of a similar nature.

>> Seek professional assistance (from a doctor, therapist, lawyer, or clergy member).

>> Try to see the positive side.

>> Focus on the problem, not your emotional reaction.

>> Be patient. Don't look for the quick fix.

>> Persist. Keep trying no matter how long it takes to reach a solution.

>> Accept feelings of uncertainty while you work toward a solution.

>> Develop several options for problem solving.

>> Keep communication lines open.

>> Be willing to compromise.

>> Be optimistic.

IN THIS CHAPTER

» **Getting up and moving**

» **Creating a positive sleep habit**

» **Surveying the role of substances**

» **Checking your diet**

» **Considering medications**

Chapter **20**

Balancing Your Body

When your body doesn't feel balanced, your moods will likely be unstable. You may feel fatigued, sad, irritable, or angry. Little things set you off. If you take better care of your body, you'll have more resilience against anger-provoking situations. Consider the following example:

> **Ricardo,** recently divorced, discovers that he needs a second job to make ends meet. Previously, he'd completed anger-management classes at his church because anger problems had ruined his marriage. Ricardo joins a men's group to keep himself focused on his recovery. He hopes to find forgiveness for his past behavior. He feels confident that his family will take him back because of his hard work and the changes he's made.
>
> Ricardo finds that his second job robs him of free time. He stops exercising, and he begins to have trouble with sleep. He feels overwhelmed by the new responsibilities of child-care, now that he shares custody of his three kids. Between working, soccer practice for his sons, dance lessons for his daughter, and homework help for all three kids, Ricardo's anger problems reemerge. He also starts drinking more to "take the edge off." He lets his diet go. His irritability with the kids increases. Ultimately, he explodes when his kids tell him, "You haven't changed at all, Daddy!"

This chapter describes the important role of exercise, sleep, substance abuse, and diet in anger management. It also discusses the option of medications for those who want to consider that approach.

Softening Moods Through Exercise

A plethora of scientific evidence supports the fact that regular physical exercise improves moods. If you choose to exercise regularly, you can expect to

>> Concentrate better

>> Sleep better

>> Show a greater interest in sex

>> Have more energy

>> Be less tense

>> Enjoy life more in general

>> Feel less alienated from those around you

>> Make decisions easier

>> Be more optimistic

>> Complain less about minor physical ailments

>> Be less self-absorbed

>> Think more clearly

>> Be less obsessive

>> Be more active

>> Be less irritable and angry

Even with all these benefits of exercise, people have many excuses for not exercising. Some of these are noted in the following sections. Understanding the excuses you're using helps you overcome them.

Making time

Okay, you might say, "Sure, I'd love to exercise, but I simply don't have the time." Understood. Today's chaotic, fast-paced world makes finding time for lots of things difficult. Many people let that fact defeat them before they even start. But research has shown that less than ten minutes of *high-intensity* exercise five or more times per week conveys significant benefits. You read that right, ten minutes per day.

TIP

If you're wondering what you can do in ten minutes a day, check out 7minuteworkout.jnj.com and download the free app. This workout takes just seven minutes per day. Even better, all you need is a wall, yourself, and a floor. There, you can't say you don't have time now.

Before you undertake any exercise program, especially high-intensity (which the 7-minute plan certainly is), check with your doctor. And if you hurt during the session, stop. Pain (as opposed to normal soreness) is a signal that something is wrong.

If you have bad knees, joint problems, or other health concerns, you can modify your exercise program accordingly. If your health problems are complex, a physical therapist will no doubt have good ideas to help you bring exercise back into your life.

Finding the motivation

If your issue with exercise isn't that you don't have the time but rather that you aren't motivated to keep up with an exercise program, start by reviewing the benefits of exercise noted earlier in this section. Furthermore, many people find that "activity monitor" devices help keep them going. Most of these devices track your steps and heart rate; some even alert you when you've been sitting too long, which happens to be a real health hazard.

You can also recruit an exercise buddy to keep you going. It's a lot harder to let a friend down than yourself. Both you and your friend should consider making a chart to record your progress week to week. Finally, signing up for a class, such as spin or Pilates, at your local gym may inspire you and keep you accountable.

If you make exercise a rule rather than a "possibility," you're more likely to keep at it. Get moving. You'll feel better if you do.

Reviewing the types of exercise

Some people are able to carve out the time and find the motivation to work out regularly, but they're just not sure what to do. They wonder how intense and frequent their exercise routine needs to be. Or they think they must have the perfect routine. These are basically needless concerns. Consider the following:

>> **It doesn't matter what type of exercise you choose.** I once heard someone ask a friend of mine who owns and operates a gym, "What's the best kind of exercise?" His response was, "The kind you'll agree to do!"

>> **It doesn't *have* to be strenuous to be effective.** The key is that you incorporate it into your lifestyle so that it's not just an add-on that you do only when you have time or feel li̶k̶e̶ ̶

TIP

When it comes to using exercise to enhance mood, the best regimen is a combination of the following:

>> Aerobic exercise, such as walking or jogging, for endurance

>> Weight-lifting for strength

>> Balance exercise for stability

>> Stretching exercises for flexibility

It's pretty hard to feel angry after a tough workout. Try it and see for yourself.

Getting Enough Zzzs

Have you ever seen a child out in public, screaming and thrashing about, totally at odds with everything going on around him? The child is likely tired and angry, and nothing his parents do suits him. But if he can hold still for one second, he falls into a deep sleep, hanging on his mother's arm like a rag doll.

Fast-forward this scenario 20 or 30 years, and you see countless adults doing the same thing: acting cranky because they're exhausted and behind on their sleep. Poor and inadequate sleep increases irritability, which is a crucible for impending anger.

The following sections talks about the vital role that rest and proper sleep play in anger management. You find out how to maintain good sleep hygiene. With this information, you won't always find yourself getting up on the wrong side of the bed.

What sleep can do for you

Contrary to what you may have always thought, sleep is *not* a waste of time. Sleep is an essential tool in the human nervous system's effort to survive. Sleep plays a restorative function, both physically and psychologically. It helps you recover from the events of the previous day and prepares you to meet tomorrow's challenges. Most important, sleep restores lost energy.

Perhaps the easiest way for you to appreciate what sleep does for you is to see what happens when you're sleep deprived. The following are just a few symptoms of chronic sleep deprivation:

>> Suppression of disease-fighting immune system function (in other words, you're more likely to get a cold or the flu)

>> Increased irritability

>> Impaired creativity

>> Difficulty concentrating

>> Impaired memory

>> Obesity

>> High blood pressure

>> Reduced problem-solving ability

>> Inefficiency at work

>> Being prone to accidents

>> Driver fatigue

>> Road rage

>> Pessimism and sadness

>> Early signs of diabetes

>> Slurred speech

>> Lower tolerance for stress

>> Impaired coping abilities

>> Slower reaction time

>> Impaired decision-making abilities

>> Rigid thought patterns (not being able to look at a situation in more than one way)

>> Hallucinations

>> Emotional outbursts

>> Increased potential for violence

>> Reduced muscle strength

>> Loss of stamina/endurance

WHY TORTURE YOURSELF?

The Geneva Convention, the United Nations Convention on Torture, and Amnesty International all consider extended sleep deprivation a form of torture, which should be outlawed by all civilized societies. Yet, ironically, millions of people torture themselves willingly day after day by not getting the proper amount of sleep. Who is there to protect them from themselves?

TIP

To figure out if you're suffering from sleep deprivation, ask yourself the following eight questions. If you answer yes to *three or more*, you're definitely behind on your sleep.

>> Is it a struggle for you to get out of bed in the morning?

>> Do you often fall asleep while watching TV?

>> Do you fall asleep in boring meetings at work?

>> Do you often fall asleep after eating a heavy meal?

>> Do you have dark circles around your eyes?

>> Do you typically sleep extra hours on the weekends?

>> Do you often feel drowsy while driving or riding in an automobile?

>> Do you often need a nap to get through the day?

WARNING

People who suffer from attention deficit/hyperactivity disorder (AD/HD), sleep apnea, alcoholism, or clinical depression, as well as those who do shift work, are at *high risk* for sleep deprivation.

Rating the quality of your sleep

Even more important than the number of hours of sleep you get is the quality of your sleep. Just because you spent eight hours in bed doesn't necessarily mean that you got a good night's sleep. Ask anyone who's slept off a big night of drinking whether she feels refreshed when she wakes up the next morning. Odds are, the answer is no.

TIP

To determine the quality of your sleep, all you have to do is rate how rested and refreshed you feel on a 10-point scale, where 1 is "not at all" and 10 is "extremely rested." Concentrate on how you feel when you first wake up in the morning (before you even head off to the bathroom!). Record your sleep quality for a period of ten days and then figure out your average (add up all ten numbers and divide by ten). This number will tell you whether you're usually getting a good night's sleep. If your average sleep rating is 7 or above, you're in good shape. If your average rating is below 7, you may be in trouble.

Sleep quality is directly related to *sleep hygiene*, which means maintaining healthy sleep habits (just like oral hygiene is maintaining healthy habits for your teeth and gums). Some examples of *poor* sleep hygiene include the following:

>> Taking daytime naps lasting for two or more hours (with the exception of some people with health conditions or the very elderly)

>> Going to bed and getting up at different times from day to day

>> Exercising just prior to bedtime

>> Using screens shortly before bedtime

>> Using alcohol, tobacco, or caffeine in excess, especially as bedtime nears

>> Participating in some kind of stimulating activity (for example, playing video games or watching a violent show) just prior to bedtime

>> Going to bed angry, upset, or stressed

>> Using the bed for things other than sleep and sex (like work or watching TV)

>> Sleeping in an uncomfortable bed

>> Sleeping in an uncomfortable bedroom environment (one that's too bright, too warm or cold, too noisy, and so on)

>> Actively engaging in important mental activity while in bed (This isn't the time or place to rehearse the speech you're going to give at tomorrow morning's staff meeting.)

Improving the quality of your sleep

Improving the quality of your sleep is one area where you can definitely make a difference. Rather than continuing to be a victim of poor sleep (in other words, exhausted and irritated), and before considering the use of sleeping pills, begin practicing some good sleep hygiene. The following sections show you how.

Avoid stimulants and alcohol

The two main stimulants that most people should avoid four hours prior to sleep are caffeine and nicotine. Both activate the central nervous system — your brain — and promote alertness, which isn't what you want to do when you're getting ready to go to sleep.

TIP

Although alcohol isn't a stimulant, it frequently impairs sleep quality as well. Alcohol is also associated with emotional outbursts like anger, which is hardly conducive to good sleep. On the other hand, many people have a glass of something alcoholic before bed with no adverse effect. But others find that doing so impairs the quality of their sleep.

Set up a pre-sleep routine

Your nervous system craves routine. It works best — and to your advantage when it comes to being healthy — when you carry on day to day in much the same way. *You* may find living a routine life boring, but your *body* loves it!

So if you're looking to get a better night's sleep (and you want to manage your anger), you need to have a consistent pre-sleep routine. That routine should begin as much as four or more hours before you actually try to go to sleep. After your afternoon or early evening workout, stop using caffeine and drinking alcohol, and eat your last big meal of the day. It's also not good to go to bed on an empty stomach. An hour or so before you go to bed, have a light snack such as, for example, some yogurt or a piece of fruit, not six slices of pizza or an ice-cream sundae!

Design a restful space

When it comes to creating a sleep environment with reduced stimulation, it's not just a matter of what you eat, drink, and smoke that counts. It also includes the physical environment itself. Ideally, you want a place to sleep that doesn't just make getting a good night's sleep *possible* but very likely.

TIP

Here are some tips on how to create a positive sleep environment:

>> **Use curtains and window shades to cut down on intrusive light from the outside.**

>> **Avoid temperature extremes.** Most people sleep better in a cool room. You may have to experiment to find the best temperature range for you.

>> **Use earplugs if the person sleeping next to you has a snoring problem.**

>> **Use background noise, such as a ceiling fan, a radio on low volume, or a sound machine, to mask more disruptive sounds.**

>> **Spend some money on a good mattress.** You want one that fits your body size (you don't want your feet hanging off the end of the bed) and provides adequate support.

Eliminate competing cues

The human brain works on the principle of *association*, which means that if two things occur together in time and space often enough, your brain makes a connection. When that connection is made, one part of that association will trigger the other. (That's why when you walk past an ice-cream store, you may suddenly crave a hot fudge sundae.)

Your brain should have only one connection — one thought, one impulse, one craving — when it comes to the sleep environment and that is: "Hooray, *finally*, I can get some sleep!" If you're saying, "What about sex?" don't worry: Sex is the one other activity that the brain can connect with the bedroom, but sleep is the primary reason for being there.

You may have a problem getting to sleep in your bedroom simply because your brain has too many connections to other activities that *compete* with sleep. For example, your bedroom may be the place where you do any of the following activities:

>> Watch television

>> Argue with your spouse

>> Eat late at night

>> Work

>> Listen to loud music

>> Study for a class or upcoming test

>> Talk with your housemates about something upsetting from the day

>> Ruminate about your to-do list

>> Ruminate about someone you're angry with

>> Plan for tomorrow

>> Roughhouse with your pets

>> Have late-night phone or texting conversations

If using your bedroom as a multipurpose room sounds familiar, no wonder you have trouble sleeping and are tired — *and irritable* — all the time. These are all activities that you can and should do elsewhere. Where? Anywhere but where you sleep. Your bedroom should be a place of sanctuary, a place where your mind and body can rest and recover.

What if you live in a studio (one-room) apartment? Try to separate your sleeping area from the rest of the room with bookshelves, a screen or room divider, or something similar. Then vow to keep your non-sleep activities to the other areas of your space.

If you've spent more than 20 minutes in bed without sleeping, get up for a while. Do some necessary but boring task that doesn't get you cranked up. Don't go back to bed until you feel *really* tired. Even get up again if you don't fall asleep in another 20 minutes or so. Your mind needs to associate your bed with sleep, not non-sleeping.

Distance yourself from work

For many people, work has become an all-consuming daily activity (some argue that it's an obsession). If you're not actually at work, it's on your mind and in your home. In fact, the most likely competing cue (see the preceding section) that interferes with your sleep is work. With so many people working from home during the pandemic, the separation between work and home has become even more difficult.

If work fills your every waking moment, you need sufficient time to disconnect or unplug your mind from work activities before you can have any hope of getting to sleep. Start by pulling away from all things work-related a couple of hours prior to sleep. If that seems impossible, at least give yourself one hour of separation time between work and sleep, but keep in mind that more is better. You're likely to gain in efficiency the next day what you lost in time working the night before.

Unclutter your mind

Another reason you may have difficulty getting a good night's sleep is that your mind is too cluttered with psychological "junk" at bedtime. The instant things get quiet and the room darkens, your brain focuses on all the unsolved problems, grievances, anxieties, worries, and frustrations that make up your psyche. Some people find that journaling about these issues for 20 minutes or so an hour or two before bed helps them calm down and feel ready to sleep.

As part of your pre-sleep routine, try writing down things you have in mind *to do* the next day. (Keep a notebook handy by your bedside table just for this purpose.) That way, the list will be there for you in the morning and you won't have to toss and turn all night, worrying that you'll forget.

CONSIDERING SLEEPING PILLS

Many people, frustrated from days, weeks, months, or years of bad sleep, think that sleeping pills are a good option. Using sleeping pills to get a good night's sleep (and reduce fatigue and irritability) may work for you, but you should consult your doctor first. Many types of sleeping pills produce negative side effects (daytime drowsiness, anxiety, nighttime wandering, memory problems, and rebound insomnia when you stop taking them). Plus, using sleeping pills may only reinforce the idea that you're a victim of a disorder over which you have no control, which is far from true. Nevertheless, some people manage to take sleep medications under a doctor's care without negative, untoward effects.

Another type of pill that might help you get a good night's sleep, but without the usual concerns about addiction and rebound effects, is an antidepressant. Antidepressants can be prescribed at lower dosages to promote sound sleep. Consult with your physician before deciding whether taking antidepressants to help with sleep is appropriate in your case.

Even less of a risk than sleeping pills or antidepressants is the natural hormone, melatonin. You can purchase melatonin over the counter. Discuss this and any other supplements you take with your primary care provider.

Knowing what to do when good sleep eludes your best efforts

Sometimes even after creating a sleep-conducive environment, establishing a good pre-bedtime routine, unplugging from work issues, and eliminating sleep-competing cues (see previous section for more on these), you still can't sleep well. What now? The next three sections tell you what to do when sleep eludes your best efforts.

Cast catastrophizing aside

One of the most common interferences with sleep can be found inside your head. You may hear various thoughts that make you even more miserable and far less likely to sleep. Here are some common *catastrophizing* thoughts:

>> "Tomorrow's an important day; I'll be a mess if I don't sleep."

>> "I can't stand it when I don't sleep."

>> "I know the baby will wake me up at 3 a.m., and I'll be exhausted tomorrow."

> » "If I don't get enough sleep, I'll be irritable and grouchy all day."

> » "I hate it when I don't fall asleep right away."

Who could fall asleep with thoughts like that echoing through their brains? But there's an alternative. You can start repeating some de-catastrophizing thoughts, such as these:

> » "I don't like it, but I've gotten through many days without sleeping the night before. It's not the end of the world."

> » "If the baby wakes up, I can cuddle with him while he feeds and that always feels nice."

> » "With time and practice, I can get a better sleep in general, but everyone has occasional sleepless nights."

In other words, the more crucial you consider sleep to be, the more likely sleep will be disturbed. You can get better sleep but, meanwhile, relax and don't catastrophize.

Sleep less to sleep better

Sleep less to sleep better, you ask? Actually, studies show that people with sleep problems tend to stay in their beds for *as long as possible* in hopes of getting enough sleep. The problem with that approach is that your brain learns to disconnect your bed from sleep, which is quite the opposite of what works for good sleep.

So instead, try going to bed an hour or two *later* than you have been, even though that may seem counterintuitive. Doing so increases the chances that you'll fall asleep sooner and sleep more efficiently.

REMEMBER

If you're tossing and turning for very long, get out of bed. You need to associate bed with sleep.

Seek sleep therapy

If you try all these sleep suggestions and still suffer from insomnia, it's time to step up your game. Start by going to your primary care provider and discussing your problem. She may recommend that you go to a sleep clinic to evaluate your sleep and determine whether you have *sleep apnea* (a condition in which your breathing starts and stops throughout the night) or other issues hindering your sleep, such as medications, gastric reflux disease, and restless leg syndrome.

Even after physical causes for your sleep problems have been ruled out or treated, you could still have insomnia. In that case, seek a cognitive behavior therapist who treats insomnia. Cognitive behavior therapy works very well for this problem (see Chapters 5 and 6 for more on the principles of cognitive behavior therapy).

Determining Whether Substances Are Messing with Your Anger

This section shows you how to effectively manage anger by creating a less anger-friendly *internal* environment: the environment within your body. It also describes how common chemical substances, such as nicotine, caffeine, and alcohol affect your body (and your anger). And it lays out the connection between impulsivity, anger, and substance abuse.

Connecting your anger and substance intake

If something is legal, some people tell themselves it can't harm them. But common sense tells you otherwise. Substances of various types exert effects on the body that trigger anger. For example, cigarettes are legal, but everyone knows that nicotine is an addictive drug and that smoking leads to the untimely death of millions of people. Alcohol is legal, but when it's used in excess, it contributes to everything from domestic abuse and fatal traffic accidents to heart attacks and liver disease. And caffeine, perhaps the most popular common-use drug of all, is certainly legal but can interfere with sleep and raise blood pressure.

One big problem is that most people don't think of common-use chemicals as "real" drugs — certainly not in the same way they think of heroin, cocaine, amphetamines, and marijuana. They consider them "safe" drugs that have no ill effects on their health and well-being. Most people don't really know the connection between the "chemistry of everyday life" and emotions such as anger.

The following so-called "harmless" chemicals, as it turns out, can lower your threshold for anger arousal in a number of ways:

>> **Caffeine and nicotine stimulate the central nervous system, making it more reactive to environmental provocation.** *Translation:* If your nervous system is ramped up, you'll have a harder time staying calm when that guy on the freeway cuts you off.

>> **Alcohol, even in small quantities, can cloud or exaggerate a person's perceptions, causing an intoxicated person to misread the actions and intentions of others.** *Translation:* If you've had too much to drink, you may think your girlfriend is flirting with that bartender when she's really just asking where the bathroom is.

>> **Alcohol tends to make people less inhibited (emotionally and behaviorally), allowing them to feel and act in ways they wouldn't if they were sober.** *Translation:* When you're sloshed, you're much more likely to lash out or throw a punch at someone you're upset with. (Bars have bouncers for a reason.)

>> **Alcohol can affect your mood, especially in terms of depression, which in turn affects emotions such as sadness and anger.** *Translation:* If you've ever ended up crying into your beer stein only moments after you were toasting your friends, it may be because the alcohol has wreaked havoc with your mood.

Moderating your substances

First you're hooked on anger, and then you become hooked on substances. In addition, caffeine and nicotine are stimulants that have the capacity to overstimulate your nervous system, thus making it easier for you to get angry the next time you get frustrated or provoked. In effect, you end up in a vicious cycle where anger leads to chemicals and chemicals lead to anger.

Stopping or cutting back smoking

Smoking is a *habit* (a predictable behavior that is conditioned to repeat itself without any conscious, deliberate thought or intent on the part of the smoker). Smokers light up basically because they have the urge to do so, and that urge is stronger at certain times of the day than others. As a starter, try eliminating your favorite cigarette of the day whenever it occurs. If you can eliminate the strongest urge in your day, it will make all the other weaker urges throughout the day easier to overcome.

TIP

After you decide which your favorite cigarette of the day is, develop a plan of action for outlasting the urge. As part of your plan, you may want to

>> **Spend the time you normally allocate to smoking a cigarette on some alternative form of pleasure.** Despite its health hazards, there is no denying that smokers derive pleasure from ingesting nicotine. So what you're looking for here is a substitute.

- » **Talk yourself through the urge.** One good mantra is "This, too, shall pass."

- » **Rely on a higher power to help you find the strength to resist the urge to smoke.** Do you have sufficient faith in yourself to overcome the urge to smoke?

- » **Lie back, close your eyes, and engage in some positive imagery.** Give your mind something to do other than focus on smoking a cigarette. Picture yourself doing something you enjoy where you typically don't smoke.

- » **Have a piece of hard candy rather than a cigarette.** This strategy works with anger, so why not smoking?

- » **Take a minute for some journaling.** This is a perfect time to spend a minute or two — as long as it takes for the urge to pass — to write down how you're feeling at the moment. It's okay to confess that you miss having a cigarette!

The smokers who are the most successful in quitting (or cutting back) are those who devise their own self-help program. So if you're committed to this as part of your overall anger-management program, then the odds are in your favor. Don't be afraid to be creative! Think outside the box. You never know what might work. For more help quitting, see *Quitting Smoking & Vaping For Dummies* (Wiley).

Counting your caffeine

TIP

If caffeine seems to trigger anger in you, try the following:

- » Switch from coffee to tea as your beverage of choice. (Both have caffeine, but tea has less.)

- » Alternate between caffeinated and decaf coffee.

- » Try drinking "half-and-half" coffee, which is half caffeine, half decaf.

- » Cut back on your use of over-the-counter medications that contain caffeine.

- » Instead of than caffeinated soda, order seltzer water in restaurants. It's trendy!

- » Give up soft drinks altogether. Many contain caffeine, and almost all of them are really bad for you, including diet versions.

LETTING THE IMPULSE PASS

Call it an urge, a craving, a hunger, whatever. You ingest most substances based on impulse. An impulse is your body's way of signaling you that it wants (or needs) something, and your job is to satisfy that impulse. The whole process is mindless.

Some people have too many impulses to eat, and they end up obese. Some have too many urges to consume alcohol, and they end up alcoholics. Some have too many urges to smoke cigarettes, and they end up with lung cancer. Some have too many urges to buy things, and they end up broke. The number of urges you have throughout the day to do something reflects just how much a part of your life is defined by that want.

The good news about impulses are that they're transient: They come and go, passing through your nervous system if you let them. Each time you experience the impulse but don't act in a way that satisfies it, the strength of the impulse weakens just a bit. If you're a smoker, think of your favorite cigarette. Each time you *don't* smoke that cigarette, it becomes a little less important until one day it's not your favorite cigarette at all. The same strategy works when you're trying to get sober: Each time you intentionally put yourself in a situation where you always drank alcohol in the past and *don't* drink, the connection between that place and alcohol weakens until you can go there with no urge to have a drink whatsoever. (That's why traditional 28-day in-patient sobriety programs generally don't work. They isolate you from the real world for a few weeks until you dry out and then send you right back out there where the situational urge to drink is just as strong as ever. You don't have a chance!)

Adopting a new drinking style

TIP

Unless you have a definite drinking problem, a few common-sense rules about how to drink responsibly will hold you in good stead. Here are a few ideas to get you started:

» **Avoid drinking alone.** Married people are less likely to smoke, drink, and drink heavily than unmarried people. As crazy as this may sound, you're also less likely to abuse alcohol when you're in good company than when you're by yourself.

» **Eat plenty of food before you drink and while you're drinking.** Food absorbs alcohol and lessens its effect on your nervous system (especially high-protein foods such as meat and cheese).

» **Alternate between alcoholic and nonalcoholic drinks.** That way, you'll cut your alcohol intake by half.

>> **Drink slowly.** Aggressive drinkers drink everything faster and, as a result, end up having more drinks. Try to make each drink last one hour (the approximate time it takes for your body to process the alcohol).

>> **Volunteer to be the designated driver once in a while.** Your friends will love you, and you'll feel much better than they do in the morning.

>> **Never drink when you're in a bad mood.** Remember: Even though most people think of alcohol as a stimulant (it loosens you up and gets the social juices flowing!), it's actually a depressant. The truth of the matter is that after a brief period of euphoria, your mood will take a downturn.

WARNING

If you do all of the preceding list and you still drink too much, consider seeking professional help.

Curbing Consumption Cravings

Diet and patterns of eating also contribute to anger problems and vice versa. If you're on an overly restrictive diet, you just may find yourself more irritable than usual. On the other hand, following an anger outburst, many people turn to food to calm themselves down.

The food all too many people turn to is *sugar*. Sugar feels great — for a little while, that is. However, studies show that blood sugar level spikes are followed by sudden drops in blood sugar levels, which set up more cravings.

WARNING

Other studies show that people make terrible decisions when their blood sugar levels plummet. And explosive anger is rarely anything but a bad decision.

Try the following guidelines to maintain more stable, healthier levels of blood sugars throughout the day:

>> Eat slowly.

>> Eat lots of fruits and vegetables, but whole foods, not so much juices.

>> If you eat carbohydrates, make sure they're whole and complex.

>> Eat small meals but consider having a small, healthy snack or two during the day.

Looking at Medication Options

Most anger-management programs don't address the issue of medications. In part, that's probably because medications aren't actually a way of managing your anger. And studies on the effectiveness of medications for anger have been somewhat inconsistent. However, you should know that medications may be an option for some people, especially when other emotional disorders, such as depression or anxiety, accompany their anger. Or when violence is part of the picture, medications may play a role in treatment.

Some of the major classes of medications prescribed for people with anger problems include the following:

>> **Atypical antipsychotics:** These are powerful drugs that tend to sedate patients. They can have serious side effects, such as problems with glucose metabolism which increases risks of diabetes.

>> **Antipsychotics:** These are older versions of atypical antipsychotics. They're used when patients lose touch with reality, experiencing hallucinations, delusions, or paranoia. This class of medication has extremely serious side effects, including abnormal, irregular muscle movements, spasms, a shuffling gait, and intense feelings of restlessness.

>> **Antidepressants:** This class of medication is especially effective for the times that depression and anger coexist. Many of these medications also have significant side effects, such as weight gain, nausea, and fatigue.

>> **Antiseizure medications:** These medications sometimes help reduce major mood swings and uncontrolled outbursts. Side effects can include fatigue, nausea, and confusion among others.

>> **Beta blockers:** These medications are usually used to treat high blood pressure. However, they can be helpful in decreasing the physical components of anger because they block the action of norepinephrine, which accompanies anger outbursts. Side effects are usually less than those of the preceding medications but can include fatigue and lightheadedness.

WARNING

Anti-anxiety medications, such as the benzodiazepines, are sometimes used to treat anger problems. However, they can cause disinhibition, which angry people often have too much of to begin with. Furthermore, they can easily cause dependency (requiring increasing dosages over time) and addiction.

WARNING

Medications for anger problems should be obtained by experts in prescribing psychotropic medications. Not all primary care physicians feel comfortable in prescribing medications for this purpose. Consider seeing a healthcare provider who specializes in prescribing medication for anger.

Chapter **21**

Building Social Support

uman beings are social animals. Like dogs, people are what are commonly referred to as *pack* or *companion* animals. Living alone isn't part of human nature. That isn't to say that you can't survive all by yourself; it just means that you'll find it much more tedious, burdensome, and difficult to do so, especially when life becomes stressful.

Developing solid social support can go a long way toward helping you maintain a positive outlook and improving your long-term chances of successfully managing anger. It's much harder to feel like a victim when you have a group of people who you believe are truly *there for you*. And when you're surrounded by people who care, there's less to be angry about. Finally, study after study has convincingly demonstrated that social support reduces your risks of adverse cardiovascular events, dementia, and improves overall health.

This chapter gives you ideas for increasing both the size and quality of your social support system. It describes steps for building your relationships and also shows you how to enhance the benefits you derive from having the right people around you.

Building Quality, Not Quantity, Support

Often, people confuse social *support* with a social *network*. Support has to do with the *quality* of your relationships with those closest to you — family, spouse, friends, children, neighbors — and, at its best, reflects a state of intimacy or emotional connection with others. A *network*, on the other hand, simply defines how *many* such relationships you have (the quantity).

Some people have a rich support network, with only a small number of individuals. Others have a zillion friends and acquaintances yet are hard-pressed to name one they can call on in a time of need. Of course, it's great to have casual acquaintances in your life — people you hang out with once in a while — as long as you have strong support in other relationships. These more enduring and *meaningful* relationships are the ones that protect and sustain you during hard (more stressful) times.

TIP

Here are a few ideas on how to start assembling your support team:

1. **Make a list of people you can call on when life becomes too stressful.**

2. **Next to each name, list whether these people are local (within driving distance) or long-distance (only an email, text, or phone call away).**

3. **Make a note of how long it's been since you had contact with each person — two days, six months, or longer than that?**

   If it's been too long since you last touched base, call or drop each person a note, text, or email, and reconnect.

4. **Decide what type(s) of support you can get from each member of your team.**

   Examples include

   - Emotional support: A hug, the chance to vent

   - Tangible support: Transportation, fixing something for you

   - Informational support: Advice, counsel

   - Appraisal feedback: Constructive criticism, praise

5. **Think about what type of support you can give to the people on your list (it's a two-way deal after all). And let them know you're available for them.**

If your list shows that your life is already full of connected, *meaningful* relationships, then that's outstanding! But if you come up a little short, the following sections give you ideas for other ways you may find new people to populate your support system.

TIP

Friendships take time and effort to develop. Be patient. Look far and wide. You may have to meet quite a few people before you find two or three who meet the criteria for being able to provide real support. Even a single, intimate friend can be an invaluable enhancement to your life.

Volunteering

Volunteering has rich potential for connecting you with new, interesting people and experiences. Start by asking yourself what interests and talents you have. Next, do an internet search on "volunteering" in your local community. You're likely to find a plethora of organizations and people who both need help and match your personal expertise. When you volunteer, you're not only benefiting the organization or person, but you're also doing the following:

>> Improving your health

>> Feeling valued and appreciated

>> Expressing your gratitude

>> Developing new skills

>> Networking

>> Beefing up your résumé if that's something you need

>> Making a contribution to society

>> Improving your social skills

>> Combating depression

>> Improving self-esteem

>> Making yourself happier

>> Showing yourself that you can make a difference

>> Seeing that other people have more problems than you

>> Increasing your sense of empowerment

>> Focusing on others, not just yourself

>> Realizing that others have experienced unfairness just like you

TECHNICAL STUFF

When people feel upset about injustice, suffering, or discrimination experienced by others, they sometimes feel what's known as *moral outrage*. Moral outrage can actually be a good thing when it motivates people to help those who suffer from unfair circumstances. People with anger about injustice, unfairness, and inequality volunteer with passion, enthusiasm, and altruism, which are not exactly ingredients that go into making a soup of toxic anger. (See Chapter 11 for more about moral outrage.)

Volunteers, generally speaking, make up a pool of potentially good friends. That's because volunteers have committed themselves to the well-being of other people. Furthermore, lots of people volunteer not only to do good, but also to meet other people. In the process, volunteers typically obtain an increase in their sense of purpose and meaning in life. (See Chapter 22 for more information about purpose and meaning.)

TIP

You may think that you don't have enough free time to consider volunteering. Of course, time pressures could represent one of your anger trouble spots. But even if that's the case, you can probably wrangle an hour per month for volunteer efforts, and you're not likely to regret it.

Participating in self-help groups

Self-help groups abound if you look around a bit. Obviously, you may want to consider such groups for assistance in certain areas of your life, such as anger management. However, self-help groups may also give you a variety of possible friends. After all, you start off the bat with something in common. Specifically, anger-management self-help groups consist of people interested in dealing with anger management and improving their lives. These groups are typically not run by licensed professionals so you want to be sure that they aren't simply a bunch of people who gather to gripe and complain.

WARNING

A few individuals in anger-management self-help groups may be so early in their work on anger that they wouldn't make a good choice as a friend or confidant. Proceed with some caution and care. Be especially cautious of anyone recently mandated to attend by the court system or who has an admitted history of violence.

Self-help groups for anger management exist online. However, if you're looking for possible friends, you want to find groups that meet in person with some frequency. You can find local anger-management groups (that meet in person) online at `https://angermgt.meetup.com` or by searching for "anger management near me." You can also find anger-management self-help groups through churches, the newspaper (they do still publish these!), senior centers, and local universities' and colleges' continuing education programs.

TIP

Most people have various issues and concerns in their lives, including anger, anxiety, depression, relationship problems, grief, and so on. Consider joining a self-help group for problems you may have other than anger.

Looking for friends

You can also find friends by, well, looking directly for friends. You may have a few acquaintances whom you haven't explored as possibilities for becoming close friends. Changing acquaintances into friends will take some effort on your part. But you can dig down deep, reach out, and invite someone from your neighborhood, school, or work to do something with you.

Start with something small: coffee, a walk, or a brief visit. Realize that if someone doesn't show interest, it likely has nothing to do with you and much more to do with his too-full calendar.

TIP

Most people need to make numerous invitations before finding anyone who would make a really good friend. Expect turndowns. Persevere.

Hosting block parties

Many neighborhoods have block parties from time to time. These get-togethers sometimes include what's known as a *neighborhood watch*. Neighborhood watches help decrease crime in your neighborhood by having neighbors look out for each other and report suspicious activities to the local police.

Sometimes representatives from the local police and fire departments will attend a neighborhood watch gathering if asked. They will listen to neighbors' concerns. Neighborhood watches build a sense of community and increase people's interest in keeping the neighborhood safe. They also provide yet another source of meeting potential friends.

If your neighborhood doesn't yet have a formal neighborhood watch, you could consider organizing one. The local police department will likely assist you in that process. But if you're not ready for such an undertaking, consider simply holding a neighborhood block party. Here are a few ideas on how to hold such a party:

>> Start an organizing committee by inviting a few interested neighbors to join you for a meeting.

>> Figure out convenient times and places for your first party. Most people prefer early evening, after work.

>> Decide whether to have a potluck where people bring one or more dishes to share or a picnic where everyone brings their own food. If this initial effort succeeds, maybe you'll want to try something more adventurous in the future such as a barbeque or a catered event.

>> Communicate to your neighbors about the party through email, flyers, and word of mouth. Consider collecting a list of emails of everyone you can and ask others to contribute names and emails as well.

>> Sit back, enjoy, and visit with your neighbors. You just may make a new friend or two.

Of course, if there are restrictions on parties in your neighborhood such as during the pandemic, then a neighborhood party would not be a great idea. Check with the local authorities about any obstacles that might interfere with a large event, especially if alcohol or legal marijuana are involved.

Conversing wherever you are

You no doubt cross the paths of possible friends every single day, but you just don't know it. You likely walk through your day while barely noticing the strangers around you. Maybe it's time to try something new.

I like to encourage people to practice their conversational skills in situations that have *low importance*. In other words, try conversing with people you're not likely to become close friends with, like maybe the postal clerk, someone in front of you in the grocery store line, or someone you pass while walking your dog. Here are a few conversation openers:

>> **Comment on the weather.** It's really hot today; how have you been staying cool? Do you think we'll ever get rain again? What do you think of this incessant wind?

>> **Ask a question about the area you're in.** Got any suggestions for good restaurants around here? I'm looking for a new place to walk; do you have any ideas? What's your favorite grocery store around here?

>> **Tell someone something about yourself.** I just moved here from the Northwest; got any advice for a newbie? I had the greatest time last weekend because my 13-month-old son just started to walk.

>> **Comment or question people about their devices or gadgets.** I see you have the new Isotope 6000 phone. How do you like it?

Talking about current events in politics is a bit risky, no matter what "side" you are on. Stay away from controversial topics when trying to make small talk. Learning to connect with others comes before trying to change minds.

You'll probably engage in a couple hundred brief (or longer) conversations before a true friend emerges from the process. However, you'll also gain social skills and finesse that will serve you well at parties, meetings, and other gatherings.

In any conversation, try to ask a question or two — or three or four. People love talking about themselves, and you may learn something surprisingly interesting. That's how friendships start.

Joining a gym

Chapter 20 extolls the value of exercise for anger management. Although working out at a gym is great for keeping the lid on anger, it's also a place to meet and make new friends. There are also meet-up hikes and other opportunities for social engagement found online that do not include joining a gym.

Practice social skills with as many people as you can, like those at the front desk, other members, and people in classes (yoga, spin, and so on). If a conversation gets going and you start to establish a gym relationship, consider going for coffee or juice after your next workout. Take it from there.

Prioritizing Friends

Friends won't just beat a path to your door on their own. You can't merely start a conversation or two and expect a lifetime friendship to come out of it. Furthermore, busy lives make it difficult to find room for friendships. Most people work all day and cram in errands as they can.

So if you want new friendships, you have to *prioritize* making and keeping friends. That means you have to understand that friends indeed can make you happier and less angry to boot. The following sections provide you with a few skills you'll need in your quest.

Emphasizing listening over talking

There's an old adage to the effect that you can't learn by merely talking, you learn only when you're listening. This truth is particularly germane when you're trying to make friends.

You simply must ask lots of questions. Truly listen and ask follow-up questions. Don't make your conversation like a ping-pong match where you say one thing, your friend chimes in with one item, and it goes back to you. Rather, actively explore topics. Ask about your friend's views, feelings, and values. Here's an example of a ping-pong conversation (not what you want):

Rob: What'd you do last weekend?

Gene: Not much. I cleaned the garage.

Rob: I went to the casino and won $1,000.

Gene: Great. I went to that new restaurant down the block.

> **Rob:** I've never won that kind of money.
>
> **Gene:** I had grilled chicken, pretty good, too.
>
> **Rob:** I think I'll go to the casino next weekend, too.
>
> **Gene:** Yeah, and you know, they have good desserts, too.

You can see that Rob and Gene just pinged and ponged back and forth. No exploration, no dialogue, no connection. See what happens when they take an explorative approach.

> **Rob:** What'd you do last weekend?
>
> **Gene:** Not much, I cleaned the garage.
>
> **Rob:** Not much? Really? I never get around to that. How'd you get yourself motivated?
>
> **Gene:** Well, I decided to have a garage sale and needed to get it organized.
>
> **Rob:** When are you having the sale? You need any help?
>
> **Gene:** Actually, that would be great. Do you have just an hour or two Saturday to help me set it up? That's all I need.
>
> **Rob:** Sure. I have a bit more time than that if you want. Would you mind if I brought a couple items of mine to sell, too?
>
> **Gene:** Terrific. You help me and we can go out for lunch Sunday. I'll buy with the proceeds.

As you can see, they listened and connected and offered support for each other. Sounds sort of like friends, huh?

Asking for what you need

If you're like most people, you have lots of potential support that you never fully take advantage of. What possible good does the help of other people do you if you don't accept it?

Earlier in this chapter, you'll find a suggestion that you make a list of supportive people in your life. Allowing others to help you when you need it actually makes friendships closer and stronger.

REMEMBER

Having people who support you isn't enough though. You have to *accept* that support when they offer it. If volunteering and helping others gives you pleasure, why would you want to deny others the same pleasure? Don't deny others the joy that comes from giving to you.

Empathizing with others

People who struggle with anger often spend too much time thinking about themselves (which is covered in Chapter 7). Self-centered thoughts disconnect you from other people. These thoughts make it easier to become angry with others because everything seems more personal.

Empathy helps you connect. Empathy occurs when you're able to think about and feel concern for the wants and needs of other people. In other words, you find a way to put yourself in other people's shoes. You step out of your own space and take another person's perspective. Usually, when you do that, you become less angry and make a better friend.

TIP

If you haven't spent much time empathizing with other people, it will take you some time and patience to learn how to do it. Play with the concept; try being empathetic when you're not angry first. Listen to and understand where other people are coming from. Refrain from judging.

NEIGHBORS HELPING NEIGHBORS

A flourishing movement in many communities across the United States focuses on neighbors pitching in to help senior citizens remain in their homes for as long as realistically possible. To accomplish that goal, volunteers organize themselves into villages (non-profit agencies). Their goals include connecting members to vetted services, such as handymen and painters, and providing help with everyday tasks, such as replacing out-of-reach light bulbs or providing transportation to medical visits. In addition, the village movement offers classes, social activities, and lectures.

Where I live in Corrales, New Mexico, the organization here is called Village in the Village, because Corrales itself is considered a village. Volunteers have offered computer technical support and respite care. During the pandemic, volunteers delivered masks and hand sanitizer and also picked up groceries and prescriptions for shut-in seniors. Organizations such as these are just one more way to connect with other people and make a difference in the world.

IN THIS CHAPTER

» **Living a valued life**

» **Making gratitude a daily habit**

» **Immersing yourself in meaningful pursuits**

» **Staying positive and showing compassion**

» **Striving to be humble**

Chapter **22**

Finding Meaning and Purpose

W hen angry thoughts fill your mind, there's little room for focusing on more meaningful, productive pursuits. The reverse is also true: When you focus on living a purposeful, value–driven life, there's far less room for anger. In other words, *doing good* keeps you from *feeling bad*. Consider the following example:

Rachael and **Crystal** grew up in a poor family. Their father spent much of their childhood in prison for domestic violence and a series of drug-related charges. When he lived at home intermittently, he frequently was abusive to the kids and their mother. Their mother struggled with drug addiction and remained emotionally unavailable to the kids much of the time.

Both kids had behavior troubles in school. By high school, their paths diverged. Rachael joined a gang. She dropped out of school, used illegal drugs, and was arrested the first time at the age of 14. Crystal, on the other hand, had an aunt who took special interest in her. Her aunt frequently questioned Crystal about what she wanted her life to look like. Crystal eventually decided to go into social work. She wanted to make a difference in the world. She wanted her work to help others avoid the problems she experienced growing up. Her life had purpose and meaning.

This chapter helps you evaluate the extent to which you're living the life you really want to live. What made Crystal turn her back on her difficult childhood and move forward? She set a goal of living a purposeful life. To do that, she had to examine her values, interests, and direction. You can do that too.

Putting Your Values at Center Stage

Take out a sheet of paper and write the word *I* on the first line. Then spend 15 minutes writing an essay about your life up to now; include anything and everything you think is relevant and important. Stop at the end of 15 minutes (set a timer if necessary) and read what you wrote. Try to be as objective as you can. Try pretending you're reading about someone else's life.

After you've finished reading what you just wrote, answer the following questions:

>> How much of your life essay is about *you* versus other people?

>> How much of your essay has to do with your work?

>> How much of your essay has to do with financial successes or failures?

>> Does the essay sound like a life story in which the person feels satisfied and content?

>> Would you say that this essay is about someone who has a sense of purpose or meaning in life?

>> How much of the essay is about what you have *gotten* from life versus how much you've *given* back?

>> If this were, in fact, another person's life story, would you want to trade places with that person?

If your essay has a healthy balance between references to yourself versus references to others, if work and financial success (or failure) aren't the sole focus, if your essay portrays a reasonably content person whose life is full of purpose, if there is balance between *getting* and *giving,* and if you'd actually want to live that person's life, you can be fairly sure that you're living a meaningful and value-driven life.

If you answered otherwise, take a long, hard look at yourself and think of ways that you can change your story. Repeat this exercise once a week for the next six weeks, each time asking yourself those same questions afterward, and see if you're beginning to move beyond a self-centered life. If you work at changing the focus of your life, the focus of your essay should change as well.

Writing Your Own Epitaph

No matter how old you are, you can start thinking right now about how you want your tombstone to read. In other words, what kind of statements would you like to be made about the purpose of your life? What values and characteristics would you want people to remember about you? What would you like your life's *signature statement* to be?

Take a look at all the epitaphs in Table 22-1 and, as honestly as possible, choose the one that you think the people in your life say is accurate about you.

TABLE 22-1

The Tombstone Test

Unanchored to Values Here lies a person who . . .	Anchored in Values Here lies a person who . . .
. . . made a fortune.	. . . was a friend to everyone.
. . . was feared but respected by all.	. . . cared deeply about family and friends.
. . . hated to be late for anything.	. . . could be trusted.
. . . was a mover-shaker.	. . . was a real team player.
. . . wasn't afraid to be angry.	. . . had an abiding curiosity about life.
. . . multitasked with the best.	. . . loved passionately.
. . . left this world without expressing positive feelings of love and caring.	. . . left this world satisfied.

TIP

After you've chosen your epitaph, ask yourself if that's how you *want* to be remembered. If the epitaph that others think is most accurate for you happens to be in the "Unanchored to Values" column, maybe it's time for a change. For example, if the epitaph that most accurately describes you is, "Here lies a person who made a fortune," you can begin to enrich your life with new friendships or perhaps explore charitable giving that you find meaningful.

If your "Unanchored to Values" epitaph is "Here lies a person who was feared but respected by all," you can volunteer to help someone learn how to read and people can respect you for helping others rather simply because they're afraid of you.

Acquiring the Gratitude Habit

Anger has a lot to do with feeling that you're not getting what you want (or what you feel entitled to). You're not getting recognition at work or making the money you feel you should. Your kids don't show you the respect you feel entitled to as a parent. Your dog doesn't come when you call him. So you get mad. Gratitude, on the other hand, has to do with being thankful for what has already been given to you.

TIP

Start each day with a prayer or practice of gratitude. Make a mental list of all your blessings — people, events, whatever — and recite them to yourself (silently or out loud) so that you remember the good things that have been bestowed on you and you are, indeed, thankful. And then see if you don't feel a sense of inner peace as you take on the challenges of the day.

Being grateful has benefits. People who appreciate the blessings of life find life to be more satisfying. Overall, those who express gratitude have fewer physical complaints, sleep better, feel more connected, and generally express more optimism than people who don't express gratitude.

REMEMBER

You can feel grateful about big stuff and even really small stuff. Whether you win a million-dollar lottery, fall in love, catch a subway just in time, or find a great parking spot, all these types of events provide you with an opportunity to experience and feel grateful. What matters the most is acquiring the gratitude habit.

PUTTING GRATITUDE TO WORK

Gratitude is a positive emotion that occurs when people believe that they've benefited from something or someone. For example, when you get a flat tire and someone stops to help, you feel grateful. Or when you get a compliment, a pay raise, or an unexpected gift, you're likely to feel grateful. You may also feel grateful about the nice weather (or snow if you're a skier), good food, an engaging book, or seeing someone you love smile.

Professors Emmons and McCullough asked one group of research participants to write five sentences about things they were grateful for daily for two weeks. Another group wrote about daily hassles, and a third group wrote about neutral events. The group that wrote about things they were grateful for was more likely to help others, felt better, and even exercise more.

Finding Flow

Do you ever get so involved in something that nothing else seems to matter and you lose track of time? This is the question that Dr. Mihaly Csikszentmihalyi (don't even think about trying to figure out how to pronounce his name) has asked countless numbers of people in his studies of what he calls *flow*, which is a state of consciousness that occurs when you find yourself immersed in one of those "best moments of my life."

Csikszentmihalyi, interestingly, finds that only 20 percent of people answer yes, that this happens to them on a daily basis. Fifteen percent say no, that it never happens, and these, I'm willing to bet, are the folks most likely to experience chronic anger.

So how do you get into this healthy state of mind? Actually, it's not that difficult.

>> **Flow comes from active involvement in some aspect of daily life.** Flow isn't some mystical, magical, spiritual state that falls over you — if you're lucky — like mist from the heavens above. It comes only when you're actively involved in life. Passive activities like watching TV or listening to music won't do the trick. For me, writing books provides a frequent state of flow (some days are, well, better than others). For you, it may be a hobby like stamp collecting, birdwatching, experimental cooking, gardening, chess, or recreational sports like jogging, volleyball, or tennis.

>> **Flow requires positive motivation.** Flow is a byproduct of a *want-to* activity. If you don't really *want to* play golf today, and you're just doing it because your boss wants you to, you may shoot a low score, but you won't likely experience flow. A few fortunate people, like me, find flow in work, and for that, I am extremely grateful.

>> **Flow requires your full attention.** Flow requires a full commitment on your part. Your mind can't be elsewhere while you're actively engaged in something that has the potential to produce flow. Mentally speaking, you and the activity have to be one.

A client who suffered from extensive pain throughout his body every minute of the day for over 20 years put it this way: "When I can't stand the pain anymore — when it's absolutely killing me — I go up into my computer room and get *into* the computer. I don't get *on* the computer, I get *into* it. I get lost in there, and for a couple of hours, I am completely pain-free."

>> **Flow activities have to be challenging.** Doing something that is easy, that doesn't take much in the way of skills, energy, or concentrated effort, won't produce flow. Flow comes from activities that are challenging, even though they may seem effortless when you're doing them. Repetition makes people dull. If you start out achieving flow from a particular activity, over time, if you don't change the activity in some way to make it more challenging or complex, it will lose its effect.

>> **Flow comes from activities that produce immediate reward.** You achieve flow in the *process,* not in the outcome. It happens while you're actively engaged, not later on down the road. Whereas most of the rewards in life come from sustained effort (think nose to the grindstone), flow occurs in the here and now. And it begins to subside as soon as you stop whatever you're doing to produce it.

>> **Flow activities don't always present themselves, so sometimes you have to create them.** People say all the time, "I just never seem to have the time to do the things I really enjoy. I can't remember the last time I had an opportunity to sit and play the piano — my favorite thing. I wish God would just give me a day off."

What is less common is something to the effect of, "I know the dishes need to be washed and I still haven't vacuumed the downstairs, but, what the heck, I'm going to stop and play the piano a while. I need to get into the flow."

Make time for flow. Make it a priority in your life. Be one of that top 20 percent of the population that understands what Dr. Csikszentmihalyi is talking about.

>> **Flow comes from knowing yourself.** You experience flow when you commit yourself to spending time in your favorite activity. So what is your favorite activity? You may not be able to readily answer that simple question. That's in part because you don't know enough about yourself to actually know what your favorite activity is. Spend some time experimenting with different activities that appeal to you a little bit and see which ones you have the most fun with.

Table 22-2 lists examples of activities that are likely to produce a state of flow and some that are less likely to do so.

Ask yourself the following questions:

>> What is my favorite activity?

>> What do I do that is effortless?

>> What is it that I like to do that makes time stand still?

TABLE 22-2   **Activities Likely and Unlikely to Produce Flow**

Activities Likely to Produce Flow	Activities Unlikely to Produce Flow
Working or studying at something you're very interested in	Doing housework
Preparing a creative meal	Mindlessly eating that meal
Traveling	Watching TV
Taking part in interesting hobbies	Sitting and feeling bored
Playing recreational sports	Resting and relaxing
Playing a musical instrument	Passively listening to music
Having conversations with interesting and stimulating people	Having idle conversation
Writing a book about anger	Responding to copy editors (no offense, guys!)
Taking part in creative activities	Doing mindless activities
Researching and digging deeply into a fascinating subject on the internet	Mindlessly surfing the internet

TIP

Now, make sure you engage in an activity likely to produce flow at least once a week.

Flow and anger are incompatible emotions. When you are in a state of flow, anger has no room to exist.

REMEMBER

Searching for Healthy Pleasures

One thing is for certain: Human beings are creatures who constantly need and seek pleasure. Without a sufficient amount of joy and pleasure in your life, you'll inevitably end up feeling irritable, moody, tense, and, worst of all, dull.

Seeking pleasure in everyday life is just as natural for your brain as avoiding pain. That's right: The rather large, extremely complex brain you have operates on what's called the *pain-pleasure principle,* and it continually strives (with or without your help) to strike a favorable balance between the two.

REMEMBER

The brain doesn't distinguish between healthy and unhealthy pleasure. From a neurological standpoint, it's all the same. The good news is you can achieve the same high from running a marathon as you can from smoking pot. The former is an example of healthy pleasure (pleasure without adverse consequences); the latter, not so much.

If you're like most people, you have a bit of experience with unhealthy pleasures such as eating too many sweets, drinking too much alcohol, taking in too much caffeine, gambling, driving above the speed limit, having unprotected sex, and/or engaging in shop-'til-you-drop consumerism. But do you often engage in *healthy pleasures?* Here's a list of possibilities:

>> Attending a jazz festival

>> Savoring a cool glass of lemonade

>> Hiking in a lovely meadow

>> Walking your dog

>> Going to an interesting museum

>> Spending some time at a dog park

>> Savoring a piece of chocolate

>> Watching birds cavort through the trees in the springtime

>> Enjoying an especially interesting meal

>> Helping someone less fortunate

>> Seeing the Grand Canyon for the first time

>> Riding in a hot air balloon

>> Spending a week on a tropical island

>> Watching your favorite football team score the winning touchdown in the last second of the game

>> Looking at clouds

TIP

Spend some time (it doesn't have to be much) each day indulging in some form of healthy pleasure. Careful, you might get addicted!

Looking at the Glass as Half Full

Positive psychology is the study of the principles and concepts that lead people to feeling happy, satisfied, and fulfilled. Optimism has been widely cited as useful in this quest. Thus, it's often thought that people who believe reasonably good outcomes will likely occur frequently persist in the face of challenges.

Intuitively, people with anger issues may seem to have insufficient optimism. But that doesn't appear to be the case. Becoming more optimistic could be a good thing at times, but it won't do a lot to reduce your anger.

WARNING

Excessively optimistic people may actually increase negative future outcomes. For example, an excessively optimistic person may underestimate the risk of the future health consequences of unhealthy behaviors, such as overeating, drug use, and unprotected sex. In addition, overly optimistic people may become angry and upset when things don't come out as well as they expected.

Practicing Compassion

All world religions, regardless of their differences, have one thing in common: They teach and preach compassion. When the Bible talks about doing unto others as you would have them do unto you, it's not talking about anger and violence; it's talking about love of your fellow human being (or, for that matter, your cat!).

Table 22-3 highlights some differences between two opposing ways of treating other human beings: compassion and revenge.

TABLE 22-3

Revenge Versus Compassion

Revenge	Compassion
Is born out of anger or hatred	Is born out of love
Has the goal of hurting someone	Has the goal of helping another person
Heightens conflict	Eases conflict
Is judgmental	Is nonjudgmental
Says, "They're wrong"	Says, "They need help"
Says, "I'm against them"	Says, "I'm for them"
Is destructive	Is constructive
Plots to punish someone	Releases the desire to punish someone

TIP

Make a pact with yourself not to let a day go by without finding some way in which you can show compassion to your fellow humans. You might be surprised at how small acts of compassion — a kind word at exactly the right time — can salvage someone's day. Professor Shelly Taylor at UCLA sees such acts as examples of what she calls "tending and befriending," a form of positive psychology, that allows everyone to better survive hard times. (Interestingly, this trait is much more common in women than it is in men. Maybe this is why women live much longer?)

Being Humble: It Helps

Developing a sense of humility is yet another antidote to toxic anger. Being humble is the opposite of

>> Being arrogant

>> Feeling entitled

>> Seeing yourself as superior

>> Adopting an attitude of contempt toward all those you see as not as good as you are

All these opposites of humility tend to incite anger. Have you ever met a truly angry person who was humble? Unlikely.

Reputedly, Dr. Hans Selye who, when asked why he wasn't stressed by the infirmities of his advanced age (hobbling up and down from a stage to lecture about stress) and the fact that not everyone in the medical profession agreed with the conclusions of his life's work, replied simply, "Because I never took myself that seriously." Selye's response is a good example of humility.

Try getting involved in a community task without being the person in charge. Find some fairly menial ways to make the world a better place. Beautify your community by collecting trash on the side of the highway. Or spend a day working for Habitat for Humanity.

If the concept and emotion of humility eludes you, consider going outside and stargazing for a while. Ponder the vastness of the universe and the smallness of each individual person. All of us are a small part of a far greater creation.

7

The Part of Tens

Chapter 23

Ten Ways to Deal with Angry People

Imagine that you're at the grocery store parking lot. You back out slowly and somehow tap the bumper of a car that suddenly appears behind you, seemingly out of nowhere. You suspect the car was moving too fast, but you don't really know. You stop and open your car door to check for damage.

The other driver charges out and runs up to you shouting, "What the *&%#!? You idiot! What the %&@# were you doing? Don't you even bother to look? What's wrong with you?"

His face is red; he's standing really close to you. You see his hands balled up. You feel your heart racing and palms sweating. You're not sure who's to blame, but you sure don't want this situation to get out of hand. What started out as a minor fender bender starts ratcheting up, and you're not sure what to do. How can you bring the heat down?

This chapter gives you ten techniques for cooling down situations that threaten to ignite when you don't want them to. In all but the rarest of cases, you'll feel better and come up with more effective solutions when you *contain* conflict rather than give anger a free rein.

WARNING

When faced with an angry person, you want to do everything you can to avoid escalation. Heated arguments and even violence can erupt when escalation climbs. And escalation can happen really fast if you're not careful.

Apologizing and Listening Deeply

You might be wondering, why apologize if it wasn't my fault? What do you have to lose? Apologizing just might stop the anger in its tracks. You don't have to admit that you did something wrong; just make a general apology for what happened. For example, you might say, "Gosh, I'm sorry this happened."

When people attack, your best defusing strategy is to listen. Really listen. Give the angry person some time to completely express his frustration. The ideal way to show that you're listening is to paraphrase what's been said. For example, start with one of the following phrases:

>> "So it sounds to me that you're saying . . ."

>> "If I'm hearing you right . . ."

>> "I get a sense that you're saying . . ."

>> "Correct me if I'm wrong, but I think what you mean is . . ."

TIP

After using one of these phrases, tell the person how you heard what was said. If the person agrees you got it right, you can move on. If not, ask for a restatement of what was said so you can better understand the person's intent.

Controlling Pace, Space, and Breath

Arguing in parking lots and other open spaces merely increases the chances of escalation. You can bring those risks down by moving to another, more contained space, such as a nearby coffee shop or the inside of a store. Locations such as these usually inhibit people from getting physical or verbally abusive.

Here are a few more ideas for containing a potentially explosive interaction:

>> **Suggest that the two of you sit down in chairs.** Doing so equalizes height and has a calming effect.

>> **Notice where the exit doors are located just in case.** Don't put yourself in a position where your exit path is blocked. You'll feel more relaxed that way.

>> **Attempt to maintain a distance of about two arms' length away from your adversary.** This provides just a bit of extra safety.

>> **Control the speed of your speech.** Slow down the pace. Insert pauses. It's much harder to rage against someone who speaks slowly and with pauses. Control the rate of your breathing, too.

WARNING

It can be really tempting to get caught up in the rapid-fire pace of someone you're arguing with. That response is rarely helpful and usually results in rapid escalation. Be careful.

Asking for Clarification

Many arguments occur when two people simply fail to understand what each other is trying to say. Rather than *assume* you know what the argument is about, why not be sure by asking for clarification? You can restate what you think is going on, but say that you want to be sure that you have it right. Ask about or query the other person regarding any part of your communication (or the other person's) that you think may remain unclear. Consider this example:

> **Amantha,** a dental hygienist, works three days a week. She helps with her elderly grandparents almost every day that she isn't working. Her sister takes the responsibility when Amantha works. **Terrence** works at the same dental office as a hygienist. He says to Amantha, "It must be nice to work only three days a week. I asked for four days, and they wouldn't let me cut down to that. You have some sort of special relationship with the boss?"
>
> Amantha, who feels exhausted from all she does, angrily responds, "How dare you accuse me of sleeping with the boss!"
>
> Terrence replies, "Whoa. I didn't mean to imply that. I was just kidding. I was curious, though; why did they let you have that schedule?"
>
> Amantha says, "I think it's because I told them at the interview that I take care of my elderly grandparents the other four days of the week. It's exhausting work."
>
> Terrence apologizes, "Oh, I get it. I'm sorry for implying some kind of favoritism was going on. It must be tough for you."

Terrence accomplished a lot by simply asking Amantha for clarification as to why she landed that schedule. If he had not done so, things could have gotten ugly fast.

Finally, ask for *more* information. That's right; ask for more about what's upsetting the person. Rather than get defensive, query about additional concerns by asking questions like these:

>> "Okay, I think we're clear on that, is there more that's bothering you?"

>> "Do you have additional things that are bugging you?"

>> "Do you think there's more to this situation that's upsetting you?"

>> "Is there something more you'd like me to hear?"

Don't worry; you'll have your chance to present your side after things calm down. When you rush into presenting your case, you increase the likelihood of escalation. Take your time.

WARNING

Sometimes angry people switch gears rapidly from ranting and yelling to stony silence. If that happens, don't insist on more information right then. Suggest another time to talk.

Speaking Softly

Have you ever listened to the voice volumes of people while they're arguing? You probably can't think of many times when arguments proceeded at a soft volume. A soft, patient voice tone and volume keeps emotions in check. It's basically as simple as that, so pay close attention to your voice volume when an argument threatens to break out.

TIP

If someone you're speaking with uses a high volume, it's okay to say, "You know, it really helps me understand you better if you speak a little more softly. Would that be all right with you?"

Connecting

When you feel *disconnected* from people, it's far easier to feel angry with them. On the other hand, even a small bit of connection can dampen hostile feelings. You can start by asking angry people what their names are. Then use their names a number of times during your encounters.

Another way of connecting is to offer something edible (a muffin, a mint, whatever) or something to drink like tea or coffee or even water. When you offer people something, they typically feel a desire to reciprocate in some way; at the very least, they'll be less likely to explode. Furthermore, it's kind of hard to yell if you have something in your mouth!

Dropping Defensiveness: Verbally and Nonverbally

Defensiveness communicates an intense need to guard against criticism or other hostilities — whether real or imagined. Defensiveness increases, rather than decreases, the chances that someone may attack you verbally or physically. That's because defensiveness is a weak response, whereas non-defensiveness communicates strength and confidence.

Facial expressions, body language, posture, and what you say all can increase or decrease defensiveness. Consider trying the following non-defensive strategies:

>> **Put a curious look on your face.** Slightly raise your eyebrows, and tilt your head a bit. Look genuinely interested in the other person's perspective.

>> **Put on a Mona Lisa smile.** You're aiming for a kind expression, not sarcastic.

>> **Nod your head.** Even if you disagree with the person's views, nodding shows that you're listening — not necessarily agreeing, but listening.

>> **Turn a bit to the side.** A slight turn demonstrates that you're not trying to provoke or confront.

>> **Give choices, not all or none.** Most arguments can have more than one solution. Try to find multiple possibilities that you can live with and toss them out to the person.

>> **Ask the person whether there's something you can do to help the situation.** You don't necessarily have to agree to the request, but offering to help can bring down the heat.

Finding Agreement Where You Can

No matter how obnoxious or outrageous a person's viewpoint may be, you can almost always find a sliver of agreement. Express partial agreement with phrases such as the following:

» "I can see how you might look at it that way."

» "Sometimes that's probably true" (even if you don't think it is at the moment).

» "You may have a point" (even if you doubt it, it's always possible).

TIP

See Chapter 8 for more information about assertive communication styles, including finding agreement with the technique of disarming.

Expressing Understanding

When dealing with an angry person, show that you understand by empathizing with the other person. Be careful to avoid saying you know exactly what the other person is feeling. Obviously, you don't for sure. You can empathetically toss out a possibility but allow the person to disagree. For example:

» Thank the person for expressing her views honestly.

» Tell the person that you understand how upset he may feel.

» Refrain from judgmental statements about the other person. That doesn't mean you agree with the other's viewpoint, but it shows you at least have respect for her as a person.

Developing Distractions

Distraction involves abruptly changing the subject or focus of attention onto something else that's unrelated to the conflict at hand.

WARNING

Most disagreements *don't* call for distraction. For example, if someone argues about getting short-changed, you wouldn't want to change the subject. However, you could turn to distraction when the dispute involves any of the following:

>> A child, especially when in places where disruptive behavior would be problematic, such as a religious ceremony

>> Someone who has mental impairments, such as dementia or limited intellectual functioning

>> Someone who's impaired from legal or illegal drugs and has impaired reasoning

So if distraction is called for, you could try one or more of the following techniques:

>> Point to something in your surroundings and comment on it. For example, "Look at that amazing cloud formation" or "Do you see that huge crack in the ceiling?"

>> Bring up another topic entirely, such as the weather or the news. Make a comment like "Can you believe how fast this cold front has come on?"

>> Take out your smartphone and show the person an interesting picture or even send a text to the person if you know the number.

Considering a Timeout

Sometimes a resolution will elude you. The argument goes round and round and fails to progress. You see no solution in sight. When that happens, it's time to stop. Here are a few suggestions:

>> "You've given me a lot to think about. Can we touch base on this again tomorrow?"

>> "I'm afraid I can't process everything that's being said. Can we take another run at this later?"

>> "What we're talking about is really important, but I have somewhere I have to go to in a few minutes. How about we pick this up again in the morning?"

>> "We don't seem to be getting anywhere right now. I need a timeout. Let's talk further another time."

WARNING

Don't get caught up in feeling you must come to a resolution immediately. If things aren't getting anywhere or if you feel unsafe, it's best to terminate the conversation and get out. Not all situations are resolvable. Do try again if you feel there's a reasonable chance of success but not if it looks impossible.

TIP

You can use the excuse of needing to use the restroom to slow things down or even escape a difficult or dangerous situation. Most people can't get themselves to refuse a request to use the restroom. Just declare that you're going there. If need be, call for help.

Chapter **24**

Ten Ways to Decrease Anger with Compassion

A nger, whether directed at you or your own anger directed at others, is not a pleasant experience. Most people feel drained and down after an episode of anger. Instead of responding to bouts of anger with more anger, consider compassion. Compassion involves kindness and understanding as a reaction to yourself or others. In this chapter, discover how compassion can serve as an antidote to both givers and receivers of anger.

Embracing Acceptance

People suffer. Suffering is an inevitable part of life. Babies fall down and hurt themselves, young kids get bullied, teenagers feel awkward, and people get sick, lose loved ones, have accidents, and eventually die. Sorry, but it's true.

Understanding that you will, at times, suffer and that other people suffer too is accepting reality. In addition, accept that the world is not always fair, you don't always get what you want, and some things will never change. Accepting reality decreases ineffective and self-sabotaging anger.

At the same time, joy, love, and beauty are parts of life. Good things also happen to people. Take the time to enjoy the life you have when you can. Appreciate friendships and family. Look upward to the stars.

Looking for Commonalities

Most people are looking for a secure life, a roof over their heads, meaningful pursuits, dignity, and good relationships. There's plenty of research that suggests that after people have those basic needs met and feel reasonably content, even great increases in income do little to improve their sense of happiness.

At the same time, most people struggle with something. It could be anger, depression, anxiety, obesity, relationship problems, addiction, financial hardships, abuse, or something else. Have compassion for others as well as for yourself. Focus on how most people want the same things out of life.

Practicing Acts of Kindness

Acts of kindness signal the brain to release feel good neurotransmitters. It's difficult to be angry when you are feeling so good. Kindness to others spurs those who receive or witness kind acts to pay it forward. People who practice charity are happier, healthier, and tend to live longer. There are thousands of small ways to improve someone else's day. Think of a few and you'll feel better too.

Listening More

Take time to listen to others before reacting. Extroverts can be great at entertaining. They may engage others with jokes and stories, but when people have problems, they turn to those who listen. Compassion comes from carefully listening to people's experiences. People who listen deeply to others are less prone to anger.

Forgiving

Apologize more. Forgive yourself and others with abandon. Holding a grudge means that the grievances of the past live with you in every present moment. Being angry and regretful with yourself keeps you an unhappy and unpleasant person. Wipe the slate clean. Start each day with hope and optimism — not anger.

Saying Thank You

Being polite goes a long way to make you less angry. Find a way to increase your use of words of appreciation. Acknowledge small kindness throughout the day. Be sure to say thank you to those who provide service such as waiters, drivers, and clerks. Say thanks to your spouse for everyday chores, to your kids for doing their homework, to yourself for not losing your temper. Good manners matter.

Becoming Less Judgmental

There is a saying about the word assume, that perhaps you know: Assume makes an "ass" out of "u" and "me." To assume means that you know something about someone or something without really knowing the whole story. Then you take that assumption and make a judgment.

Imagine you are shopping and someone knocks into you almost pushing you over. You might assume that the person is a rude jerk. But perhaps that person has just received a call about an accident at home, or is having a stroke, or even a bathroom emergency. On the other hand, perhaps the person is a rude jerk. You just don't know. Don't make judgments that you haven't been able to check out; it simply causes undue upset.

Having Fun

If you are angry all the time, you may have a hard time figuring out pleasurable activities. The same is true if you are the recipient of considerable anger. In both cases, fun is incompatible with anger. Make a list of pleasurable activities. You deserve to have a good time, do something for yourself. It will help decrease your anger.

WARNING

If your idea of a good time is getting drunk or high with your friends, but you usually end up getting into an argument over politics, then maybe you should rethink the situation. Similarly, if you love tennis but get furious when you lose or miss a shot, then maybe tennis isn't for you. Pleasurable activities don't work if they get you worked up. Find something else.

Smiling and Saying Hello

I live in a small village outside of Albuquerque, New Mexico. People here are friendly. They wave to each other, say hello, and even during the reddest and bluest times of recent politics, were largely helpful and nice to each other.

When visitors come from the east coast, they usually comment on the friendliness of the people of New Mexico. When I travel to the east coast, it takes me awhile to realize that everyone isn't mad at each other. Sometimes I forget and say hello to someone walking by and get weird looks.

It doesn't take much to smile or nod your head at a passerby. Don't take it personally if the nod isn't reciprocated.

Opening More Doors

When you get a chance, hold a door open for someone coming through at the same time. It's not much, but the small gesture of kindness is often greatly appreciated. Being nice makes you feel nice. Opening doors for others may help you open your own small world to greater peace. We could all use some of that right now.

Chapter **25**

Ten Anti-Anger Thoughts

Anger management is a case of mind over matter. What you have in your mind matters because it spells the difference between being full of anger versus anger-free. This chapter offers you ten thoughts that will help you manage anger — yesterday, today, and tomorrow.

No One Can Make You Angry Without Your Participation

Every time someone says, "He (or she or they) made me mad," I want to speak up and tell that person how absolutely wrong this is. When people say that, it's their way of trying to make other people responsible for their emotions. No circumstance, person, or event has that power over you. You aren't a car that can be started by another person's key — and you should be glad about that.

What *is* true is that external events can (and do) provide you with opportunities to become angry. The unfortunate part is that people embrace this opportunity all too readily. You can, *if you want,* choose not to lose your temper. Either way, the choice is yours.

The next time — and there will be a next time — you find yourself facing an opportunity to become angry, remember this comforting thought: No one can make you angry, no matter how hard he tries, unless you decide to let him.

There are many degrees of anger. Don't beat yourself up if you occasionally lash out with annoyance or irritation when frustrated. Just try to calm down and carry on without losing your cool.

What Goes Around Comes Around

You've probably heard numerous sayings like "What goes around comes around" and "You reap what you sow." Most of them coming out of the mouth of someone who has felt harmed or hurt by someone else. These sayings serve a purpose: They remind you that life is, by and large, a two-way street.

There is a certain *reciprocity* to human emotion; in other words, anger begets anger, fear engenders fear, and one act of kindness is often followed by another. People respond in kind to whatever you throw out there. Throw out anger and you get back anger. Throw out love and you get back love. Emotions work just like a boomerang.

If you want others to treat you positively, begin each day by creating positive karma. Ask yourself the following questions:

>> Who can I care about today?

>> Who needs my understanding, not my judgment?

>> How many kind remarks do I want to offer others today?

>> To whom can I be sympathetic?

>> How many people can I hug before the sun goes down?

>> How often can I say *please* and *thank you*?

>> How happy are people when they see my smiling face?

Then see how difficult it is for you to get angry.

It's Only Money

Far too often, people get upset or even angry because something goes wrong, and it has a monetary consequence. If the cost is minimal, they get irritated. If the cost is more than they can (or want to) bear, they fly into a rage.

Does this sounds like you? If so, what you need to consider is that it's only money. It's not the end of the world or civilization as you know it. It doesn't mean that your life is ruined forever. It's only money. For example, say your kid or spouse wrecks the car; do you find yourself asking

>> "How much is that going to cost?"

>> "How's the car?"

>> "How much damage was there?"

>> "Is the car drivable?"

>> "How much will our insurance rates go up?"

The more *important* questions — the ones you should be asking — are

>> "Are you okay?"

>> "Are you hurt?"

>> "How are you?"

>> "Are you dealing with it okay?"

The rest is only a matter of money and metal.

REMEMBER

It's all about priorities. Discover that your love and concern for people are far more important than the "cost" of *anything*. As financial guru Suze Orman often declares, "People first, money second, and things third."

Other People Are Not the Enemy

From an evolutionary standpoint, anger serves a purpose. It's a means to an end: survival. Emotions were built into your nervous system to help you adapt to life so that you can live long and well. Anger has a single purpose: to protect you from your enemies, those who threaten your very existence. But who are these enemies, and how many do you have?

If your kid comes home with a D on his report card, is he your enemy? If your wife isn't as interested in sex as you'd like her to be, is she your enemy? If someone ahead of you in the express-checkout line at the grocery store has 11 items rather than 10, is she your enemy? Is everyone who gets in your way, inconveniences you, or beats you at poker your enemy? If so, then you're going to be angry a lot!

TIP

Reserve the status of *enemy* for those people who truly threaten your physical safety. Think of the rest of them as *people* — son, daughter, spouse, or a person who doesn't see fit to obey the rules in the checkout line — not enemies. Unless the lady in the checkout line pulls out a gun and asks you for your wallet, she's just an annoying person, not an enemy, and not worth getting angry over.

Life Isn't Fair and Never Will Be

When life goes the way you want it to, you call that fair. When it doesn't, you call that unfair. You decide what's fair and what's unfair. In other words, you're the ultimate judge. How you think about what happens to you is what determines how angry you get. Every time you think "unfair," do you resort to anger?

Think about fairness. What is it? Who passes it out? Are all bad events unfair? Why? Many people think there's a spiritual, unknown plan for what happens to them and the world. Others believe that there is simply no explanation for random events — both good and bad.

TIP

So maybe the answer is to stop thinking about whether what comes your way today is fair or unfair and just deal with it as best you can — without being judgmental, which is where the anger comes in. Try it.

Also, remember to be grateful even when life doesn't go the way you want it to. Gratefulness about small things improves moods.

Energy Is a Limited Resource

It takes energy for you to be angry, it takes energy for you to stay angry, and it takes energy for you to do all the things you do to express or relieve anger. Too much anger can leave you *utterly exhausted*.

MAINTAINING VITALITY IN OLD AGE

Research shows that as people age, they consistently report fewer episodes of anger, experience less intense anger, and get over anger more quickly. Maybe that's because the angry people die off early. Or maybe it's because those who survive have discovered one of the great lessons of life: It takes energy to preserve life. And you have a lot less energy at your disposal in the second half of your life as you do in the first half. So people are forced to become good stewards of energy as a way of ensuring vitality.

Are you sure you want to devote so much energy to one emotion or, for that matter, to emotions in general? You don't have an unending supply of energy; you can use it up like any other resource. Where you spend your energy pretty much defines your day. If you put most of it into tasks, at the end of the day, you feel productive. If you put most of it into anger, at the end of the day, you feel angry, defeated, exhausted, and unproductive.

REMEMBER

As long as you're alive, you're spending energy on something. The question is, "What are you spending it on?" Is your energy working to benefit you or someone you care about, to improve your lot in life or the lives of others, or is it simply wasted? Your decision, your choice.

We're All Human After All

Thinking of yourself as *superior*, or better than other people, is an open invitation to anger. Anger tends to flow downhill toward those you regard as inferior: as sillier, stupider, and less important than you are. You tell yourself, "They (the lesser people) deserve what they get when they make me mad."

Psychologists use the label *narcissism* to describe people who feel unusually superior to other people. The narcissist is one who has a grandiose view of herself; she sees herself as a "special" person, a person whose opinions should carry more weight than others, and a person who feels that all the other people are just there to cater to her needs — in other words, the *queen bee!*

The same is true in marriage. According to marriage expert Dr. John Gottman, as soon as contempt enters the relationship, the marriage is doomed. Contempt goes along with a feeling of superiority, and it goes way beyond ordinary criticism of your partner. The intent behind it is to demean, insult, and psychologically harm your so-called loved one.

TIP

Settle for just being an *ordinary*, nothing-special person. Then you can relax.

This Isn't the Hill You Want to Die On

Just as in war, as you struggle your way through life, you must invariably decide which objectives — hills, goals, or issues — are worth dying for and which ones matter less. The more things matter (the more of an emotional investment you have in something), the angrier you get when things don't go your way. Frequent intense anger is bad for your health. It pays to be selective in the battles you choose to fight.

TIP

Reserve the right to fight as few battles in your life as possible, and live to fight another day.

Nothing You Can Achieve in Anger Can't Be Achieved Without It

Anger can be used constructively in some instances, but anything you want to achieve in life can be yours without anger.

Somewhere along the line, people forged an association between getting mad and getting things done. And now the anger comes automatically when you're faced with obstacles, challenges, and problems. It's what experimental psychologists call *superstitious reinforcement*. In other words, people *think* that anger is vital to their day-to-day survival when it's really not.

TIP

Try to remember the last time you got angry. What was the problem that led to your getting mad? Could you have dealt with this problem in any other way without needing to be angry? Be honest. Did your anger help or hinder your ability to resolve the problem? Most likely, anger was a hindrance.

WARNING

At some time in the history of humankind, anger no doubt served a purpose, mainly through its connection with physical survival. But in today's world, anger has nearly outlived its usefulness. Too often, anger is nothing more than a bad habit passed down from one generation to the next.

You're Not Entitled to Anything

If you discover one thing from reading this book that will help you manage anger better, it's this: You're not *entitled* to anything. A sense of entitlement is the root cause of much of the anger in today's fast-moving, complex world.

According to the dictionary, an *entitlement* is anything you have legal claim to, like the title to a piece of property. Historically, it was something that English kings granted noblemen for their loyal service. Yet today, if you're like many people, you apply the concept to just about every facet of your everyday life.

Here are some common examples of things people have a false sense of entitlement to:

>> Consideration from everyone, all the time

>> Peace of mind

>> A world where everything is fair

>> Cheap gasoline

>> Prosperity

>> People who agree with their political views

>> The respect of their peers

>> Having their ideas, beliefs, and opinions valued by everyone

>> A good night's sleep

>> A car that always starts first thing in the morning

The problem with a sense of entitlement is that it conveys a sense of obligation, certainty, and predictability. For example, your adolescent kids will, without question, always do what you ask of them because *they owe you* that courtesy for bringing them into this world. And what happens if they don't see it that way? You get angry. And what does getting angry accomplish? Generally, not much, at least not much that's good.

TIP

Forget the entitlements and instead negotiate successfully for at least some of what you want (not demand) out of life: a raise, a promotion, respect, love, and recognition. It makes life flow a whole lot easier.

Index

A

abuse. *See also* past events, letting go of anger from
  domestic violence, 122, 204–205
  morally righteous response to, 38
  as trigger, 28–29
acceptance
  in children, 198
  embracing, 323–324
  of finality of being wronged, 247–248
  of past events, 230–231
  of relapses, 250–252
  strategies for, 130–132
acting in opposition to feelings, 64–65
acting on impulse, 274
action stage of change, 40
activity monitor devices, 277
acts of kindness, 324
adaptive anger, 23
adaptive thinking, 72, 96–98
addiction to stress, 265
ADHD (Attention Deficit Hyperactivity Disorder), 189
aggression
  avoidance versus, 170
  brooding, effect on, 142
  general discussion, 18–19
  genetics, role in childhood anger, 185
agreement, with angry people, 320
air rage, 7
alcohol
  anger triggered by, 287–288
  avoiding before sleep, 281–282
  drinking responsibly, 290–291
  risks associated with, 43–44
alexithymia, 11
allies, 63
ally, anger as, 21–24
alternative perspectives, 36–38
Alzheimer's Disease, 135

anger
  choosing, 8–9
  defining, 8
  getting help with, 13–14
  myths about, 10–12
  as primary emotion, 12–13
  words describing, 235
anger facilitators, 212–213
anger profile. *See also* anger triggers
  co-occurring problems, 33–34
  expression strategies, 16–20
  frequency, intensity, and duration, 32
  overview, 15–16
  positive side of anger, 21–24
  style, identifying, 20–21
anger rumination, 142
anger style, identifying, 20–21
anger triggers
  abuse and attacks, 28–29
  avoiding, 62–63
  in children, 200
  dishonesty and disappointment, 26
  events, 68–70
  events, feelings, and thoughts, connecting, 72–75
  existential threats, 29
  overview, 24
  physical problems, 28
  prejudice and discrimination, 27–28
  situations or contexts, 31–32
  stress, 259
  struggling relationships, 27
  threats to self-esteem, 26–27
  time pressure and frustrations, 25–26
  tracking, 29–31
  unfair treatment, 25
  warning signals, awareness of, 56–59
angerholics, avoiding company of, 62–63
anger-specific meditation, 138
angry drinkers, 44

overview, 287

smoking, quitting, 288–289

diet and eating patterns, 291

exercise, 275–278

medications, 292

overview, 275

sleep

alcohol, avoiding before, 281–282

amount of, 285–286

benefits of, 278–280

catastrophizing, avoiding, 285–286

competing activities, eliminating, 283–284

environment for, designing, 282

improving quality of, 281–284

overview, 278

pre-sleep routine, setting up, 282

rating quality of, 280–281

sleeping pills, 285

stimulants, avoiding, 281–282

therapy for, 286–287

uncluttering mind before, 284

work, distancing from, 284

body, effect of anger on

fatigue, 42

high blood pressure, 44

high cholesterol, 45

obesity, 44

on-the-job injuries, 45

overview, 10, 12

road rage, 45

smoking risk, 42–43

substance use risk, 43–44

suppressing anger, 19

body scan meditation, 137

booster sessions, 253

boundaries, setting healthy, 209

breathing meditation, 136

breathing techniques, 61, 65

brooding

aggression increased with, 142

costs of, 141

delayed, 142–143

disengaging from, 143–147

general discussion, 140–141

self-analysis, 141

buffering complaints, 118–119

built-in resource, anger as, 22

burnout, avoiding, 267–269

bystander effect, 217

C

caffeine

anger triggered by, 287

avoiding before sleep, 281–282

cutting back on, 289

calming down, 255

candy, sucking on, 65–66

career, impact of anger on, 45–48

caregivers, stress in, 261

carrying capacity for stress, 265

catalyst for new behavior, anger as, 22

catastrophes, turning into challenges, 272–273

catastrophic stress, 266

catastrophizing, 80–81, 285–286

catharsis, 120, 218–219

causal connections, establishing in journaling, 235–236

causes versus events, 70–72

CD (Conduct Disorder), 33, 189

challenges, turning catastrophes into, 272–273

changing

cost-benefit analysis, 48–52

critical costs of anger

on career, 45–48

on health, 42–45

on relationships, 48

distorted thinking

checking evidence, 86–87

diversity, seeking, 90–91

extremist words, moderating, 87–88

friend perspective, taking, 88

re-evaluating intentions, 91–92

reformulating, 92–96

rethinking, practicing, 96–98

tolerance, increasing, 89

overview, 35

stages of change, 39–41, 250

ten reasons for not, 36–38

chemical substances

alcohol

anger triggered by, 287–288

avoiding before sleep, 281–282

frailty of human nature, accepting, 245

Fredrickson, Barbara, 177

frequency of anger, 32

Freud, Sigmund, 34, 120

friend perspective, taking, 88

friendliness, developing, 326

friendships
  angerholics, avoiding, 62–63
  childhood anger from conflicts in, 188
  developing, 294, 296–297, 298
  effects of anger on, 48
  feedback from friends, 254–255
  with gym members, 299
  with neighbors, 297–298, 301
  prioritizing, 299–301
  in self-help groups, 296
  support from, 14
  from volunteering, 295–296

frustration, 25–26, 199

fun, having, 325–326

future events, anger over, 70

G

gender differences, anger over, 165–166

genetics, role in childhood anger, 185–186

global ratings, 81

gossiping, 17

grammar, in journaling, 234

Grandma's rule, 199

gratitude, 306

grief, 251, 267

grudges, 18, 32

gyms, making friends at, 299

H

handwritten journals, 238–239

hardiness, cultivating, 269–273

health. *See also* exercise
  effects of anger on
    fatigue, 42
    high blood pressure, 44
    high cholesterol, 45
    obesity, 44
    on-the-job injuries, 45
    overview, 10, 12
    road rage, 45
    smoking risk, 42–43
    substance use risk, 43–44
    suppressing anger, 19
  health disparities, anger over, 165
  meditation, benefits of, 134
  problems with, as trigger, 28
  stress, effect on, 260

healthy pleasures, searching for, 309–310

help from others, 13–14

high blood pressure, 44

high cholesterol, 45

high-intensity exercise, 276–277

home environment, 31, 189–191

hostility, 18–19

humility, 221–222, 312

humor, 62

hurt, relapses due to, 250

I

"I" statements, making, 112

I-can't-stand-its, 85

icons, used in book, 3

ignoring bad behavior in children, 196

illegal immigration, 157

illness, as trigger, 28

"I'm fine" response, avoiding, 126–127

imaginal exposure, 148–149

immigration, 157

impotence, 23–24

impulses
  acting on, 274
  letting pass, 290

incentives for managing anger, 255

income inequality, 164

individualism, 105

inequalities, anger due to, 163–165

inflated self-esteem, 11

informational support, 14

injury, relapses due to, 250

injustice, responding to, 156–157

insomnia, 285–287

intensity of anger, 32

intentions, re-evaluating, 91–92

intermittent explosive disorder, 33

internet rage

  anonymity, role of, 216–217

  cyberbullying, 217–220

  echo chambers, 219–220

  overview, 215–216

  social media and depression, 219

  viral emotions, 218

interpersonal violence, 122

interruptions, as trigger, 25–26

intimate partner violence (IPV), 204–205

intimate relationships

  anger towards partner, managing, 207–209

  angry partners, responding to, 210–213

  angry partnerships, 205–207

  effects of anger on, 48

  facilitating anger, avoiding, 212–213

  healthy boundaries, setting, 209

  mental traps, eliminating, 210–212

  online dating and politics, 159

  overview, 203

  victimization, avoiding, 213

  violence in, 122, 204–205

intimidation, 204

intolerance, 89, 90

invigorating anger, 22

involvement, sense of, 271–272

IPV (intimate partner violence), 204–205

irrational thoughts about relapses, 253

irritability, 17, 201

J

journaling

  audience in, 233

  causal connections, establishing, 235–236

  emotions during, dealing with, 237

  first person, using, 233–234

  grammar, not worrying about, 234

  handwritten versus digital, 238–239

  judgement, suspending, 237–238

  by laid off workers, 46

  negative, focusing on, 234–235

  overview, 232–233

  quiet place for, finding, 239

  reflection after, 239

  for smoking cessation, 289

  timing, 236–237

joy, 13

judgement

  avoiding, 325

  in journaling, avoiding, 237–238

  judging thought distortion, 83–84

jump-starting anger management

  acting in opposition to feelings, 64–65

  anti-anger actions, engaging in, 63–66

  avoiding triggers, 62–63

  awareness, increasing, 56–59

  candy, sucking on, 65–66

  distraction strategies, 63–64

  overview, 55

  reactions, rethinking, 59–62

K

keeping cool, 19–20, 193

kind acts, practicing, 324

L

laid off workers, journaling by, 46

laughter, 272–273

learned reaction, anger in children as, 186

letting go of anger, 231

letting go of what might happen strategy, 146–147

life essay exercise, 304

lifeguards, personal, 254–255

lightening up, 62

limits for children, setting, 194

listening skills, 299–301, 316, 324

long-haulers, COVID-19, 28

looking at clouds strategy, 144–145

Losada, Marcial, 177

losing as only option, 163

loss, relapses due to, 251–252

loving-kindness meditation, 137

M

Maddi, Salvador, 269

magnifying, 81

maintenance stage of change, 40, 250

village movement, 301
violence
  domestic, 122, 204–205
  as trigger, 28–29
viral emotions, 218
volume of voice, 126, 318
volunteering, 295

W

walking away from conflict, 162–163
walking meditation, 137
walking slowly, 64, 104
Warning icon, 3
warning signals, awareness of, 56–59
watching the news exercise, 149
win-win solutions, seeking, 191
wise mind, finding, 132
wishing stress away, 274
women
  anger in, 10
  assertiveness in, 127
work
  anger triggered at, 31
  assertiveness at, 179–180
  career, impact of anger on, 45–48
  civility at, 179–180
  counterproductive work behavior
    avoidance versus aggression, 170
    by disgruntled employees, 171–173

identifying, 168–170
overview, 47–48, 167–168
person versus organization, 170–171
by self-centered employees, 173–175
ego, putting on shelf, 102–103
negotiating skills, 175
on-the-job injuries, 45
during pandemic, 169–170, 176
positive work environment, developing, 176–179
sleep, distancing from to improve, 284
writing exercises
  after walking away to cool down, 123
  for disgruntled employees, 172
  epitaph, writing own, 305
  journaling
    audience in, 233
    causal connections, establishing, 235–236
    emotions during, dealing with, 237
    expressing anger in, 124
    first person, using, 233–234
    grammar, not worrying about, 234
    handwritten versus digital, 238–239
    judgement, suspending, 237–238
    negative, focusing on, 234–235
    overview, 232–233
    quiet place for, finding, 239
    reflection after, 239
    timing, 236–237
  life essay, 304

About the Author

Laura L. Smith, PhD, is a clinical psychologist. She is a past president of the New Mexico Psychological Association. She has considerable experience in school and clinical settings dealing with children and adults who have anger problems. In fact, she worked for four years at the Juvenile Detention Center in Albuquerque, New Mexico, where she was called upon to help a wide variety of offenders, most of whom had significant issues with anger and aggressive behavior. She presented workshops on cognitive therapy and mental health issues to national and international audiences.

Dr. Smith has worked on numerous publications together with her husband Charles Elliott, PhD, who is now retired. They are coauthors of *Quitting Smoking & Vaping For Dummies; Borderline Personality Disorder For Dummies,* 2nd Edition; *Child Psychology & Development For Dummies; Anxiety For Dummies,* 3rd Edition; *Obsessive Compulsive Disorder For Dummies; Seasonal Affective Disorder For Dummies; Anxiety & Depression Workbook For Dummies;* and *Depression For Dummies,* 2nd Edition (all published by Wiley).

Dedication

I dedicate this book to Charles H. Elliott, my partner, best friend, and husband. We will always be the coauthors of our lives.

Author's Acknowledgments

I want to thank the outstanding team at Wiley. As usual, their expertise, support, and guidance was of immeasurable help. Thank you to Kelsey Baird for her encouragement during the initial planning for the book. Project manager extraordinaire Tim Gallan answered questions, helped with editing, and kept the content on point. Thank you also to Joseph Bush for his particularly insightful input.

A special acknowledgment to Charles Elliott, coauthor of the 2nd Edition of *Anger Management For Dummies*. Despite his retirement, he was always available for an edit, an idea, or more importantly, another cup of coffee. I'd also like to acknowledge the contribution of W. Doyle Gentry, who passed away in 2013. He wrote the first edition of this book, and many of his ideas have flowed through subsequent editions.

Publisher's Acknowledgments

Acquisitions Editor: Kelsey Baird
Development Editor: Tim Gallan
Technical Reviewer: Joseph P. Bush, PhD
Proofreader: Debbye Butler

Production Editor: Tamilmani Varadharaj
Cover Image: © Epoxydude/Gettyimages